Praise for *Wargaming for Leaders*

*"The simulation on HIV/AIDS exceeded all our expectations . . . [and]
resulted in some very innovative partnerships. I was deeply impressed by
the energy and commitment of the participants, who came from four
continents and included people from China. The outcome was the commitment to try to collaborate in innovative ways, building on the expertise of each sector. This sort of creative thinking could pave the way for
genuine progress in reversing this terrible epidemic. . . . We hope to try
to repeat the simulation model in other countries with emerging epi-
demics, such as China and Eastern Europe, as well as in Africa."*

> —RICHARD C. HOLBROOKE,
> president and CEO of the Global Business Coalition
> on HIV/AIDS, Tuberculosis and Malaria; former U.S.
> ambassador to the United Nations

*"Fascinating stuff. These wargaming techniques allow participants to
develop scenarios that can lead to unexpected and remarkable outcomes.
The wargames described in this book, particularly those on national
security and energy issues, often suggest a future no one could have imagined in advance. Public policymakers should take note."*

> —NEW MEXICO GOVERNOR BILL RICHARDSON,
> former U.S. ambassador to the United Nations; former
> U.S. Secretary of Energy

*"Over the past several years, I have personally participated in several
wargames to find solutions to the health challenges facing our country.
These simulations can accomplish in a day or two the kind of practical
problem solving and consensus building that too often takes months or even
years. If your organization hasn't put these methods to work, you should."*

> —NEWT GINGRICH,
> former speaker of the U.S. House of Representatives;
> founder of the Center for Health Transformation

WARGAMING
FOR
LEADERS

STRATEGIC DECISION MAKING FROM THE
BATTLEFIELD TO THE BOARDROOM

MARK HERMAN

MARK FROST

ROBERT KURZ

New York   Chicago   San Francisco
Lisbon   London   Madrid   Mexico City   Milan
New Delhi   San Juan   Seoul   Singapore
Sydney   Toronto

1 2 3 4 5 6 7 8 9 0   DOC/DOC   0 1 0 9 8

ISBN: 978-0-07-159688-6
MHID: 0-07-159688-7

Interior design by Lee Fukui and Mauna Eichner

This publication is designed to provide accurate and authoritative information in regard to the subject matter covered. It is sold with the understanding that the publisher is not engaged in rendering legal, accounting, or other professional service. If legal advice or other expert assistance is required, the services of a competent professional person should be sought.

> —*From a Declaration of Principles Jointly Adopted by a Committee of the American Bar Association and a Committee of Publishers and Associations*

McGraw-Hill books are available at special quantity discounts to use as premiums and sales promotions, or for use in corporate training programs. To contact a representative, please visit the Contact Us pages at www.mhprofessional.com.

This book is printed on acid-free paper.

CONTENTS

ACKNOWLEDGMENTS

A wargame is built on the dedicated efforts of many individuals. Over the past 20 years, thousands of leaders have contributed their creativity and commitment to make the wargames we stage for organizations in both the public and private sectors a remarkable success. We sincerely thank each of these individuals for their enthusiasm, engagement, and candor in taking on some of the most complex problems our governments, businesses, and public face. The stories on the following pages reflect the generosity of our clients, participants, and colleagues.

Without the support of our partners at Booz Allen Hamilton, this book would not have been possible. We especially wish to express our gratitude to Booz Allen chairman Ralph Shrader, who encouraged our groundbreaking efforts at the World Economic Forum, and to Joe Garner, a senior vice president at the firm who provided ample encouragement as we took on this book project.

We extend our most sincere gratitude to Mike Ruby for his perspective and perseverance in pulling together a sometimes overwhelming amount of information into a cogent, compelling narrative. A first-class reporter and writer, he gave shape to the innumerable memories and insights we've gathered over the years from our work.

Many of the stories in this book draw on the memories of our partners Mark Gerencser and Bill Thoet, and of core members of our wargaming staff—Bob Statz, Mark Jacobsohn, Larry Hamby, Andrea Beck, Eliot Goldberg, Bob Mayes, Nicole Weepie, Nicole Monteforte, and Tracy March. And our gratitude to Rosie Schwartz,

Melanie Olmsted, and Jolene Sawvel, who managed the daily miracle of keeping our schedules on track so that we could continue to serve our clients while focusing on this book.

No wargame is a light undertaking. Each takes weeks of intense preparation. Many Booz Allen professionals contributed extraordinary commitment and passion to helping our clients explore innovative solutions to the Herculean problems that plague their businesses, industries, and communities. We cannot name them all here, but each of them knows that their contributions were invaluable.

Our early successes in wargaming were realized through the pioneering efforts and encouragement of our colleagues Charley Beever, Marty Bollinger, Paul Branstad, John Harbison, Barry Jaruzelski, Dan Lewis, Skid Masterson, John McCarter, Joe Nemec, Bruce Pasternack, George Thibault, and John Treat. In recent years, Heather Burns, Joan Dempsey, Chris Kelly, Janet Lyman, Mike McKeon, Susan Penfield, Robin Portman, Don Pressley, Ghassan Salameh, Gary Schulman, Steve Soules, Reggie Van Lee, Rich Wilhelm, and Charlie Zuhoski have helped extend Booz Allen's run of impactful wargames through their generous support and efforts. As well, we thank our corporate communications team—especially Randy Rothenberg, Marie Lerch, Amy Bernstein, Janine Cornecelli, Cynthia Baker, and Melanie Pontier—for their assistance in conceiving and launching this book.

Our warmest thanks go to our wives—Carole Herman, Paula Frost, and Pamela Alexander—for their great patience, tolerance, and understanding in allowing us to embark on one great wargaming adventure after another.

MARK HERMAN
MARK FROST
ROBERT KURZ

INTRODUCTION

It was two o'clock in the afternoon, only a few hours after Americans had awakened to the news that Saddam Hussein's military forces had invaded Kuwait, and we already had assembled a team to take on the Iraqi dictator. Our "battlefield" was a conference table in suburban Virginia, within hailing distance of the Pentagon and the nation's capital across the Potomac River. Our war council included a few colleagues from our firm, Booz Allen Hamilton, and several experts from the National Defense University, especially its Institute for National Security Studies.

We knew what Iraq had done that day in early August 1990. We had mustered our forces to ask why Saddam had acted, what he intended to do next, and what the United States and the other good guys could do about it.

Before us on the table was "Gulf Strike," a board wargame Mark Herman had designed for hobbyists seven years earlier. It was one of the dozens of commercial wargames that he had authored, a reflection of his fascination with military history dating back to the age of 12, when he mapped out his first wargame, on the Battle of Balaclava. The Charge of the Light Brigade wasn't top of mind on August 2, 1990. Instead, we were concerned with Saddam's Republican Guard and what was then the fourth largest army in the world.

We had divided our participants into teams representing the nations and interests in the game. Before them was a detailed map of the countries in the region, with pieces or symbols representing various military, transportation, and economic assets.

Iraq's military had provided the opening real-world scenario in this wargame, but why? Money was plainly a key motivating factor, the players agreed. Saddam was deeply in debt to Kuwait, and seizing the tiny emirate would erase the red ink and give him access to a rich state treasury to boot. He also would gain control of Kuwait's oil wells, expanding his influence in the OPEC oil cartel.

One scenario, then, was that Iraq would consolidate its gains and hold Kuwait, advancing no farther. "Kuwait isn't exactly beloved within the Arab world," one of the members of our group said, acknowledging a resentment on the Arab street for a perceived arrogance among oil-rich Kuwaitis. "Maybe Saddam figures his stature in the Arab world will grow, and there'll be no outcry if he stays put."

Sure, and pigs fly. The key to the crisis, the players felt, was Iraq's huge neighbor to the south, Saudi Arabia. The Saudis sat on the richest oil fields on the planet and produced more crude than any other member of OPEC.

A second scenario was that Saddam would secure Kuwait and then, in relatively short order, invade Saudi Arabia, aiming to grab the prodigiously productive oil fields in the kingdom's eastern province. If he was successful, Saddam Hussein would gain effective control of OPEC production and the global price of crude—the oil weapon writ large. Assembling a military force to stop him couldn't happen overnight, but could he be checked to buy some time? And if so, exactly how?

Wrestling with such critical questions on this particular day was hardly a casual exercise in our professional specialty. We had received a phone call that morning from Andrew Marshall, the legendary director of the Office of Net Assessment (ONA) in the U.S. Defense Department. Andy Marshall had run ONA, a kind of internal think tank at the Pentagon, for nearly two decades. (Now in his eighties, he still runs it.) The group Mark Herman heads at Booz Allen had built a reputation for the quality of its wargaming work for the Defense Department. What Marshall wanted was a quick-reaction wargame on the Iraq crisis, and he wanted it fast. The results certainly wouldn't dictate the U.S. government's action in the weeks and months ahead, but the knowledge and reasoning employed by the players around that conference table might well contribute to the mix.

○   ○   ○

W argaming, a creative tool for replaying military history or trying to anticipate battles to come, goes back thousands of years to the ancient conflicts documented in countless books and other accounts. Sun Tzu, the Chinese military philosopher whose writings in *The Art of War* 2,500 years ago have found a modern audience among contemporary business executives, certainly was an early practitioner. More recently, Benjamin Franklin encouraged his fellow Americans to play chess, the better to learn about their own defenses. But chess, as intoxicating as it can be, is a wargame only in a limited sense. When a game of chess begins, the two opponents have complete information: All the warriors are on the chessboard, and they can be moved only according to a strict set of rules.

Modern wargaming—what we and our colleagues do for our clients in the military, large corporations, and nonprofit organizations around the globe—differs in one essential way: The participants do not have complete information when they play one of our wargames because we design wargames to reflect the real world; in the real world, decision makers almost always are forced to make choices that are based on *incomplete* information. An economist, Thomas Schelling, got a Nobel Prize in 2005 for his work applying game theory to the interactions of people and nations. A central point of his "impossibility theorem" states: "One thing a person cannot do, no matter how rigorous his analysis or heroic his imagination, is to draw up a list of things that would never occur to him."

The genius of modern professional wargaming is that it embraces the impossibility theorem and provides a methodology to get at the things that one leader, no matter how visionary, cannot grasp on his or her own. How? Not by relying on computers, which we use mainly in a variety of supporting roles. Instead, we bring together the real experts on the issue at hand and allow them to "experience" the future in a risk-free environment and find answers to questions that had not been on their radar screens before they began the wargame.

The experts can be several dozen senior officers in the military or a similar number of executives at a transnational corporation or a group drawn from the public, private, and civil sectors who come together to solve a problem too big for any one of them to handle alone. This is what we call a megacommunity. We stage the wargame, but it is the players who take an opening scenario designed by us to build a story about the future—how a battle might unfold, how a corporate strategy might play out over time—because they live it as a kind of virtual experience.

The power of these minds interacting with one another—what we call "cognitive warfare"—leads to unexpected and often startling outcomes. As you will see in this book, our wargames for government, corporations, and nonprofit groups address many of the vital issues facing leaders in the public and private sectors in the United States and around the world. We do not promise miracles; we leave such matters to a higher authority. Also, what happens in our wargames does not necessarily reflect the organizational policies or real-life reactions of the participants. However, there is no question that the creative and visionary act of cognitive warfare produces powerful results. If you are a decision maker in any organization or enterprise, large or small, public or private, or if you aspire to leadership, ask yourself this question: If I could look into a telescope and glimpse the consequences of a course of action before the point of no return, before committing blood and treasure, would I do so?

○　○　○

Looking into that telescope, of course, was exactly what Andy Marshall wanted us to do on that day in August 1990. The players in our wargame had made enough moves on the conference room tabletop to feel confident that it would be difficult to stop Saddam if he moved immediately to take Saudi Arabia's oil fields. But assuming that Saddam wouldn't move immediately, we might have a window of opportunity. We generally agreed that the Saudis would have to request formal help from the United States and that Washington certainly would provide it. How, when, and in what form that help would arrive were still matters of debate.

At one point, after we had covered the possible scenarios and variations of them, Mark Herman asked everyone to sit back and respond to the toughest question: Okay, friends, what do you really think will happen? This would be a gut check, informed by expertise and, more important, wisdom.

In modern warfare, there is something called "dominant battlespace awareness," or DBA in military shorthand. DBA is essentially the *science* of war: the satellites, the unmanned aerial vehicles, the acoustic sensors—all the spycraft and technology brought to bear that permit one side to know where the other side is positioned. DBA is important, but it isn't as important as "dominant battlespace knowledge." DBK is the *art* of war, and it's what usually is determinative. It is the dimension that tries to reveal an enemy's intentions and whether, for example, its apparent leverage is vulnerable to feints, bluffs, and small countermeasures. That was what Herman wanted his colleagues to address.

One of our players, the National Defense University professor Phebe Marr, was and remains an Iraq expert who actually had sized up Saddam Hussein in person. Phebe's answer to Herman's question was electric: Saddam was a bully boy, she said, a coward who would take what he could get if no one stood in his path. But it wouldn't take much, at least initially, to stop him in his tracks. The right words from Washington, backed by relatively small military gestures at the beginning, would freeze him in the hot Kuwaiti desert. Do that, she said, and he won't move on Saudi Arabia. His hesitance in turn would give the United States and its allies critical time to try diplomatic means of persuasion even as they prepared for war in the Persian Gulf.

○   ○   ○

You know what happened next as well as we do. What you don't know is the wargaming that we and our colleagues continued to do for the Pentagon during the Desert Shield buildup of allied forces and the Desert Storm offensive to remove Iraqi troops from Kuwait. Eight years later, in 1999, we found ourselves hard at work on another wargame, "Desert Crossing," that we designed and staged to examine what might happen in Iraq if Saddam Hussein's regime collapsed either internally or from military action by the United States and its allies.

The outcomes of our Iraq wargames will be covered mostly in the first section of this book, which focuses on our work for the U.S. military over two decades. The second section of the book will take you through wargames for commercial clients that illuminate both common and unusual concerns of large corporations in an increasingly complex and competitive environment. The third section places you in virtual jeopardy through global-crisis wargames that examine some of the challenges we all face in the post-9/11 world: terrorism, of course, and threats to port security, public health, and financial institutions.

We end with a chapter on a wargame especially designed and run for this book. This game's objective was at once simple and complex: Drawing on our internal specialists and a few invited experts, we aimed to assess the post-Iraq environment for the American defense, homeland security, and intelligence communities; those communities played and continue to play central roles in the ongoing fight against terrorism. The game's results should resonate with government policymakers and elected officials, strategic planners, and military experts in the United States and other democracies who are focused on what may prove to be one of the great challenges of the twenty-first century.

The glue binding these sections and chapters together is cognitive warfare. In today's world of asymmetric conflict, security threats, remorseless competition, and economic uncertainty, there is an even higher premium on road testing the plans and strategies of large institutions, whether they are governmental organizations, transnational corporations, or emerging megacommunities that are trying to come to grips with global crises. Wargaming has emerged as a strong tool for such purposes, giving "players" an opportunity to look into an imagined future, learn from what they see in that risk-free environment, and apply those findings to shape the real world in which they live.

This book is for anyone interested in testing assumptions, mitigating risk, and revealing the unintended consequences of decisions yet to be made.

PART I

MILITARY
WARGAMES

DESIGNING THE MODERN WARGAME: THREE KEY MOVES

I t is an axiom of modern life that change is the only constant, and the pace of change certainly has accelerated, presenting new challenges to institutions throughout society. At one time, the velocity of decision making may have seemed adequate to tackle most crises; today, a crisis can spin out of control even if the correct decisions to contain it are made in what once was considered good time. You will see that phenomenon at work in some of our wargames. For example, we have wargamed an outbreak of avian flu several times in several places and learned that authorities would have a pandemic flu on their hands before decisions could be made to bring it under control. As we will see later in this book, the takeaways from these pandemic flu games can inform planning for the real-world crisis if it arrives.

A wargame is not the answer to every problem or challenge. The issue may not be large enough or may be addressed better by one analyst or a small team of analysts. A CEO or an army general

As a general rule, a successful wargame requires two conditions. First, we and our client must be able to identify a clear objective or, in military parlance, a concept of operations. Second, it is crucial that there be key groups with different equities—interests that are at real or imagined odds with one another, based on arguments over strategic or tactical plans, data, or institutional culture.

may get all she needs for a smart and informed decision by asking her people for the top three courses of action, with the pros and cons for each course.

Also, a wargame probably is not appropriate for teaching the equivalent of first principles. Once we had a prominent government agency ask us to design and conduct a wargame to address one of its problems. It turned out that the agency was having some difficulty rolling out a Six Sigma program. (Six Sigma is the renowned quality-control methodology for sharply reducing defects in processes and systems. It was pioneered at Motorola, but perhaps its most famous disciple was former General Electric CEO Jack Welch, who brought Six Sigma to GE in the 1990s.)

The government agency wanted an interactive exercise for its Six Sigma training program, and some of its people thought a wargame would be just the thing. However, there really was nothing to wargame: no stakeholders at the agency fighting over turf, for example, and no wrestling over strategy. This seemed to us perfectly straightforward, a case in which traditional training was the answer. We explained our thinking, and the agency went back and focused on the real issue: training the people who would inculcate Six Sigma throughout the organization.

Our wargames can be intricate affairs, with many moving parts—occasionally, too many. A few years ago an insurance company that was expanding rapidly and diversifying its offerings wanted to know whether we could wargame its future. The company probably had two or three dozen different products and was eager to operate in 50 or more countries. Specifically, its top people, anticipating this huge expansion overseas, proposed that we apply wargaming principles to the whole shooting match. Impossible, we said, unless the project could be divided into a series of wargames that narrowed the scope of each game. But that would take much more time and probably cost more money than traditional market analysis. Sometimes, especially when large, fundamental questions are on the table, an appetite suppressant is prescribed medicine to make the wargame work.

When does a wargame make sense? As a general rule, a successful wargame requires two conditions. First, we and our client must be able to identify a clear objective or, in military parlance, a concept of operations. Second, it is crucial that there be key groups with different equities—interests that are at real or imagined odds with one another, based on arguments over strategic or tactical plans, data, or institutional culture. In the military, the U.S. Army, Navy, Air Force, and Marines; the Office of the Secretary of Defense; the Joint Chiefs of Staff; and combat commanders can all take different positions on issues, whether the nation is at peace or at war, and those interservice arguments or rivalries can paralyze decision making.

Imagine a debate about nothing less than the future of the nation's force structure. Some*one* or some*thing* must serve to narrow the disagreements and build a rough consensus on a way forward. That is a perfect situation for what we do because wargames can drive change by the very nature of the process. The game allows military officers or civilians—or corporate executives or leaders in the nonprofit world—to work in a contested environment of their own creation; they can test overarching strategies and specific plans before committing their organization, its people, and its resources to a course of action from which there is no turning back. It is a way to experience the future without the risks attendant in the real world.

The planning, research, design, and preparation of wargames (see Figure 1.1) begin with a conversation or series of conversations with our client's core group of decision makers or policymakers. They have come to us with a problem they want addressed, but we

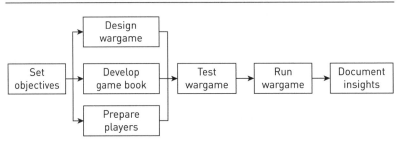

FIGURE 1.1
The phases of a wargame

need to drill down to identify the critical objective of a prospective wargame. If the client is a corporation, we often sit down first with senior executives, including the CEO, and ask: What is it that keeps you up at night? What really worries you looking forward?

We expect candor from clients and usually get it, but on rare occasions we learn of a hidden agenda only after the game is afoot. Once we did a game for a company that had enjoyed a near monopoly in its business but recently had encountered a serious competitive challenge from two other firms. The CEO wanted a wargame that tested the new competitive environment. It turned out that all the players on the "home" team and on the two competitor teams were selected carefully from upper-middle management. The CEO, who did not play the game but attended all the briefing sessions, clearly wanted to see how the company's future leadership operated under pressure. Never let them see you sweat? Forget it: The younger executives were visibly nervous, as one could tell from the perspiration on their brows. However, it would have been better if the CEO had given us a heads-up before we designed the game; we probably would have tweaked it to serve his hidden objective more effectively than the simple perspiration test did.

We need to know with as much precision as possible what the client hopes to achieve from the game. It can be ratification of an existing strategic plan, identification of a plan's potential weaknesses, the wisdom of a new-product introduction, an assessment of a program for major change in military procurement, or the implications of a terrorist incident at a major port in the United States, Europe, or Asia. Clarity of purpose is essential because a wargame cannot be all things to all people. The idea is to build the game to meet a set of objectives that challenge the client and meet the client's expectations at the same time.

Often the process requires multiple meetings over several weeks. A few years ago, for example, a large automotive company hired us to wargame the impact of the "Block Exemption" in Europe. The European Union had deregulated various facets of the automobile business. Importantly, the EU had opened up the aftermarket for parts and service. Before the Block Exemption, new car buyers were required to get their parts and service from the dealers. That was no longer the case, and the new situation meant that automobile manufacturers were facing a wide range of potential competitors. Would parts manufacturers open up their own shops and service centers? What other companies—retailers such as Carrefour—might try to get in on the action? It took us five weeks of meetings, sometimes with 10 to 12 senior people twice a week, to nail down the scope of the game. How many teams would play? How many market segments would they represent? What geographic markets would we try to cover?

A wargame often takes at least 6 weeks and as many as 12 weeks—occasionally even more—of preparation. We realize that one size doesn't fit all in wargaming; everything we do is made to order, and that requires customized research, sometimes a lot of it. In one case, also in the automobile industry, our client, a U.S. parts manufacturer, wanted us to wargame the global market for its products at a time when electronic systems were beginning to sweep through the industry. To build the game, we had to research the technologies, examine what the car companies had on the drawing boards looking forward six or seven years, and develop profiles of how the new electronic systems were likely to be integrated into the vehicles. It took a team of five Booz Allen people, working fulltime, nearly 16 weeks to complete the research work and begin to frame the wargame.

Members of a game's design team argue among themselves as the work moves closer to the finished product. One rule of thumb is that the first construct of a wargame is both brilliant and wrong, prompting us to tear it apart and rebuild it until we think we've got it right. Even then, we always run a test game, using our people and the client core group as participants. In effect, we wargame the wargame. It is not unusual for our clients to be unnerved by this exercise, because a test game amounts to an extension of our internal argumentation by other means. However, a client's participation is crucial because it helps us examine the granularity of the game: whether the level of detail is right, whether the approach is appropriate for the people playing the game.

If the test reveals weaknesses or anomalies we didn't anticipate, we revisit our methodology, fix what's broken, and run a second test game or a third or a fourth—however many it takes to produce the virtual reality we seek when we take the game live for a client. For example, we did two wargames for a capital goods manufacturer. We tested the first, which was to be played by middle-management executives and centered on cost cutting and product quality, and found that we had not plugged in enough numbers. We retooled the game and played it out.

The second game was to be for senior management, including the CEO, and we found through further test games that the detailed number crunching in the first game was not transferable to the second. We had to widen the lens and reflect the bigger picture. The objective for game 2 was to examine how the corporate brain trust viewed the U.S. marketplace for its products. We challenged the senior executives to describe their three big priorities for the ensuing two-year period. For each priority, they were to tell us what they were trying to do, how they expected to make it happen, how it would affect unit sales and revenues, and how it would change costs and capital investment. In effect, the testing between the two games altered the approach to the second.

The way the real game is played varies with the client and the game's objectives. Military games can involve a few dozen uniformed and civilian participants or as many as several hundred, and can be a single game played in a day or a series of games played episodically over many months. However, most wargames for the government, commercial clients, and nonprofit groups play out over two days with anywhere from 50 to 100 participants and simulate a period of time in the future: a few months to a decade or even more in certain types of military wargames.

Older wargames were played on tabletops or other flat surfaces, with distances and topography adjusted to scale and with moves required of the players. Modern wargames usually are played in moves, too. The typical game consists of three moves, the first of which is a reaction to the world as it is or to a scenario or environment supplied by our design team. Why three? Through trial and error, we have learned that a three-move exercise provides the flexibility to develop and complete the game without placing an unreasonable burden on the players' time. Three moves, furthermore, give the players enough experience with the possible scenarios to get to the endgame and envision a resolution.

Booz Allen wargamers serve as the control group during the game, adding new information or scenario shifts—"injects" in our parlance—as the subsequent moves unfold. In a military or business game or a game on a major public policy issue, teams of competitors, adversaries, or stakeholders react to the initial scenario—for example, a major regulatory change in the commercial airline business, the imminent auction of wireless leases, a different approach to missile defense, or the deaths of a few people from avian flu in two large cities.

Team members come from the client: uniformed and civilian personnel in military games, executives in business games, invitees in games we cosponsor with nonprofit groups. We and our client determine which teams will be represented and who will play on each one; we generally mix it up so that many participants get the chance to walk in someone else's shoes by playing an adversary or competitor. Teams usually meet in separate rooms or at separate tables if the game is staged in a huge ballroom. As the game proceeds, teams designate a spokesperson to brief everyone else in a plenary session after each move. There is plenty of opportunity for interteam communication and no small amount of confusion as the participants grapple with alterations in their virtual environment supplied by control.

Our wargaming, as we indicated earlier, has deep historical roots that stretch back millennia, but it also has a contemporary context in the broad field of simulations for the management of large enterprises. These management games basically trace their beginnings to the Massachusetts Institute of Technology. In the early 1960s, social scientists and computer scientists at MIT began experimenting with mainframe computer languages to create rehearsal spaces for what they thought of, even then, as a new form of thinking—what we have come to call artificial intelligence.

No one did more to advance this use of computer-based learning than Seymour Papert, a mathematician and computer scientist at MIT, where he cofounded the Artificial Intelligence Laboratory. Papert is a disciple of Jean Piaget, the enormously influential Swiss philosopher whose work on the way children think laid the groundwork for the field of developmental psychology. Papert used Piaget's teachings as the basis for his own theory of learning, which he called constructionism. Papert defines constructionism as "giving children good things to *do* so that they can learn by doing much better than they could before." He theorized that people constantly build and revise mental models of their world on the basis of their accumulated experience. As he put it in his groundbreaking book *Mindstorms* (2nd edition, Basic Books, 1993), children are "builders of their own intellectual structures."

Constructionism, then, is the idea that the most effective way to pick up new concepts is through direct experience, in which one makes sense of the theory by "constructing" it out of one's own practice. Scientists were open to constructionism because of their laboratory experiences, in which they assimilated theory through experiments; the more they replicated the uncertainty in an experiment by not being sure of the answer, the more likely they were to learn.

These management games basically trace their beginnings to the Massachusetts Institute of Technology. In the early 1960s, social scientists and computer scientists at MIT began experimenting with mainframe computer languages to create rehearsal spaces for what they thought of, even then, as a new form of thinking— what we have come to call artificial intelligence.

In business, Outward Bound and other experiential programs applied the same principle to problems such as team management, in which people learn to grapple with uncertainty by being thrown into unfamiliar circumstances, albeit in an environment where they cannot do harm to themselves or others. However, there were only a limited number of business problems that an Outward Bound program could help people solve. It could not help people with strategy, finance, or choosing from among technologies. It was not until the advent of the computer that such testing grounds could be set up in virtual space rather than in the wilderness.

Papert coined the term "micro-world" in the late 1970s to describe any computer-based simulation space. The earliest examples of microworlds, using a computer language Papert had designed called Logo, were designed to teach school kids about math. The children were able to program the environment, see what happened, and then hone their understanding of the fundamentals of mathematical relationships. Papert used a turtle as the locus for his approach. It is a computer-controlled object that can be a physical toy or a digital representation. The child moves the turtle by typing commands into the Logo environment. "Forward 50" moves the turtle 50 steps forward. "Right 90" makes the turtle spin 90 degrees. The children then learn to program the turtle by teaching it to obey new commands.

The Logo turtle embodies Papert's approach. "Intellectual activity does not progress, as logicians and designers of school curricula might want us to believe, by going forward step-by-step from one clearly stated and well-confirmed truth to the next," he wrote in *Mindstorms*. "On the contrary, the constant need for course corrections, which I call 'debugging'. . . , is the essence of intellectual activity." It is not hard to see how the idea of microworlds migrated into the business realm to cover the whole spectrum of digital and live simulations in which individuals can experiment with responses and strategies to build their understanding of the dynamics that govern the real world in which they operate.

At the same time that artificial intelligence and microworlds were gaining traction, so was the field of system dynamics, an approach to understanding the behavior of complex systems, that is, systems that interweave with and affect one another over time. As our former colleague Art Kleiner describes in his book *Age of Heretics: A History of the Radical Thinkers Who Reinvented Corporate Management* (2nd edition, Wiley, 2008), Jay Forrester, a pioneer in that field, had grown up on a cattle ranch in Nebraska, experiencing firsthand the power of the forces of supply and demand, shifting prices and costs, and the various other pressures that affect ranching. An electrical engineer with a degree from MIT, he had designed servomechanisms (automatic control devices), radar controls, and flight training computers for the Navy during World War II. After that, he worked with the team at MIT that built the first digital computers.

In the 1950s, the thirty-something Forrester abandoned computer design to join MIT's Sloan School of Management and apply his knowledge to the real problems of business. There he met with managers from General Electric's household appliances division who were plagued by a problem common throughout manufacturing: They couldn't figure out why their Kentucky plants had to work three and four shifts a day in some years and had to let go of half their workforce in others. Forrester rejected the usual explanation of business cycle fluctuations. Instead, to better understand GE's dilemma, he reached back to the feedback control systems he had worked with during and just after the war.

He talked to the managers about how they made their hiring and inventory decisions and, using what he called "simulation using pencil and paper," worked through the way each decision would play out at the plants. Even if orders were constant, he realized, the GE approach to hiring and inventory would lead to employment instability. This was the birth of system dynamics.

Wargaming is not brainstorming, although some have made the comparison. Competition, a central feature of most military and commercial wargames, is not common in brainstorming.

Using his theories of dynamic feedback behavior and system dynamics, Forrester pioneered the use of "flight simulators" for management education. These devices, as the name implies, give managers a chance to test their strategies without bringing down the entire company. Perhaps the best known is Forrester's Beer Game. The game is played on a board by teams of managers or students and concerns the production and distribution of beer over the course of a year. Each team consists of players representing one of four roles in the supply chain: manufacturer, retailer, wholesaler, and distributor. Each "week" in the game, the team, limited to incomplete information about the market and the supply chain (just as most managers are in the real world), must deal with the vagaries of consumer behavior and the gamut of production and distribution delays.

Further complicating matters, teammates are not allowed to communicate with one another except through the numbers of the orders they place, and so they are unable to synchronize and broaden their understanding of the situation and coordinate their responses, much the way supply chain managers often struggle in the real world. As pressures mount, players are tempted to act in their own interests and against those of the team, and that can drive up costs.

Over the course of the game, each player collects whatever

Wargames often can lead participants to recalibrate perceptions about their competitive or political environment.

"data" he or she has to work with and then shares the information with the rest of the team during a debriefing at the end. The debriefing is when the "aha" moments occur, when players confront their false assumptions about their business and see how their actions have led to unwanted or unintended consequences. They see how their behavior affects the behavior of their teammates up and down the supply chain and learn that the mental models they have of their industry's dynamics, from the relationships among business partners to customer behavior, often can be off-base.

Simulations like the Beer Game serve to heighten players' consciousness of their own behavior in a variety of circumstances and encourage them to examine their decision-making processes. If you become aware of your own decision making in a game, your skill at decision making supposedly accelerates.

Wargaming clearly taps into some of the same insights: that leaders usually work with imperfect information and, given the opportunity to test ideas in an environment that simulates the complexity of their fields of practice, can gain insights and make strategic breakthroughs that lead them to rethink their entire approach to their work. But as you will see in the pages that follow, modern wargames of our design turbocharge these concepts and empower the players to take them in directions that lead to startling and often prescient conclusions. In the process, the games become nothing less than a remarkable and unique weapon in the strategist's arsenal—to lead, compete, and win.

Wargaming is not brainstorming, although some have made the comparison. Competition, a central feature of most military and commercial wargames, is not common in brainstorming. Also, wargames usually have adjudication: There are winners and losers. Brainstorming can be a valuable experience, but it is a bit like playing chess against yourself, akin to scenario planning, in which you think of things that support your viewpoint or strategy and tend to discount things that get in the way of your strategy because you believe they cannot happen in the real world. In a wargame, with teams playing different points of view in parallel, these affronts to your strategy can and do happen, providing insights that participants otherwise would not get.

Those insights, flowing from plausible scenarios in the game, can drive change in the real world. We had one client, a global financial institution, that wanted to wargame a new approach in its information technology organization. It had begun to outsource support for its desktop computers, but the chief information officer's group still was providing support for the bank's business units, such as commercial lending. The chief information officer's people had written a new organizational manual, and the game allowed players from the bank to play out the new roles and responsibilities. It was chaos: Manual or not, hardly anyone in information technology could fathom the new rules and relationships. Here is a typical exchange:

"What do you mean I don't talk to the PC suppliers? I always talk to them."

"Not anymore. Bill over here does that. You need to work with the business units."

At the end of the first move, the CIO and his deputy practically got into a fistfight. The next morning, we called a time-out so that we and the clients could spend a couple of hours talking through the problem. We found that their concept of operations wasn't working because it wasn't clear enough to the people who would have to carry it out. To make a long story short, they talked it through and identified the bottlenecks, and then we played the rest of the game. By the end of the day, all the players were on the same page; their positions, at odds when the game began, had aligned, and they now had a shared vision of how they would work together in a reorganized IT group.

Wargames often can lead participants to recalibrate perceptions about their competitive or political environment. At the turn of the last decade, an international packaged goods company hired us to do a wargame on what was seen as an emerging threat— Internet retailing, which was still in its infancy at that time. Narrowing the scope of the game, we agreed to focus on one country because the client felt confident it could extrapolate its "learnings" throughout Europe and North America. The client even provided a couple of business models to create an online presence; in those models, Internet channels would funnel the company's products to businesses that might use them, for example, dry cleaners and Laundromats. However, in the game, it became clear that the company really worried that it was going to lose touch with the final consumers of its products because big retail grocery chains would drive customers to their house brands in part by promoting them on the Internet.

As we played out the game, the threat turned out to be an opportunity. The company realized what it probably knew intuitively: Its brands had power in the marketplace. The threat was, in fact, a strategic opportunity to work even more closely with retailers and to redouble efforts to deepen the relationship with consumers.

In the end, games often produce astonishing results that lead to change in the real world. Game scenarios need to be plausible, not predictive, but outcomes sometimes foreshadow what will happen in a few weeks, months, or years. Consider the following:

- A major oil company needed a strategy for crude oil supplies in the Pacific Rim. The wargame revealed that an existing joint venture with another global company, previously ignored, might be the key. After the game, the company ramped up the joint venture, which became central to its Pac Rim strategy.

- A pharmaceutical manufacturer was considering vertical integration to gain greater direct access to customers. A wargame underscored the value proposition of vertical integration; shortly after the game, the company acquired a pharmaceutical benefits manager—a so-called PBM—in a multi-billion-dollar deal. Other pharmaceutical companies quickly followed suit.

- A national defense–related wargame in late 1998 suggested the changing nature of potential threats to the United States; the game concluded that homeland security would become increasingly important in an environment where nonstate actors could translate real or imagined grievances against America into terrorist attacks. Little more than two years later, the U.S. Commission on National Security/21st Century—the Hart-Rudman Commission, named for its cochairs, former Senators Gary Hart and Warren Rudman—completed its work. It recommended a new National Homeland Security Agency; two years after that, in the wake of 9/11, the Department of Homeland Security was created.

- A wargame on the increasingly clogged air traffic system that was conducted in early November 2007 raised a security-versus-convenience issue. In the game, participants playing the U.S. military were asked by those playing commercial airlines whether military airspace could be used, especially during peak demand periods. No way, the military said—not at a time of ongoing threats of terrorism. Two or three weeks later, the president of the United States announced that the military would allow its airspace to be used over the heavy-travel periods between Thanksgiving and the New Year.

As you will see in the following chapters, wargames can produce fascinating and useful results that can influence an organization's behavior—even if a decision is reached to do nothing at all.

CHAPTER **2**

A DECADE OF COMPETITIVE STRATEGIES

I n July 1947, an article of nearly 7,000 words was published in *Foreign Affairs*, the influential magazine of the Council on Foreign Relations, under an unusual author byline: X. The writer, most insiders knew, was George F. Kennan, then 43 years old, a veteran diplomat who was fluent in Russian and was an ardent anticommunist. The article, adapted from a classified cable Kennan had sent to Washington a year earlier, was titled "The Sources of Soviet Conduct." In it, Kennan analyzed the Soviet Union under Joseph Stalin, who by then had ruled Russia for a quarter century, and set down what would become the cornerstone of U.S. foreign policy for two generations. A short summary at the top of X's long article said it all: "Soviet pressure against the free institutions of the Western world is something that can be contained by the adroit and vigilant application of counterforce at a series of constantly shifting geographical and political points, corresponding to the shifts and maneuvers of Soviet policy, but which cannot be charmed or talked out of existence."

Fast-forward nearly four decades. Cold War containment of the Soviet Union, born in the late 1940s, was still at the core of U.S. policy in the mid-1980s, but change was coming. At the Pentagon, we were conducting wargames under an umbrella called Competitive Strategies, an initiative that flowed in large measure from the analysis of Andrew Marshall, head of the Defense Department's Office of Net Assessment. Marshall and others believed that the competition between Washington and Moscow—not only in military affairs but in the economic and political spheres as well—required measures to maximize our strengths and minimize our weaknesses; that effectively would serve to magnify the Soviet Union's weaknesses and minimize its strengths.

The goal was to keep the Soviets off balance—reacting to what we were doing or what they *thought* we were doing—and unhinge their military strategy. Stealthy aircraft, for example, demonstrated our technological superiority at the same time that it imposed economic costs by forcing Moscow to invest even more in what already was an extensive homeland defense network. The increasing sophistication of cruise missiles was another breakthrough, and of course there was missile defense. Taken together, these and other elements of Competitive Strategies completely flummoxed Moscow's military planners, whose spending, as you will see later in this chapter, already was breaking the back of the Soviet empire. In our view, Competitive Strategies played a big role in bringing down the Soviet Union without a shot being fired.

We want to focus on one series of Competitive Strategies wargames in this chapter and then turn to another, related wargame that in many respects capped our work for the U.S. Defense Department in the 1980s.

On March 23, 1983, in a national security speech carried live on television and radio, President Ronald Reagan teased listeners in his first paragraph with a reference to a decision he said he had made that "offers a new hope for our children in the twenty-first century, a decision I'll tell you about in a few minutes." Nearly 4,000 words later, the actor turned governor turned president returned to what he called "a vision of the future" with a rhetorical question: "What if free people could live secure in the knowledge that their security did not rest upon the threat of instant U.S. retaliation to deter Soviet attack, that we could intercept and destroy strategic ballistic missiles before they reached our own soil or that of our allies?"

With that, Reagan unveiled what came to be known as his Strategic Defense Initiative (SDI), or Star Wars in the shorthand adopted by skeptics, late-night comedians, and the media. Reagan's argument was that the concept of mutually assured destruction (MAD)—the crude stability derived from the prospect of mutual annihilation in the event of nuclear war—was a perversion and no way to defend a free people.

The fact that SDI would be dismissed as wildly expensive, destabilizing, and a devastating strategic failure was understandable. Missile defense had been a subject of debate ever since the Soviet Union got the bomb in the late 1940s. The central issue was leakage. The Soviets had an estimated 15,000 nuclear warheads by the early to middle 1980s, and the conventional wisdom held that any shield arrayed against them would have to be virtually perfect. The prospect of even a few missiles getting through was unthinkable in light of the destructive power of the hydrogen bomb. MAD indeed might have been mad; still, it had achieved a nuclear standoff that had lasted nearly four decades.

But was the conventional wisdom flawed? If you were able to shoot down, say, 99 percent of Soviet incoming missiles, would that be useful? What about 98 percent or 95 percent or even 50 percent? In short, how much defense would make a difference? And that was not the only issue. The second big question was how the other side would respond. In any war, cold or hot, the enemy has a vote. Would a U.S. defense system alter Soviet behavior? In the 1970s and 1980s, Glenn A. Kent, who retired from the U.S. Air Force as a lieutenant general in 1974, studied that question and argued that defenses deployed against nuclear weapons would roil calm waters, that perturbations in an otherwise stable environment were unstable by definition. In the event, governments ought to think twice, or maybe three times, before taking the potentially fateful step because it would be very difficult to know in advance how the other side would react.

It may threaten comfort zones to think of nuclear war and nuclear defenses as subjects for games, especially when they are conducted under the auspices of one of the governments with a finger on the button, but that is precisely why wargaming even the most troubling issues must be done. We cannot make this point too often or too emphatically: A wargame probes an imagined future for teams with a stake in the outcome and does it in a risk-free environment, before a critical decision can be made in the real world. Is any potential conflict more significant than nuclear war?

Andy Marshall apparently did not think so; that was why he charged us with developing SDI wargames as part of the Competitive Strategies initiative. Full disclosure: Coauthor Mark Herman also regards Andy Marshall as an informal mentor, someone from whom he has learned much during more than two decades of their association.

At Marshall's direction, we designed two separate series of SDI games that were played starting in 1987. The first: How much defense is necessary to make a difference in the enemy's offensive planning? The second: How will the enemy respond? You're probably wondering why we didn't combine the two into one game. Good question. The answer is that we wanted to isolate each issue and then look at the results together. On defense, the idea was to wargame the way the Soviet Union would act assuming a space-based missile defense at varying levels of protection. On deployment, the idea was to wargame what the Soviets might do when the United States put its first defensive weapon into space. How would they behave? The two series of games overlapped, but they were conducted as separate exercises.

These games were played in a large Pentagon conference room

featuring just two teams: Blue, representing the United States, and Red, representing the Soviet Union. Each team had about a half dozen players, with the cast of characters drawn from a mix of military officers and government rocket scientists assigned to the SDI office. At times, there also were some participants from what was then called the Strategic Air Command (SAC). Although the man himself was not present, the shadow of Edward Teller, father of the hydrogen bomb and a staunch advocate of missile defense as a science advisor to President Reagan, seemed to linger in that room.

We approached the first game—to examine how much defense was enough—with a hypothesis. We would start at the bottom, with no U.S. defenses against Soviet missiles, and then work our way up in subsequent games. The hypothesis was that we would begin to start seeing real effects when Blue's space-based defenses could shoot down about 50 percent of incoming Soviet intercontinental ballistic missiles (ICBMs). However, even with all the intellectual candlepower in that room, no one really knew. This was Schelling's impossibility theorem writ large: None of us as individuals could imagine what we did not know. That's the thing about wargames: We create the environment, the players engage, and what comes out of team play often surprises and even stuns everyone involved.

It is important to provide some brief background here on the ghoulish business of superpower nuclear warfare. Each side had what was called a single integrated operations plan (SIOP), which established a hierarchy of targets in a full-scale nuclear war. A prime target for the Soviets probably was what we can call our strategic military and political leadership, and Washington, D.C., almost certainly was at or near the top of the list in the same way that Moscow almost certainly was at or near the top of the U.S. hit list. Each side's strategic rocket forces were doubtless prime targets, and so on.

An operations plan also would dictate the sequencing of missiles fired to prevent unnecessary duplication. Adjustments would have to be made on the basis of the "hardness" of the target—that is, how much concussive power, or overpressure, the target could withstand and still survive. American ICBM missile silos, for example, are very hard: They are designed to withstand a nuclear blast, and so it might require several strikes to knock one out. In the end, it becomes a matter of mathematics: so many warheads to accomplish objective A, so many to accomplish objective B, and so on. This dispassionate drill sounds like something out of *Dr. Strangelove* because one finds oneself calmly talking about the destruction of a good part of planet Earth, but in a wargame, you have to suspend disbelief. You can't fight the scenario.

We played the first game assuming that the United States had no missile defenses. In an unfettered exchange, the United States would be reduced to a nuclear ruin, and the Soviets would have used just half of their 15,000 warheads. Russia would be a smoking cinder, too, and the United States still would have plenty of warheads left. But the point of the game was U.S. defense; with none, the gamed outcome was sadly predictable.

It was time to enter what-if territory. What if Blue had a protection level of 15 percent? In other words, Blue could shoot down Soviet ICBMs carrying 2,250 warheads. We regarded this scenario almost as a test game because it was widely felt that the result would be close, if not identical, to the result of the no-defenses game. How could a defense capable of destroying a mere 15 percent of Moscow's arsenal of 15,000 warheads possibly serve as a deterrent of any kind?

Here's how: The Soviet Union—the Red team in our game—examined its operations plan, its list of target priorities, with the knowledge that Blue had the capacity to shoot down 15 percent of its available warheads. (Most Soviet ICBMs carried multiple warheads, as many as 10 in some cases.) The operations plan had designated X number of warheads to take out a target set encompassing the U.S. strategic military and political leadership. But Red calculated, on the basis of its own experience and its knowledge of America, that the United States almost certainly would do whatever it could to protect its leadership with defensive weapons.

After all, if the leadership could survive an initial blow, it could carry on the war. As a result, Red reasoned that it would take *4X* warheads to overwhelm U.S. defenses and destroy the American strategic leadership.

Next, Red looked at its second priority, U.S. strategic nuclear forces, and concluded that they too would be designated for protection by Washington. What had been *Y* number of warheads to destroy targets in Moscow's SIOP needed to be multiplied to *4Y* warheads if success was to be guaranteed.

Red continued to move down its list of targets, calculating which ones might be defended by American space-based weapons and which might not be. Keep in mind that zero defenses led to the destruction of the United States and still left the Soviets with half their nuclear arsenal. But in the wargame, even the capacity to take out a mere 15 percent of Red's incoming warheads made a world of difference. Because of its concern about taking out high-priority targets that might be defended, Moscow had to add to its original operations plan in almost every case. With Blue's 15 percent defenses, Red exhausted its entire nuclear arsenal less than two-thirds through its target list. At that point, its cupboard was bare. There was no reserve capacity.

Shock does not do justice to the reaction among the players in that Pentagon conference room. The great insight that was not obvious before took everyone by surprise. Red, without knowledge of what was protected, had to assume that almost everything was defended. The necessity of a perfect defensive shield was shattered. We played some additional games with defenses in the 30 to 40 percent range, but it really wasn't necessary to go much further. The point was that even what was regarded as a modest defense against nuclear weapons could have a significant impact, to our advantage. Strategically, it meant the Soviets might countenance defensive arms, however reluctantly, because they could not afford to act otherwise. This concept gave new life to Reagan's SDI initiative.

Think about the strategic picture today, when the United States and its allies face countries potentially hostile to their interests—

The point is that deploying defenses creates instability even today.

North Korea and Iran come to mind—armed with, or intending to arm with, one or two or three nuclear weapons. In theory, an enemy with a single nuclear weapon could hold the United States or one of its allies hostage if, say, it threatened to launch its missile at a major city. But assume the United States has a half dozen defensive missiles, as it does now on Kodiak Island in Alaska, and assume they have been tested and are deemed reliable. That might alter the equation. A hostile power could launch, guaranteeing massive U.S. retaliation, but would that power risk a launch if success was unlikely or even an open question, especially when even a failed attack would invite a devastating U.S. response?

○   ○   ○

The deployment wargame posited a system of space-based defensive systems. Based on work done by Glenn Kent and the Rand Corporation, we thought the question to examine was how the Soviet Union would react to the deployment of the first defensive weapon. If the United States already had deployed 10 of those weapons and weathered the predictable expressions of outrage by the other side, putting up an eleventh probably would be no big deal. However, going from zero to one, we figured, would be a very big deal indeed.

We played this game several times, looking at the problem from several angles: deployment in peacetime and wartime, during a period of crisis and during a period of relative tranquility, when one side had defenses and the other did not, and when both sides had defenses.

The outcome of this series did not surprise us very much, but it did drive home how important it was for the two nuclear superpowers to work the issues. The situation was most volatile, as one might imagine, when one side had defenses and the other did not.

The perception that one side has an actionable advantage, where an asymmetry suggested the possibility of a first strike, was an inherently unstable situation. Deployment during a crisis would be foolhardy and dangerous in the extreme; it might make matters worse. However, even in times of peace, deployment would require careful management and as much transparency as possible, and even that might not be enough to forestall unintended consequences.

You might believe all this is ancient history in light of the collapse of the Soviet Union and the Warsaw Pact, and it certainly is true that tensions between the United States and Russia have diminished. But remember what happened a couple of years ago when Washington announced that it planned to place defensive missiles in Poland and the Czech Republic, two former Warsaw Pact stalwarts that are now members of NATO. The objective was not to threaten Russia in any way, the Americans said; the interceptors would provide a defense if some Middle Eastern country— read Iran—were to launch a missile at a NATO country.

Moscow went, well, ballistic. Vladimir Putin, then the Russian president, complained about "a new arms race" sparked by the Americans and ordered a modernization of Russia's strategic nuclear forces. Meanwhile, top Russian officials, including some generals, began to suggest that the defensive missiles might be on the target list in Russia's nuclear planning.

The point is that deploying defenses creates instability even today. When we put up six missiles on our own territory, in Alaska, the Russians did not even blink because the objective was well understood and the process was transparent. In contrast, the expansion of NATO eastward, to the Russian border in the case of Estonia, was regarded in Moscow as a provocation, and the defensive missiles went even further. The Russians were smart; they offered to supply the radar for the missiles, suggesting that everyone deserved to be defended. They knew the Americans would not accept, but they were making a point. We had touched a nerve, and the Russians wanted to send a signal that they were not happy.

◯   ◯   ◯

I n 1987, we were still living in what was widely perceived as a bipolar world defined by the nuclear standoff between the United States and the Soviet Union, but in fact the world was not frozen in amber. The West Europeans were getting stronger economically and militarily. "Japan" and "juggernaut" appeared regularly in the same sentence as analysts marveled at Japanese industry's amazing strides and wondered how soon it would be before Tokyo became more assertive militarily and diplomatically. Deng Xiaoping had introduced some economic reforms in China, and even the Soviet Union under Mikhail Gorbachev was at least talking about *perestroika* or the restructuring of its ossified economy.

Not surprisingly, at the Pentagon, Andrew Marshall's creative mind was mulling such changes, curious about how they might affect the relationship between the United States and the Soviet Union in an emerging multipolar world. Therefore, in the same year we started the SDI games, Marshall asked us to design and conduct a wargame to address another huge question: How will the nature of power—its very definition—change in a multipolar world in the decades ahead?

We did a series of games over nearly two years, but it was the very first one, in 1987, that produced genuinely prescient outcomes.

The cast of characters for the wargame included not only people from all over the federal government—military and intelligence officers, diplomats, economists—but also experts from think tanks such as the Rand Corporation. We divided the players into six teams: the United States, the USSR, the European Economic Community (the precursor to today's European Union), Japan, China, and the Middle East, mainly because of its importance in oil production. Our folks played control. The game also was informed by some simple economic modeling of the U.S. and Soviet economies. We'll concentrate here on four teams—the Americans, Russians, Europeans, and Japanese—because China and the Middle

East played considerably smaller roles in this 1987 game. The opening scenario was the world as it was then. To set the stage, here's what troubled the big four teams in the equivalent of move 1:

Team USA: The players on the American team worried about the U.S. economy. A harsh recession in the early part of the decade, imposed by the Federal Reserve as the cure for crushing double-digit inflation, had left a legacy of high budget deficits and a soaring national debt. Japan's growing economic power and increasing technological prowess could mean big trouble ahead for American industries such as automobiles and consumer electronics. There was talk of a looming education gap, with American kids losing out to their counterparts in Japan and Western Europe.

Team USSR: Mikhail Gorbachev was talking about change, but his objective seemed to be to relax controls to make communism more efficient. However, the economic model showed something else when it came to control versus efficiency. Lots of control meant little economic efficiency. Ease the lever on control, and efficiency increased, but it would be tough to stop easing up once efficiency started building a head of steam and moved toward unfettered markets. In short, the Kremlin could misjudge the process and lose control entirely. At the same time, the Soviet team was recognizing that the USSR, though it coveted trade with the EEC and Japan, had no real allies in the world.

Team EEC: The Europeans wanted to end the antagonism with Eastern Europe, in part because they craved the obvious investment opportunities that would spring up if the countries in the Soviet orbit were set free. They also wanted to trade more openly and aggressively with Russia. "I like Mr. Gorbachev. We can do business together," British Prime Minister Margaret Thatcher had said. But it would not be easy in the existing Cold War framework. Something had to give.

Team Japan: Japan worried about America's reaction to its economic rebirth, particularly given protectionist sentiments in certain sectors of U.S. industry. The Japanese also wondered whether America's commitment to protect them against any aggressors would remain strong, especially if China emerged as a world economic power. There was even talk of significant rearmament in Japan.

○   ○   ○

As the game moved forward, the American team made some consequential decisions. The players, realizing that American strength might be threatened by rising economic powers such as Japan, the EEC, and even China, decided it was time to reduce the rate of growth in military spending as one step in a program to cut the budget deficit and reduce the fiscal drag on the economy. The team also took steps to invest more in education and technology.

The USSR team, in many respects the linchpin of the wargame, knew that its economy was seriously stressed, not least by the weight of its military spending. A debate had raged about just how much Moscow was spending on its military. The CIA pegged the figure at roughly 20 percent of gross domestic product, more than three times what the United States spent as a percentage of GDP. That would have been bad enough. But Dr. Charles Wolf, Jr., an economist affiliated with the Rand Corporation who had examined the Soviet economy in exhaustive detail, suggested that the CIA and others had understated what the Soviets were spending. Wolf pegged the figure at roughly 50 percent of GDP. No wonder their economy was such a mess. The Soviets were vulnerable to radical change if someone pushed the right button.

Control added an inject to the evolving scenario. Romania was a Soviet satellite long under the thumb of a brutal dictator, Nicolae Ceausescu. His "death" in the wargame, however, meant that a new leader had taken power, promising to take the country in a new, more democratic direction. The inject inspired the EEC team to think the unthinkable. A designated player from the EEC came to control with a proposition: "Look, we've got to reduce the threat in Eastern Europe. Will you permit us to approach the USSR team with a proposal?" We heard the proposal and said yes.

The EEC wrote down its question—we do such things by e-mail in today's games—and handed it to the USSR team: "If Romania under its new leader wants to leave the Warsaw Pact, would you allow it to happen without intervention or threats?"

George Kennan had written that the first time the Soviet Union did not crush a rebellion in its Eastern European empire, the entire edifice would begin to collapse. In our game, Kennan's prediction proved accurate. The USSR, desperate for trade with the West and unable to afford the cost of its empire, said it would let Romania go without a bang or a whimper. In our game, that was the beginning of the end for the Soviet empire and the USSR itself.

Here's the astonishing short list of what happened in our 1987 game compared with what soon occurred in the real world:

- In the game, all of Eastern Europe opened to the West without Soviet objection. (In fact it did, starting with Poland in June 1989 and Hungary three months later. Romania? Ceausescu was tossed out in 1989, but democracy did not flower until the middle 1990s.)

- East Germany and West Germany reunited quickly, without Soviet objection. (The Berlin Wall came down in November 1989, and the Germanys reunited in October 1990.)

- The Warsaw Treaty Organization, or Warsaw Pact, signed in 1955, collapsed fairly quickly. (It did that in June 1991).

- The Union of Soviet Socialist Republics failed economically within two years and imploded politically. (It did that between August and December 1991.)

George Kennan had written that the first time the Soviet Union did not crush a rebellion in its Eastern European empire, the entire edifice would begin to collapse. In our game, Kennan's prediction proved accurate.

It is possible that some academics and government analysts were forecasting such imminent changes in the 1980s; if so, they did not have much of an audience. In fact, one of the CIA's Soviet experts, a participant in our wargame, regarded its conclusions as unrealistic and a waste of the agency's time; he left in a huff. Two years later, with thousands joyously chipping a piece of history from the falling Berlin Wall, he called to express wonder at our game's outcome and to apologize for walking out.

The collapse of the USSR and its empire also triggered something else in the game. Team USA, which had begun to tighten military spending, continued to do so in projections through the next decade and beyond. By the late 1990s, in the team's economic model, reduced military spending and a booming economy generating increased tax revenues produced actual budget surpluses. One Army colonel who was playing on the U.S. team hooted at that one: "Yeah, but we'll never have the political will or stomach to make that happen." In fact, the U.S. government did run a few budget surpluses at the turn of the last decade.

As we always say, wargames pose plausible scenarios; they do not predict. But sometimes life imitates art.

CHAPTER 3

GULF WARS (THE REST OF THE STORY)

I t is no secret that Anthony Zinni, the four-star general who headed Central Command (CENTCOM) in the late 1990s and who is now retired, became a fierce critic of the way the occupation of Iraq was handled after the fall of Saddam Hussein. As he put it in his book *The Battle for Peace*, published in 2006, in Operation Iraqi Freedom the military did its job of taking down the Hussein regime in spectacular fashion, but there was not a postwar political, economic, and social effort of equal heft because the assumption was that it would not be necessary.

His point was that assumptions were made about how the war would go and how the Iraqi people would react. But what if those assumptions were incorrect? It is always a good idea to hedge against being wrong. A wargame can test a battle or invasion plan before the first bullets are fired and the first bombs are dropped—before the order to send men and women into combat. The findings from those games do not forecast outcomes: Scenarios for wargames ought to be plausible, but they are not necessarily predictive. Still, as they did in a 1999 wargame called "Desert Crossing," wargames can raise cautionary red flags that can be factored into military plans before an irrevocable decision is made.

○ ○ ○

Phebe Marr was right, of course, when she offered her startling analysis that early August day in 1990. She effectively knew Saddam Hussein's mind, anticipating what he would do and not do perhaps even before the Iraqi dictator realized it himself.

On August 7, Operation Desert Shield began, and the first U.S. forces—F-15 Eagle fighter jets—arrived in Saudi Arabia. Hussein's army never moved on the Saudi kingdom. However, there was no way to know for certain in early August, and the Pentagon planners with whom we were working were wise to play what-if in the subsequent wargames during the American troop buildup and deployments in the late summer and fall of 1990. The initial question was: How large a commitment of U.S. forces in the region would it take to stop Saddam Hussein if his military invaded Saudi Arabia? This was in part a numbers game, matching our anticipated flow of forces into the region against an Iraqi army on the move, but the game also included elements of warfare that are not easily quantifiable. Iraqi oil money had purchased a lot of gee-whiz equipment from the Soviets: Scud and surface-to-air missiles (SAMs), MiG-23 fighters, and even better stuff. In other words, the Iraqis had high-end technology that was not as good as ours but pretty good nonetheless.

What should we assume about their ability to use that technology to its full potential? U.S. pilots fly 40 or 50 hours a month to maintain their skill levels. Iraqi pilots, we knew, flew a tiny fraction of that in training. Factor this training gap into the wargame, and you had to conclude that U.S. Air Force pilots and U.S. Navy aviators would clobber the other guys. That's exactly what happened.

The point is that wars are fought by human beings, not by machines, and wargames that do not take into account factors such as training, morale, and unit cohesion are deeply flawed. The Theater Analysis Model (TAM) we were using in 1990 was one of the first to examine these admittedly coarse metrics of combat, and it paid off.

Iraq's army was big and conventional, a Soviet-style force designed to fight on flat, open terrain. It had been battle tested in an eight-year war against Iran, and its Republican Guard—almost always, in news accounts, the "elite" Republican Guard—was supposed to be formidable. But were the Iraqis really that good? Despite its superficial resemblance to a Russian force, Iraq's army also was built for internal control of its people. We assumed the United States could bring to bear plenty of air and naval power in the short term, which probably would slow an Iraqi assault on Saudi Arabia. It wouldn't be a cakewalk for them, and the Americans might even stop their advance. Eventually, with U.S. boots on ground, the Americans and their allies would take them on in a land war. Would they stand and fight like the equivalent of the Iron Brigade in the U.S. Civil War, or were they going to fold?

The Pentagon was gaming these questions with different simulations: TAM in our group and other models in individual services in the Pentagon. TAM did not really calculate casualty numbers, but some of the other models did. At one point, a guy playing one of the other games walked into our space. His group had played out the same scenarios we had and had concluded that if the Iraqis attacked a combined American-Saudi force, they would take Saudi Arabia and we would suffer 30,000 casualties. That was what his model said.

Interesting, but we didn't quite see it that way. He asked what we thought about casualties. He was pressing hard for numbers, so we tried to calculate as best we could, and in our model we couldn't even get to 2,000 casualties. We told him that the results would be 2,000 casualties max and we'd hold. His reply is not fit for print here, but Mark Herman was heard to say that his own parents were in fact married when he was born.

It was getting testy, to put it mildly. This was a fundamental disagreement: They said 30,000 casualties and the American-led force

The point is that wars are fought by human beings, not by machines, and wargames that do not take into account factors such as training, morale, and unit cohesion are deeply flawed.

loses; we said fewer than 2,000 and the United States and its allies win. We were working for an Army colonel who was in charge of our Pentagon wargaming group, and he wasted no time putting it on the line. We didn't tape him, but he got pretty cranked up. To paraphrase: "I've been a U.S. armored cavalry regiment officer and I've trained my whole life in this kind of warfare, and I'm telling you we can do this." Pointing at the interloper who had brought bad tidings to our deliberations, he said: "Your model's not capturing it correctly." Here's a key piece: His support for our conclusions turned in part on the critical assumption that the Iraqi army just wasn't all that good and that Saddam Hussein, for all his delusions of grandeur, was no Saladin. It's a bad general who gets his men into a fair fight. We and the Army colonel working with us had concluded that given the right combination of forces and tactics, America's good generals wouldn't be waging a fair fight at all.

The outcome of Operation Desert Storm proved the point: U.S. battlefield fatalities numbered 147—to be sure, 147 too many, but a fraction of our projection.

◇   ◇   ◇

In late 1998 United Nations weapons inspectors, frustrated by Saddam Hussein's delays, pulled out of Iraq, and four days later, under General Zinni's direction, the United States launched Operation Desert Fox. The bombing and missile campaign hurt Hussein, but his regime did not collapse. It was clear, however, that at some point either the regime would implode or Saddam would do something that would require American intervention to take him down. The first three phrases of an Iraq war plan would be the easier parts. Phase 1 would be war preparation, phase 2 would be deployment, and phase 3 would be decisive actions to bring the regime to an end.

A wise author once put together a construct on the three elements of armed conflict. One is the principles of war: the things military philosophers and strategists going back to Sun Tzu have written about and that endure to this day. Another is the instruments of war: the technology that is always changing, from rocks and blunt instruments to fighter jets, cruise missiles, and even nuclear weapons. Then there is the context of war, which is dynamic, layered, and often not easily accessible.

It was the context of war that concerned General Zinni. He knew that the outcome of a war against Saddam would not be in doubt: Iraq's armed forces would be no match for American military strength, speed, and technology. What concerned him was phase 4: the aftermath. He had testified on Capitol Hill, expressing his worries about a possible invasion of Iraq: not the winning of the war but the winning of the peace. His political bosses in the executive branch were not pleased.

Zinni had raised his concerns with his military bosses at the Pentagon, asking the Joint Chiefs of Staff to conduct a wargame on post-Iraq. The Joint Chiefs were not interested. One thing led to another, and Zinni, knowing that we did wargaming work for the Joint Chiefs, asked us to design and conduct a wargame that focused almost entirely on an Iraq war plan's phase 4. In short, after the fall of Saddam's regime, what might happen next? What about issues such as security, reconstruction, humanitarian aid, economic development, and political stability? If a wargame could shed light on potential points of stress in a post-Saddam Iraq, military planners could take them into account before a shot was fired.

We and our colleagues were impressed not only with Zinni's intelligence but with his personal commitment to the wargame. A four-star general with a regional command is something like a king in his world, often insulated by a cadre of senior-officer support personnel. In that regard, he can be very much like a corporate CEO. But in the political environment of Washington, subordinate

At their best, wargames provide a nonthreatening environment in which the collective play of partici- pants can reveal unpleasant truths about a particular strategy or set of goals. So it was with Desert Crossing.

to the Joint Chiefs and the military's civilian masters, he isn't even much of a prince.

Zinni, to his credit, understood the politics perfectly and left his ego at the door. Let us give you just one exam- ple. In one of our prewargame briefings during the spring of 1999, a colonel serv- ing as one of our handlers said straight- away that his boss, of course, would be in charge of the exercise.

"Colonel, the general cannot be in charge of this wargame," Robb Kurz, one of the authors of this book, told him. "He's a prominent player, but so is everybody else." By that, Robb meant the various Defense Department assistant secretaries and deputy secretaries who also would be playing the game. In fact, Zinni would be junior to them.

The colonel looked at Robb as if he were a madman. "I can't tell him that," he said. "You've got to do it."

Robb did, telling the general when he arrived in our conference room that he was a player in the game, not *the* player, and that he needed to make his case during the game and win on the merits. "Absolutely," Zinni said without missing a beat.

We built the "Desert Crossing" wargame, staged over three days in late June 1999, to mirror the U.S. government's interagency process, that is, the procedural rules of engagement established by the president and his National Security Council at the beginning of every new administration. In practice, we established three teams representing interagency working groups and separate teams rep- resenting deputy cabinet secretaries and cabinet secretaries, a Red team representing anticoalition elements such as domestic insur- gents and neighboring Iran, and a Green team representing coali- tion forces. At its core, the game was designed to address 10 central questions posed by General Zinni:

1. What are the key U.S. decision points and conditions for intervention?

2. How do the United States and its allies manage Iraq's neighbors and other influential states?

3. How does the United States build and maintain the coalition?

4. What are the major refugee assistance challenges external to Iraq?

5. What is the appropriate role for co-opted elements of Iraqi military power?

6. How can the coalition contain Shia and Kurdish threats to the stability of Iraq and prevent fragmentation?

7. What is the U.S. role in establishing a transitional government in Iraq?

8. How can the coalition synchronize humanitarian assistance and civilian and military activities during combat and/or peace enforcement operations?

9. How do the allies reestablish civil order in the wake of combat operations?

10. What is the U.S. exit strategy and long-term presence in Iraq?

At their best, wargames provide a nonthreatening environment in which the collective play of participants can reveal unpleasant truths about a particular strategy or set of goals. So it was with Desert Crossing. Participants were playing the U.S. government at that point in time, mid-1999, and their examination of Zinni's 10 questions revealed some of the dangers, shortcomings, and missed opportunities that later would bedevil the United States in the real world during the occupation phase of Operation Iraqi Freedom.

Desert Crossing posited several possible scenarios for Saddam

Hussein's removal, including assassination, a palace coup, and a military rebellion. Each touched off events—a humanitarian crisis, sectarian fighting—that required a U.S.-led coalition to intervene, quell the violence, restore stability, and begin to move Iraq to a semblance of normalcy.

In a game of four moves representing nine months in the imagined world of Desert Crossing, the participants identified several important learnings in their "After Action Report" that addressed directly and indirectly most of Zinni's questions:

Planning
The United States cannot afford to wait until after the intervention begins to orchestrate interagency coordination and planning.

Indeed, a flexible political/economic/humanitarian plan must be developed well in advance of military action. Agencies across the U.S. government should be mobilized for the effort, and nongovernmental organizations should be used as well. "Sustaining peace often requires more complex planning and sophisticated intervention techniques than do combat operations," the report said. "If there are severe disruptions of the infrastructure that impede normal government services, if food and drinking water cannot be distributed, if reconstruction progress does not provide incentives to refrain from renewing hostilities, or if minorities perceive the social system will not protect them, then peace may be lost."

Military Action
It should be "swift, large-scale, and decisive," not only to overwhelm any remnants of Saddam's military but to demonstrate a show of force to minimize violence and ensure security.

Zinni originally envisioned an invasion force of 400,000 because he felt it was important to flood the zone—to get troops into as many cities, towns, and villages as possible. The United States went into Iraq in 2003 with considerably less than half that number.

In the wargame, the general was playing the role of a cabinet secretary; as much as possible, we wanted participants to play at a level above their normal responsibilities to challenge them to think bigger. Zinni told the group that the military takedown of Saddam's regime was only the first three innings of the ballgame. "That's not how the game ends," he said. "It's only how the game begins." Even in the best circumstances, participants in the wargame agreed, coalition forces could expect civil unrest and insurgent activity, especially in Baghdad, Basra, and other large cities. Dealing with insurgents would require a huge military presence as well as coordination with other government agencies charged with rebuilding Iraq's infrastructure and services.

Political Stability

Regime change may not enhance it; in fact,
Iraq's neighbors may try to take advantage, particularly
if there is internal fragmentation.

"What about double containment?" There it was, put on the table by one of the players on the principals (cabinet secretaries) team. For years, certainly since the end of the 1991 war against Iraq, U.S. policy in the Persian Gulf had been built on a foundation of double containment: Washington would keep a tight leash on Saddam Hussein while it also worked to contain revolutionary Iran's regional ambitions. The fact that those two regimes despised each other did not make double containment easy, but it certainly did not make the job more difficult.

What would happen, though, when the United States finally toppled Saddam's Sunni-dominated world? Iran, those playing the wargame quickly realized, was critical. If the United States and its allies were not proactive, one player said, it would be like fighting a war with Iraq that produced a hidden winner: Iran. It reminded

Mark Herman of a question he asked students at the Naval War College when he taught there: Who won the Peloponnesian War? The choices usually were Athens and Sparta, but the real winner, Herman argued, was Persia. The two powers, Athens and Sparta, that had kept the Persians out of the Aegean Sea knocked the daylights out of each other; when it was over, the Persians were the only ones left standing.

In the wargame, everyone soon agreed, Iran was a key player, perhaps *the* key player, and managing the Iran problem would be critical to the mission's success.

Ideally, the game participants said, Iran should be engaged before intervention occurs, in part to convince its leaders that the United States is not threatening its sovereignty. Indeed, lifting sanctions against Iran may be an important part of a full Iraq policy. Otherwise, Shiite Iran might feel free to meddle in Iraq, given the country's long-suppressed Shiite majority, and expand its terrorist-funding activities elsewhere in the region.

The reasoning hit many players like a blow to the solar plexus: Iran, represented in the Red team, easily could make it more difficult for an occupying force to succeed. In other words, this particular enemy had a vote. (This is another example of how principles in military wargames have applications in the commercial sector. Even the most powerful corporations must acknowledge that "the enemy"—a competing company, a government regulator—often has a vote.)

Leadership in Iraq

It's crucial to identify potential Iraqi leaders well in advance of regime change, if possible.

The Desert Crossing players concluded that United States lacked reliable information on the role of Iraqi opposition forces within the country because its humint—its human intelligence—was weak. Meanwhile, "Iraqi exile opposition weaknesses are significant," the report said.

In fact, the report's language on this point was polite. The scene inside the deputies team when its members were chewing on the question of the Iraqi opposition was less diplomatic. The discussion had turned to the identity of Iraqi opposition figures such as Ahmed Chalabi, who had left his homeland in the mid-1950s and had lived largely in exile ever since. "Well, what do we know about these people?" someone asked. Dead silence. "Well, what's their position? Who are they?" Dead silence again.

Remember, these were U.S. government people playing the game—people in a position to know the answers to such questions. But even those in the intelligence community could not respond with anything but dead silence.

Exit Strategy

The preferred "end state" for Iraq was a unified country with self-reliant political and economic systems, a stable security environment free from internal and external threats, respect for human rights and decent treatment of its own people, and recognition of its international borders and obligations.

Realizing these objectives would signal a withdrawal of the U.S. and coalition presence. However, even in the best circumstances, even if the coalition did everything right, the report concluded, it might take years to achieve that end state.

"The [Desert Crossing] scenarios looked closely at humanitarian, security, political, economic, and other reconstruction issues," Zinni wrote in one of his books. "We looked at food, clean water, electricity, refugees, Shia versus Sunnis, Kurds versus the other Iraqis, Turks versus Kurds, and the power vacuum that surely would follow the collapse of the regime [since Saddam had pretty successfully eliminated any local opposition]." In short, Zinni said, the wargame examined many of the enormous problems the United States faced after Operation Iraqi Freedom brought down Hussein in April 2003.

But in those days Zinni was unable to spark much interest in a post-Hussein Iraq. "You can't really blame [anyone] for this," he wrote. "Nobody saw Iraq as a really pressing threat. . . . Besides, we had other, more pressing crises to manage," such as Kosovo, Bosnia, the Israeli-Palestinian standoff, and more. Still, he said, somebody had to start planning for a post-Hussein Iraq. He got his people at CENTCOM on the case, but the plan "was nowhere near materializing" by the time he left in mid-2000.

CHAPTER 4

THE AGE OF
TRANSFORMATION

T he United States had designed its military and its military procurement for more than half a century for one fundamental purpose: to defeat the Soviet Union if the two superpowers ever engaged in armed combat or, at a minimum, to contain it and its empire of communist states. Along the way, the two sides fought proxy wars, or what they thought were proxy wars, around the globe, from Korea and Vietnam to Angola, Nicaragua, and El Salvador. With the collapse of the USSR and with its former satellites in Eastern Europe becoming democracies and even members of NATO and the European Union, American policymakers and military planners were confronted with questions unique in their adult lifetimes: How do we take a military fashioned largely for one purpose and redesign it to meet an entirely different set of challenges? Do we simply tweak the force here and there and modernize our equipment, or do altered circumstances require us to transform the entire enterprise? In budgetary terms, it came down to three big questions: What do I keep? What do I cut? What do I buy?

Starting in the 1990s, at the behest of the U.S. Department of Defense, we began to design and conduct wargames that addressed these questions of a large and complex military undergoing transformation in the wake of the Cold War. One such series of wargames lent special urgency to the Pentagon's Quadrennial Defense Review (QDR). The QDR is a comprehensive examination of the national defense strategy, mandated by congressional legislation, that attempts to look forward a decade. In the 1990s and in the current decade, we have participated every four years in this important exercise with wargames that are designed to address key issues raised by Congress in its QDR enabling law for each cycle. Classification restrictions, which we scrupulously obey, prevent us from providing specific details on the scenarios in the games. However, by taking you inside "Dynamic Commitment," the name given to the set of wargames we did for the 1996–1997 Quadrennial Defense Review, we can give you a real sense of the questions on the table, how the games were played, and what we and our client, the U.S. Department of Defense, learned from the exercise.

Congress had focused on a handful of key issues. First and foremost, Congress wanted the QDR to include the force structure best suited to implement the recommended defense strategy.

Congress also sought answers to some key questions: What manpower policies were required under the defense strategy to support engagements in conflicts lasting more than four months? What were the anticipated roles and missions of reserve components in the defense strategy? What reserve forces, capabilities, and equipment would be necessary to assure that those roles and missions were discharged capably? What was the appropriate ratio of combat forces to support forces—commonly called the tooth-to-tail ratio—in the defense strategy? What airlift and sealift capacity would be required? Under the defense strategy, in the event of conflict in two or more regions of the world, to what extent would resources need to be shifted among them?

The American defense strategy going into Dynamic Commitment was predicated on the proposition that the U.S. military should be prepared to fight two major theater, or regional, wars simultaneously, at least for a few months. That still had to be a part of our series of games. Indeed, the big question for us in designing the games was this: If you ran the military the way you might anticipate running it over the next decade, including the possibility of a significant conflict or perhaps two, could the force handle it?

All wargames look forward and do so in the context of pertinent history. What we needed to do was go back and examine the frequency of various kinds of missions the military had been asked to carry out over the previous decade. That decade encompassed Operation Desert Storm in 1991, of course, but it also included noncombatant evacuation operations for the State Department, Hurricane Andrew in 1992, blockades at sea in conjunction with the Drug Enforcement Administration, the training of other militaries overseas, and other tasks that fell outside the confines of the two-regional-war configuration. Our job, then, was to stress the military with wargame scenarios that exposed how well it would hold up and what, if anything, might break. Again, if you have the opportunity to learn about potential tactical and strategic outcomes in the risk-free world of a wargame, why not take advantage of it?

The Dynamic Commitment wargames were staged at our offices in McLean, Virginia, and included so many uniformed officers—up to 250—that the place at times looked more like nearby Fort Myer than like our headquarters conference center. Each of the four wargames in the series ran for two to four days. The team setup was more complicated than most. There were two principal playing teams (the Blues) and several other color-designated teams that provided support to both Blues. For example, the Silver team was in charge of oversight and arbitration, and the Gold team provided risk assessment of the two Blue teams' decisions. Two Green teams evaluated logistical and personnel decisions as well as command, control, and communications feasibility.

In planning the game, we and our military counterparts from the Joint Staff developed a bank of 50 "vignettes": scenarios of situational events or crises that required the commitment of U.S.

All wargames look forward and do so in the context of pertinent history. What we needed to do was go back and examine the frequency of various kinds of missions the military had been asked to carry out over the previous decade.

forces and might occur even during a time of a larger conflict or two. The vignettes fell into 10 categories: opposed intervention, crisis response, noncombatant evacuation operation, peace operation, humanitarian assistance, maritime sanction, a show of force, interception of illegal aliens, disaster relief, and enforcement of a no-fly zone.

The players knew the vignette categories but not the specific scenarios. When a Dynamic Commitment wargame began, we would put on the screen in the conference center a scenario directed at, say, Pacific Command. The commander of Pacific Command or a designated admiral or general then would develop a concept of operations to deal with the scenario and request from other players what he needed to deploy. For example, if the scenario involved a major opposed intervention, Pacific Command might want an armored division, an air wing, and perhaps a carrier battle group. Representatives of all the services were at the table. The Air Force might say, Well, we'll give you the Fifth Air Wing. The Navy: We'll give you the *Eisenhower* carrier group with the following ships in it, plus the Third Marine Expeditionary Unit. The Army would weigh in with the First Armored Division.

We then calculated, in the scenario, how long it would take to ramp up and get those forces where the concept of operations said they should be and how long, based on our recent history, the mission was likely to last. The stabilization of a country? Well, it might take two years. A noncombatant evacuation operation? Maybe a week or two.

The big point was that the personnel and equipment in those scenarios were not available for other duty for the duration of the missions. Those chess pieces were off the table. More than that, they would stay off the table even longer; just as there would be a ramp-*up* period, there would be a ramp-*down* after the mission's completion, especially if it was a major operation. Troops would need leave or retraining or, more likely, both; equipment would require reconditioning or replacement.

Keep in mind that scenarios overlapped with one another. That was the point: Our job was to reflect the real world as best we could by examining the past and projecting it forward not with precise replication but with creative wrinkles based on previous missions. We did not have time to use all the scenarios, but we and our military client used enough of them to learn some important lessons.

In preparation for the games and certainly during them, we literally had to keep track of where the U.S. military's people and equipment were: all the personnel units, planes, ships, tanks, artillery pieces, and much more. We didn't count the number of bullets out there, but we probably could have gotten pretty close if we'd tried. What we found was that the military did not really know where everything was at any given point in time. It had a fairly good idea, and technology was helping the logisticians get better, but there was room for improvement.

That was an important "learning" because the larger lesson was that although the force could execute the national defense strategy, the force structure was "fragile." That was the word used by three of our military colleagues—Commander Clarence E. Carter of the Navy, Colonel Philip D. Coker of the Army, and Colonel Stanley Gorenc of the Air Force—in an article they wrote about Dynamic Commitment for a National Defense University think tank. We discovered that in a stressed military, even one with superb forces and equipment, stuff breaks. What was the average time of deployments overseas for active-duty personnel? The average time reserves were called up? How often was the National Guard required to fill in for the regular Army? The numbers in Dynamic Commitment added up and raised at least a provisional red flag. As Carter, Coker, and Gorenc wrote: "Sequential deployments to smaller-scale contingencies may have cumulative, negative impacts on the all-volunteer force."

In that context, we found in Dynamic Commitment an entire

category of people and equipment we call high-demand, low-density, or HD-LD. These are things that are often very expensive—say a special satellite communications relay—and generally unneeded in abundance for any particular operation. As a result, you may not have many of them, but over a decade, with a military asked to respond to a wide range of scenarios, you need them often enough that you run out in, say, year 6. You might even have backup equipment, but chances are that it isn't as good. What about the special surveillance aircraft that are always in use? If you do not have enough trained pilots in the assignment rotation, you have a system that will break, perhaps at a moment when lives are on the line.

These are not real examples drawn directly from a specific wargame, but they suggest what we found: a range of things, people, and pieces of hardware that the military did not have enough of. We also found a bunch of items with a different kind of imbalance—an imbalance between abundant supply and so-so demand.

But it is the first category—high demand, low density—that should concern military planners. Operational units and equipment tend to become less effective in protracted periods of stress. As this book is being written, we need only examine the strain placed on our superb fighting forces in Iraq and Afghanistan. The initial wars in both countries removed an enemy from power quickly and with few problems. But the lengthy occupation of Iraq, which includes long troop deployments and asymmetric warfare as we fight insurgents, and the continuing battles against the Taliban and Al-Qaida surrogates in Afghanistan have plainly stressed the force, particularly the Army and Marine Corps.

○   ○   ○

Until Desert Storm in 1991, information and communications were important and interesting, but they were not treated with the same reverence as a major weapons system. If it came down to making the choice, military planners would never cut out a fighter program or a line of ships to make room for communications. However, Desert Storm, the Gulf War, demonstrated that command, control, and communication—C3, for short—had greater utility and mobility than previously thought. The networking of systems was beginning to prove its mettle. It was one thing to call a pilot in his or her plane and verbally issue a command. It was a different order of magnitude to move targeting and intelligence information around to large numbers of pilots or other personnel in very short periods of time—in some cases, the time it takes to make a keystroke. C3 (C4 when computers were added routinely) hadn't reached maturity, but it wasn't in its adolescence either.

The findings of wargames, with few exceptions, do not move seamlessly from a simulation in a conference room to immediate implementation and a huge change in battlefield tactics or strategy. For the most part, wargames are part of a process, persuading people that there are other ways to think about problems.

We did a series of wargames in the early and middle 1990s called "Nimble Vision," the objective of which was to examine the value of information. This is one series in which the scenarios and details are off limits, but we want to mention it briefly because the subject has grown in importance in the years since we did the games.

Information is not a kinetic force; some may consider it vacuous, something without substance. However, our charge was to see whether there was a way to measure the value of information against the value of "real" things: that fighter program, those ships, these bombs, or that personnel unit. This was not necessarily a zero-sum exercise in the sense that, say, an information network, valued highly, meant that a weapons system was destined for the scrap heap. Still, what we sought was an assessment of the impact and added value of information systems for the entire enterprise. Also, we were working in a budget-constrained universe. Depending on how the exercise turned out, the outcome might well mean buying, say, $10 billion of C3 and not $10 billion of something more tangible.

As it turned out, Nimble Vision, armed with data from the wargames, made a persuasive argument that C3 and intelligence, or C3I, had become a military force on its own terms, an asset with actual killing power, though measured in different metrics. Its use increased the efficiency and power of other killing systems, making them more valuable and certainly more dangerous to an enemy. Remember our discussion of dominant battlefield awareness (DBA) and dominant battlefield knowledge (DBK) in the Introduction? C3I ideally would combine the two to achieve unprecedented precision on the battlefield. It would bring together sophisticated electronic networks that can identify all of an enemy's positions (DBA) with the intelligence that can know an enemy's mind and anticipate the enemy's next move (DBK).

The findings of wargames, with few exceptions, do not move seamlessly from a simulation in a conference room to immediate implementation and a huge change in battlefield tactics or strategy. For the most part, wargames are part of a process, persuading people that there are other ways to think about problems. That was the case with Nimble Vision. The series of wargames did not change the world overnight. However, the wargames made a case for greater investment in C3I, and if you were to wade into the Pentagon's budget documents, you would notice a large increase in funds allocated for command, control, communications, and intelligence.

Nimble Vision left its mark. The takeaway for the military, now part of its DNA, is that information is power.

○   ○   ○

Transformation as a guiding spirit in the U.S. military has continued in the current decade and even accelerated in the aftermath of 9/11 and the wars in Afghanistan and Iraq. In fact, it's probably not much of an overstatement to say that the vast majority of our work for the U.S. military targets transformation in some way.

One of these assignments is a series of games for the Army called "Unified Quest," which we have been doing every year for more than a decade. Unified Quest may be unique in our wargames in the sense that the Army asks its men and women to look out two or three decades, paint a picture of a world that doesn't yet exist, and bring their best collective thinking to solutions for the military problems posed by that new world.

Most of the participants are midcareer people, majors and higher ranks, and the virtual world they are creating—the "Army after Next," as they came to call the exercise—is one that will arrive after they have retired, moved on, or passed away. In effect, this is a wargame about the future of their service, the legacy they have to offer their successors. They get the opportunity to free their minds and dream up new technologies and weapon systems to solve real and imagined battlefield problems. How about stealthy wheeled vehicles that can travel 80 miles per hour while they fire precision munitions at an enemy spotted by enhanced C3I networks? Can you maneuver vertically through the air along a corridor of hundreds of miles and drop a force that is immediately ready to fight? These are the kinds of questions raised in the play of Unified Quest wargames.

In fact, the future can arrive faster than a wargame's time horizon. When an innovation crops up year after year in Unified Quest, military planners want to accelerate its introduction and use; thus, ideas have an effect in the near term. The idea of putting weapons on unmanned aerial vehicles (UAVs), for example, first arose in wargames that started in the mid-1990s, including Unified Quest. By the time U.S. forces invaded Afghanistan less than a month after September 11, 2001, Predator UAVs were armed with Hellfire missiles and successfully targeted Taliban and Al-Qaida enemy operatives.

Over the years, Unified Quest has grown in size and morphed into a much more ambitious project. This sort of future think, implicit in the "Army after Next" label, remains central to the series, but the games now include the other services, reflecting the civilian and uniformed leadership's directives to bring "jointness" to military planning and exercises. Those exercises do not ignore the battlefield as it is evolving in real terms. Remember phase 4 from the previous chapter, the last stage of an Iraq war and occupation? By 2003 and 2004, it was getting fresh attention in Unified Quest and other wargames.

Our colleague Mark Jacobsohn recalls an episode in a force-on-force game from that period. Jake was taking a break in an area with a television, when a couple of Army officers wandered out of our meeting room shaking their heads. "This scenario we're wargaming is so unrealistic," one of them said. "We wouldn't do this." As Jake recalls it, the scenario had to do with variations in urban combat. The two officers glanced reflexively at the TV and a news feed from Iraq and then returned to their conversation. They should have lingered over the news clip a bit longer: There on the screen was a fairly close approximation of the scenario they had just wargamed and found unrealistic.

By that time our client, the Defense Department, had decided to go to a two-year cycle for the Unified Quest series, and that 2003–2004 cycle was particularly illuminating. The wargame, conducted during the first year of the cycle, posed a scenario in which the U.S. military, the Blue team, had to fight an enemy, take terrain, and overthrow a government. The scenario projected a time about 10 years out, and the point of the game was to test the Army's Future Combat System. FCS, which is by far the Army's biggest procurement, brings together new command-and-control and intelligence, surveillance, and reconnaissance systems with UAVs, sophisticated vehicles (non-line-of-sight cannon and mortar, for example), and more to create a networked, lethal, and lightning-fast fighting force.

In the game, using FCS, Blue performed brilliantly, overcoming the Red team's defenses and removing its leadership. End of game? Not this time. Instead of starting the next year, 2004, with a

FIGURE 4.1
The six phases of a military campaign

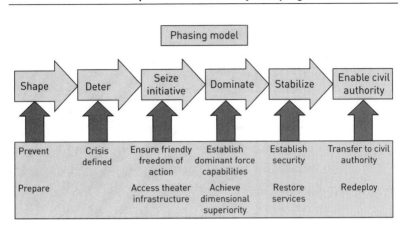

new game, we picked up the old game where we had left off. First, though, we gave Red some time to come up with a plan for a guerrilla strategy it could launch.

Our instructions to Blue in year 2: Now stabilize the region. But Blue was in trouble. It had brought a force to overthrow a government, and the FCS units had performed brilliantly. It did not bring an additional force to protect extended supply lines or fight hit-and-run insurgents. Could Blue count indefinitely on the heavy Naval and Air Force support it had received? Probably not. If this had been a chess match, Blue would have conceded. It was the first time in an Army wargame that Blue was deemed to have lost. The Blue team commander got it: He acknowledged that if had known he would have to live with the results and repercussions of his previous plan, he would have developed a different plan and brought a different force. Once again, the lessons of Desert Crossing were abundantly clear.

Unified Quest has evolved since then, increasingly focused on irregular warfare. In the process, the four phases of a military campaign have grown to six phases, only two of which involve force-on-force combat (see Figure 4.1). The six phases are as follows:

1. **Shape.** Well short of combat, joint force, interagency, and multinational operations attempt to dissuade potential adversaries and assure and firm up relationships with friends and allies. In short, phase 1 is the time for diplomacy and coalition building to see if combat can be avoided and to prepare for victory if it cannot.

2. **Deter.** The joint force demonstrates its resolve and capabilities with preparatory actions that can support subsequent phases if necessary. With the crisis defined, these actions might include employment of intelligence, surveillance, and reconnaissance assets to provide dominant battlefield awareness in real time; continued engagement of multinational partners; and coordination with nongovernmental and international organizations that might assist in noncombat activities during subsequent phases. In short, phase 2 is the time to get ready for battle and lay the groundwork for the aftermath.

3. **Seize the initiative.** The joint force executes offensive operations quickly, dislodging adversaries from their positions and creating the conditions to destroy their forces and their will to fight during the next phase. Getting access to infrastructure is important to ensure freedom of action. Crucially, the joint force tries to establish conditions for stability by providing immediate assistance to civilian populations affected by the crisis. In short, phase 3 uses the hammer even as it begins to show heart.

4. **Dominate.** The United States and its allies focus on breaking the enemy's will for organized resistance and taking control of the operational environment where combat is not taking place. This involves full employment of joint force capabilities and the sequencing of additional forces into the operational area as quickly as possible. In short, phase 4 seeks the achievement of military objectives and sets the

conditions for later phases with a large and civilian-friendly occupation force.

5. **Stabilize.** In this phase it is assumed that there is no functioning and legitimate civil government authority. The objectives here are to establish or restore security, begin widespread humanitarian and reconstruction assistance, and restore essential services. Military operations continue only insofar as they support those objectives. In short, phase 5 is intended to reduce the trauma of war and set the stage for a transition to legitimate civil governance.

4. **Enable civil authority.** The joint force supports legitimate governance, with an eye toward enabling the viability of the civil authority and its provision of essential services to the largest number of people in the region. This includes ramped-up coordination with nongovernmental organizations and international agencies. The joint force may be briefly under the control of the legitimate civil authority, but only in preparation for the end phase of the campaign, when redeployment operations are complete. In short, phase 6 makes clear to the civilian population that the joint force backs legitimate civil government and intends to withdraw as swiftly as possible.

You should think of this as a new strategic construct in a new world of irregular—or asymmetric—warfare. It is General Zinni's four-phase plan writ larger: If you do the initial two phases right, you might not have to fight; and if you have to fight and can do the last two phases right, you will not have to stay forever—and you probably will not have to come back and fight again.

5

THE U.S. NAVY AND THE POST-9/11 ERA

With a respectful salute to maritime powers going back to ancient Greece, the current U.S. Navy ranks as the most formidable fighting force ever to sail the seas of planet Earth. A single aircraft carrier battle group possesses awesome firepower: a naval air wing larger than the air forces of most countries, cruisers and destroyers armed with Tomahawk cruise missiles, a couple of attack submarines, antisubmarine capabilities, and much more. The first order of business for these ships and boats is to protect the carrier from any enemy bold enough or foolish enough to attack in the open ocean—the global commons of the Navy's world. But with the demise of the Soviet Union and the deterioration of its submarine force, today's U.S. Navy faces few real threats while it goes about its traditional business of patrolling and projecting power in blue waters around the globe.

Herman's memo found its way to Vice Admiral Arthur K. Cebrowski, an innovator who challenged orthodoxy in the U.S. military's concepts, processes, organizations, and techonologies. The analogue, he said, was to "a commercial corporate strategy for innovation."

In a post-9/11 era, however, it is worth asking whether the configuration of today's Navy remains the best way to counter new and emerging threats. That question had begun to vex some people at the U.S. Department of Defense and, frankly, some of us who do contract work for "the Building," as the Pentagon is known. Mark Herman, for one, had written a memo to Andrew Marshall, the legendary head of DOD's Office of Net Assessment, whom you met in the Introduction. The argument Herman made was that we were moving from a period of platform-centric warfare, represented by tanks, ships, and airplanes, to a period of munitions-centric warfare. Herman was suggesting that the vehicle carrying a weapon was increasingly less important in an age of "smart" bombs and other weapons systems that took advantage of breakthroughs in information technologies. These weapons—the cruise missile and the Predator drone with its Hellfire missiles are two that come to mind—can be launched hundreds of miles from a target, maneuver to avoid threats, and hone in with remarkable precision.

Herman's memo found its way to Vice Admiral Arthur K. Cebrowski, then the J6, the position on the Joint Staff in charge of command, control, communications, and computer systems. After he retired, Cebrowski was appointed director of the Defense Department's Office of Force Transformation. Cebrowski was an innovator who challenged orthodoxy in the U.S. military's concepts, processes, organizations, and techonologies. The analogue, he said, was to "a commercial corporate strategy for innovation."

Cebrowski, who had an advanced degree in computer systems management, had as president of the Naval War College conceded the fundamental differences between large corporations and the U.S. Department of Defense, but he recognized certain elements that were common to both organizations. Strategic innovation at both big companies and the world's largest military enterprise, he said, invoking Eric Beinhocker of MIT's Sloan School of Management, ought to embrace simultaneously three distinct processes:

- **A focus on core missions.** "This is basic stuff," Cebrowski wrote. "This is the realm of evolutionary changes where an organization simply tries to get better at what it is already doing."

- **A series of small exploratory steps.** This goes a bit beyond evolutionary change. It is where an organization, he said, "pushes out the boundaries of a core competency and tries to create something new." Cebrowski cited an example: the U.S. Navy's unmanned underwater vehicles for shallow water mine hunting and antisubmarine warfare. This falls into the category of a Navy core competency, but insofar as the technology makes it possible to do something the Navy could not do before, it is transformational.

- **A few big bets.** These are the things that change a military service, change the Department of Defense, and maybe even change the world, Cebrowski said. A classic example is Global Positioning System satellites, which changed the military, DOD, and civil society.

Cebrowski was particularly interested in the future of his own service, of course, and so he was receptive when Congress asked him to examine the way the U.S. Navy built and added to its fleet. The Navy's rationale for fleet architecture was a fair approximation of the old adage, "If it ain't broke, don't fix it." In practical terms, inertial tradition was at work: The Navy tended to replace carriers with the next-generation carrier, destroyers with the next-generation destroyer, submarines with the next-generation submarine, and so forth. Cebrowski's charge from Congress was to look at alternatives to that fleet architecture.

His 106-page report, coauthored with Stuart E. Johnson of the

National Defense University's Center for Technology and National Security Policy, made the case for change in the way the Navy thought about and ordered its fleet architecture. Among other things, it essentially argued that the United States was making it too easy for an enemy to detect the Navy. At a time when the Navy's budget might be shrinking, the United States had huge, high-value targets in its carrier battle groups that can represent a $30 billion or $40 billion investment—a national treasure.

As formidable as these entities are, however, they still could be tempting targets for accurate missiles fired by an enemy. Not now, when these forces are largely invulnerable, and maybe not five or ten years from now, but a determined enemy—and that could be a country or a nonstate actor—might well puzzle out weaknesses in the systems over time and develop ways to defeat them. That was one important reason the Navy had to change. No one was talking about phasing out the classic carrier battle group, but the Navy had to be a moving target; it had to innovate.

Cebrowski and Johnson argued for smaller, faster ships that could carry bigger payloads through the use of advanced materials and other technologies. The alternative fleet architecture would incorporate modular designs to allow the Navy to adapt to changing strategic or operational challenges. Network-centric warfare, a variant of what Mark Herman called munitions-centric warfare, would be an all-important governing principle. Advances in information technologies, they wrote, meant that dispersed components of a fleet, including unmanned systems, could be networked; as a result, the total power of the fleet could greatly exceed the sum of the capabilities of its individual parts.

Much of the report was aimed at confronting "asymmetric challenges"—that is, unconventional warfare threats from rogue states or terrorist groups such as Al-Qaida—but the ability to confront an adversary capable of traditional high-intensity warfare would not be sacrificed. In fact, the networked fleet could deal with new threats and old enemies with equal effectiveness. However, to get there from here, said Cebrowski, the U.S. Navy would have to move from the era of the few, the expensive, and the large to an era of the many, the cheap—well, inexpensive—and the small.

Art Cebrowski, a brilliant and wonderful guy, died in November 2005 after a long struggle with cancer. In 2006, in part because of our close association with Art, we were hired to design and conduct two wargames—one in April and a second in September—to pressure test this alternative fleet architecture against the Navy of today. The overarching objective of the wargames was to explore how the Navy could become more relevant in the global war on terrorism. Subsidiary themes included the potential efficacy of alternative-fleet architecture in missions such as humanitarian assistance, disaster relief, and noncombatant evacuations. In particular, the games were designed to identify and test potential missions for battle groups consisting of smaller ships that operated in green- and brown-water environments, that is, rivers and littoral areas close to shore.

Two teams played the critical second wargame, which built on the findings of the first. One team was the Navy of record: the Navy, already in the budget and procurement pipeline, that will be built between 2006 and 2015. The other team could trade off things in that existing Navy budget for other elements reflected in the Cebrowski-Johnson report and in the April wargame. In other words, the second team could say, for instance, that it wanted to use the money allocated to three Aegis cruisers in the existing budget to buy 30 smaller craft such as thousand-ton-displacement patrol craft or 3,000-ton littoral combat ships. ("Smaller" is a relative word. Even though it's only a third the size of an aircraft carrier, the *USS Freedom*, the first littoral combat ship, is still 377 feet in length. But it's capable of reaching speeds in excess of 40 knots (about 46 miles per hour) and operating in waters less than 20 feet deep.

The games were classified, and we cannot reveal specific scenarios, but we can give you a strong sense of what happened. For example, the fleet of the future did exceptionally well in all the scenarios that had anything to do with cooperative agreements with the navies of other countries. The reason for its success was that the smaller ships in the new fleet were configured in part for support operations. That meant you were not trying to pair up huge and intimidating elements of a carrier battle group with considerably smaller craft from a friendly third-world country; it wasn't the equivalent of the big dog and the little dog but involved a couple of roughly equal partners trying to operate together. Also, it was not a rejection of the existing Navy. What the games demonstrated in these kinds of scenarios was that for many missions—not high-end ones that involve high-intensity conflict in the middle of the ocean—the carrier battle group was simply overkill; there was a mismatch between its huge capability and a much smaller mission.

One issue, though, was how to get the smaller ships to a theater of operations and bring them back without huge cost, maintenance, and personnel issues. A key finding in the game was that you don't: The ships could stay in theater. The Navy would develop infrastructure, with the host nation's support, to handle fuel and maintenance and would fly crews in and out. The smaller vessels would become a permanent U.S. presence as long as the United States maintained solid relations with the host country. Indeed, participants in the games felt that the creation of a permanent regional presence of alternative fleet "platforms" could provide opportunities to engage a broad range of foreign partners and promote stability as well as increase operational efficiency.

There is a downside risk, of course, any time there are U.S. bases abroad, especially in the new world of asymmetric warfare and international terrorism. But barring a sharp turn toward isolationism, the American military footprint around the world figures to be substantial as far out as the eye can see. The Navy needs to do the best job it can, and these smaller ships, if they come into the fleet in significant numbers, probably can help.

How would they be used? In the games, the participants dealt with issues such as humanitarian assistance, piracy, threats to commercial shipping, and even what would be regarded as medium-intensity conflicts. This is where Cebrowski's emphasis on modularity comes in. The USS Freedom, for example, has interchangeable mission packages, giving it the flexibility to be recon-figured for different purposes such as antisubmarine warfare and surface warfare. Indeed, a modular force using easily switched-out assets would give the Navy the ability to tailor its responses to unique circumstances.

Many of the smaller ships have a so-called well deck at the stern that opens up so that even smaller craft can sail into it for mainte-nance and transportation; the well deck also can serve as a platform for helicopters and UAVs. In the games, modularity and the ability to fly were powerful factors in the green- and brown-water areas where a carrier battle group cannot operate. The participants also cited unmanned surface vehicles as critical components in the alternative-fleet package. These vehicles, enhanced with intelli-gence, surveillance, and reconnaissance features, would lead manned forces on key missions and become force multipliers be-cause they could "see around the bend" of rivers and other irregular bodies of water.

We also learned in the games that even though the U.S. foot-print overseas carries certain risks, basing these smaller ships serves as a kind of force multiplier. Remember, what the U. S. Navy is contemplating in this wargame is the potential to team up with the host country's military. Often, that country's force, particularly its navy, would not be as effective as its American guests. Let's posit for the sake of argument that country A had 10 patrol craft but be-cause of maintenance problems or substandard training, its readi-ness was only 20 percent, meaning that only two vessels in its fleet were operating at any given time. Without going into a specific sce-nario, we discovered in the game that we could add the equivalent of a shop unit to one of the U.S. ships, deliver critical maintenance support and training, and jack up the host country's readiness rate to 80 percent—a fourfold increase. Presto, a skilled U.S. Navy me-chanic capable of fixing engines and training host-country person-nel becomes a huge force multiplier.

As we always say, wargames give players the opportunity to cre-ate an environment to test plans without the risks of real-world decision making. In this particular case, what we call a build-use-build game, the Navy built a certain force structure, got to use it in a set of scenarios, examined the results, determined what it liked and did not like, and then remixed the force structure to play against a new set of scenarios.

This is conference-room wargaming, not a military exercise in the field. Under the circumstances, it was not surprising that the Navy wondered in the game how it could test the concepts of alternative fleet architecture at sea. That posed a problem. In the Navy, ships assigned to missions 60 days or longer, even if they are training exercises, are considered to be deployed. In light of the long distances involved, deployments can and usually do last much longer than the two-month cutoff. Ships assigned to missions less than 60 days are not considered to be deployed; they are said to be "working up" to an eventual deployment but are generally in fairly close proximity to their home ports, not really at sea. What to do?

Working the question in one scenario, we recommended that the Navy think about the Caribbean Sea. It offered an excellent combination of open ocean and coastal waters. Ships assigned to the task still would be relatively close to their home ports, and the Caribbean region could replicate some of the issues and problems that ships in alternative-fleet architecture might encounter when based abroad. Among other potential missions, there were humanitarian assistance operations because of hurricanes, drug traffickers and terrorist groups, and an oil-rich leader in Venezuela's Hugo Chavez who was increasingly hostile to U.S. interests.

The real-world environment of the Caribbean also might give the Navy a chance to test another finding in the wargames: the need to improve relations with nongovernmental organizations (NGOs). In areas of operation, the participants felt it would be as necessary to gain the cooperation of NGOs as it would be to gain cooperation from a local population. It would not matter whether the situation was an armed conflict or a natural disaster: NGOs and intergovernmental agency teams would head for the front, where they could provide aid and comfort to the afflicted. Through long experience, they also have efficient networks of communication and can distribute supplies. Encouraging NGO peak performance was plainly in the Navy's best interest, the participants said, even though NGOs might distrust military forces and balk at cooperating with them.

In a Caribbean test, the Navy could not use the actual ships in an alternative fleet-architecture scenario because those vessels had not been approved and budgeted, much less built. But it could approximate conditions by using some of its amphibious craft and other small ships and by inviting the U.S. Coast Guard to participate. We had been playing future forces in the game. The Navy could create the surrogate for a future force using existing vessels and then conduct normal operations in the Caribbean to examine how well this surrogate of a future force actually worked.

Wargames give players the opportunity to create an environment to test plans without the risks of real-world decision making. In this particular case, what we call a build-use-build game, the Navy built a certain force structure, got to use it in a set of scenarios, examined the results, determined what it liked and did not like, and then remixed the force structure to play against a new set of scenarios.

It takes time for the vast machinery of the U.S. Department of Defense to engage, and so we'll have to wait a bit longer to see if Art Cebrowski's vision of an alternative-fleet architecture becomes a reality. "Transformation is foremost a continuing process," Cebrowski wrote before his death. "It does not have an end point. Transformation is meant to create or anticipate the future."

In that last sentence, substitute the words "a wargame" for "transformation," and you have another version of how we explain the professional world we inhabit.

PART II

WARGAMES FOR BUSINESS

CHAPTER 6

IN THE BEGINNING

Mark Herman, the vice president in charge of the wargaming practice at Booz Allen and one of this book's authors, is an ancient history buff with multiple degrees that reflect his intellectual passion, a passion also demonstrated in the nearly 50 board games on ancient and modern wars he has designed over nearly four decades. In Mark's words:

"I got my start in the commercial world when I was a freshfaced receptionist at Simulations Publications Inc. (SPI), a company that designed wargames and made its money by binding them into a magazine called *Strategy and Tactics*. It turned out that SPI, my employer, also did wargame design work on contract for the U.S. Army. The Army, making sure that its contractor was especially well informed, had given SPI every single military manual in its library: a stack of volumes standing six feet high. With not enough design work to relieve the boredom at the front desk, I decided to read one of the manuals. To say I was hooked is understatement in the extreme: I read every volume within 30 days.

"Suddenly, this young guy, who did not know an M-16 from a peashooter before, becomes an expert in military ordnance and a lot more. Jim Dunnigan, head of SPI and a hall of fame wargamer in his own right, first put me to work redesigning a modern wargame

A military wargame was designed and conducted to test a strategy or battle plan in a virtual environment before the civilian and military leadership committed the nation's blood and treasure in the real world. A wargame for a commercial client could serve the same purpose: It could test a strategic plan, a new technology or product, or a potential acquisition or strategic alliance in advance of the company's D-Day.

system. Then he got me involved in the Pentagon work. I apparently was doing reasonably well because I attracted the attention of Braddock, Dunn and McDonald, a defense consulting firm. I was barely making ends meet in New York; when BDM offered me a job in Washington, I jumped at the chance. But one thing came first: I had to get my girlfriend on board. 'I'll go,' she told me, 'but not as your girlfriend—as your wife.' It was music to my ears.

"I was 24 years old in 1979 when I first crossed paths with Andrew Marshall, the director of the Pentagon's Office of Net Assessment whom you met in the Introduction to this book. I began to do wargaming work for Marshall under contract. My bride and I moved back to New York in 1983, and I returned to SPI. But I remained a contractor for Marshall. Other jobs followed, including a stint running Victory Games, a board wargame company; even so, I did Pentagon work as well. In early 1984, Marshall, apparently unhappy with the contract holder at the time, called and said, almost off-handedly: 'By the way, I'm moving your contract to Booz Allen.' In short order, I was a Booz Allen employee working with former Navy Admiral Skid Masterson, a computer expert, to build a wargames practice pretty much from scratch."

○　○　○

Because of the Marshall connection, our primary focus at the start of our wargaming was the U.S. Department of Defense—the Competitive Strategies games, for example, mentioned in Chapter 2 of this book. Commercial wargaming was still in its infancy as our military work was growing and maturing. In the mid-1980s, before Mark Herman was a full-time Booz Allen employee, some people at the firm had begun to think about the potential links between the two—whether our military wargaming practice might have practical and important applications in business. After all, the basic principles of a military wargame seemed easily transferable. A military wargame was designed and conducted to test a strategy or battle plan in a virtual environment before the civilian and military leadership committed the nation's blood and treasure in the real world. A wargame for a commercial client could serve the same purpose: It could test a strategic plan, a new technology or product, or a potential acquisition or strategic alliance in advance of the company's D-Day.

We began to talk to some of the firm's partners specializing in the energy, utilities, and transportation industries about the efficacy of wargaming for their clients. They were intrigued with the prospect of offering a service that might help their corporate clients glimpse the future before the point of no return. Among other things, wargaming could help ratify sound plans and strategies and, perhaps even more valuable, expose deeply flawed ideas.

Booz Allen's first commercial wargame was a case in point. In early 1987, one of our partners was trying to sell consulting services to Florida Power & Light Company, the showcase utility of the Miami-based FPL Group, Inc. It turned out that FPL's chief executive had some significant concerns on his plate. At that time, most utilities still were highly regulated; in effect, they were granted regional monopolies in exchange for tightly controlled rates. However, FPL's boss knew that partial deregulation was coming and knew that when it arrived, he probably would have to compete with another major utility on Florida's Gulf Coast. Even farther out, he speculated, what if the utility was reregulated?

He had other worries too. FPL was sole-sourcing its big transformers from a European company, and that exposed the utility to potential outages if its supplier could not deliver essential spare parts quickly. The company also had press relations problems.

What FPL learned, among other things, was that thinking outside the box sometimes can lead to foolish decisions.

Some members of the Cuban exile community in Miami were stealing electricity essentially by throwing a wire over FPL's wires; the technique worked, but too often at the expense of the thief's life—a tragedy sensationally exploited by the local and even the national media. The culprits were breaking the law, no question about it, but accidental electrocution seemed too harsh a penalty. The local media were on FPL's case, the story had gone national, and FPL's reputation was taking a big hit. This was not what its leadership had in mind when it talked about a consumer-friendly company.

Finally, FPL was worried about energy sources. It had nuclear power plants, but after Three Mile Island in 1979 and the disaster at Chernobyl in the old Soviet Union in 1986, utility executives across the United States knew that any proposal to build a new nuclear facility would be rejected categorically by regulators or smothered in long years of reviews and extended public hearings. Fossil fuels were plentiful, but oil inevitably was linked to U.S. geopolitics, natural gas faced distribution problems, and coal—an abundant source of energy in the continental United States—came with huge environmental baggage. In a few years, demand at FPL would outstrip capacity. New supply options were crucial.

When our partner mentioned the possibility of a wargame to FPL's executives, they were intrigued. They had been wrestling with these tactical and strategic issues for some time and were unsure how to proceed. Gaming out their quandaries before they committed billions to new plants seemed a no-brainer.

We spent two months researching the electric power industry, building a business model, and interviewing FPL executives. Creating the model might have been the toughest part. We always have some sort of model that we use to adjudicate the decisions made in each move and help us set up the scenario for the next move. However, this one was difficult because the variables—supply and demand, load rates, the pace of deregulation—were complex and dynamic. We built our own model, but we relied heavily on one FPL already had from the Electric Power Research Institute.

The game itself was relatively simple: There were two competitor teams (FPL and the Gulf Coast utility), a team that represented the regulators, and a team that represented the general public. The idea was to play four moves, each of which was supposed to simulate roughly three years, in other words, running through the decade of the 1990s. One lesson for us was that a simulation of four moves over four days is too long for commercial games: The players become exhausted by the mental gymnastics required, and it places too small a premium on valuable executive time. We were slow learners on this point, so it took us a while to streamline our commercial wargames. Most of them now run one day or two days, with three moves—a classic example of less is more.

What FPL learned, among other things, was that thinking outside the box sometimes can lead to foolish decisions. Going into the game, one of the utility's strategies to increase supply was to burn more coal, but there were those difficult environmental problems associated with coal. With that in mind, FPL had a plan to buy inexpensive coal in South America and send it by tanker to the Bahamas, where the company would build a huge coal-fired plant to produce electricity that would be transmitted to Florida by a cable under the Atlantic Ocean.

The team playing FPL brought that idea to the first move of the game, asking the regulatory team for permission to build the plant; it was "offshore," but FPL knew that approval by U.S. regulators would be a minimum requirement of the Bahamian government. The FPL team had been assured by a lobbying firm it had hired in Washington that the proposal would be viewed favorably by the appropriate regulatory bodies.

The lobbyists were dead wrong. When FPL announced its plan in the game, the public team went nuts and began to organize a massive protest and media campaign against what its leaders called a blatant attempt to sidestep environmental safeguards. The regulatory team, which was sensitive to public sentiment, denied approval of what one team member characterized as a "dumb idea."

In the game, it was a nonstarter, and FPL got the message: The offshore scheme also was a nonstarter in the company's real world.

FPL's executives also learned that they had to be more accessible to the public and more open in their communications. Their attitude toward the Cuban community, for example, had been that the accidental electrocutions were not FPL's problem; after all, the victims were trying to steal electricity. But they *were* FPL's problem, because people were dying and the press was crucifying the company. The game made it clear that greater involvement in the Cuban community, particularly with educational programs, would be a win-win situation: FPL would demonstrate that it cared about the loss of life, muting press criticism, and the incidence of electricity theft and accidental deaths would decline.

○   ○   ○

Fast-forward a year or so later to Peoria, Illinois, where a half dozen Booz Allen consultants had traveled to make a presentation to Caterpillar Inc., the colossus of earthmoving, construction, and mining equipment. Their mission, however, had to do with another facet of Cat's business: the heavy-truck industry and how a careful analysis of it strongly suggested that structural changes were coming. The industry was suffering from poor profitability, a consequence of cutthroat competition driven in part by deregulation and by European and Japanese expansion in the United States. There were a half dozen truck builders in the United States at the time, producing 150,000 units with little product differentiation. During the 1980s, average fuel economy had improved and prices had fallen 25 percent. It was a buyers' market. That was fine if you were Allied Van Lines or Wal-Mart; it was downright nasty if you were a seller of big trucks or a supplier to the companies that made them.

For truck manufacturers and their suppliers, it might get even worse. Greater attention to product and operating costs by truck buyers might result in consolidation among original equipment manufacturers and, potentially, a wave of vertical integration.

Vertical integration had special meaning for Cat. It didn't make the big 18-wheelers, but it did make the big engines that powered them. In fact, at that time, early in 1988, Caterpillar had roughly 30 percent of the market for big engines. However, that was a distant second to the industry leader, Cummins Engine Company, which had a market share approaching 55 percent.

The third engine company was Detroit Diesel Allison, which had been a division of General Motors until January 1, 1988. On that date, a successor company, the Detroit Diesel Corporation, was formed in a joint venture between GM and the Penske Corporation. Giant GM was the bit player, retaining a 20 percent interest; racing legend Roger Penske's company, with an 80 percent share, controlled the new Detroit Diesel. At the time, Detroit Diesel had barely 5 percent of the engine market.

Cat's Engine Division looked at the future with trepidation. The industry already was fragmented, with some players making both trucks and engines and others, such as Caterpillar and Cummins, making only engines. There had been a long-standing brand loyalty to truck makers: Fleet A or owner-operator B wanted a Mack truck or a Ford truck or one of the other four so-called OEMs (original equipment manufacturers). They also wanted the freedom to pick their engine of choice, which gave Cummins, Cat, and two or three smaller engine-only companies an opening to market and sell their products. However, vertical integration was coming to the industry, Caterpillar's executives thought, and they were worried that they would be left behind. In fact, alliances or mergers or both between truck manufacturers and engine makers would catch Cat flat-footed if it did not have in place a strategy for dealing with such structural change. Our people could help, the Booz Allen consultants argued.

The analysis impressed Cat's executives, but apparently not enough for them to close the deal and move forward with a full study by a Booz Allen consultant team. Amid the pleasantries that attend the end of an amicable business meeting, Paul Branstad, a partner based in Booz Allen's Chicago office, suggested something new: a wargame that might provide fresh insights that would be valuable to Caterpillar's management. (Note: In mid-2008, Booz Allen Hamilton, Inc. was split into two separate companies. One company, keeping the Booz Allen Hamilton name, retained the previous firm's government practice and continues to employ the authors of this book. The other company, now named Booz & Co., retained the previous firm's commercial practice.)

One Cat executive got to a pair of questions a second or two before his colleagues: "A wargame? What's that?"

The confusion was understandable because few wargames had been done for companies, even Fortune 500 giants such as Caterpillar or large Japanese and European corporations.

Our senior partners gave their Caterpillar hosts a short course in what our group had been telling them about the way wargames work and the power of creating a plausible future. "You are the ones who'll imagine this future for Caterpillar's Engine Division," one of our guys told the Cat executives. "We'll build the game structure, but your people will be playing the game, selecting the options that seem best for the teams you're on, even if it's a competitor's team."

Cat was intrigued enough to engage in further discussion; eventually, our wargamers flew to Peoria to fill in the details. Caterpillar's people liked what they heard and signed us up to design and conduct a wargame.

We spent three months learning Caterpillar Engine's business inside and out and educating the 40 to 50 company executives who would participate in deciding how the game would be played and what would be expected of them. It wasn't always easy. Caterpillar executives would have to become members of the Cummins Engine team in the game, for example, a prospect that at first put their teeth on edge. In fact, they bad-mouthed Cummins to the Booz

Allen facilitator who was briefing them before the game began. "I had to educate them to get their minds right," he recalls. 'Look,' I told them, 'Cummins has more than half the market. They make damn fine products, and they're making more money than you are. You need to play them as the company they are, not as the company you wish them to be.'"

One Cat executive got to a pair of questions a second or two before his colleagues: "A wargame? What's that?" The confusion was understandable because few wargames had been done for companies, even Fortune 500 giants such as Caterpillar or large Japanese and European corporations.

The Booz Allen partner who had brought us and Cat together thought we needed a market clearing model to make the game work. But we had a different idea. Given the number of engine-making competitors and customer segments, we decided to create a market team composed of six customer segments, an innovation that has become integral to our business wargaming practice. The participants were divided into six competitor teams that met each morning to make decisions that were based on the scenario for that day's move. The competitor teams briefed the market team on their actions over a working lunch; then the market team spent the afternoon responding to what the manufacturers had done in the morning. Our people, serving as control, took those decisions at night and calculated the financial impact in several categories, such as research and development expenditures, new products and services, and income. In other words, in the wargame, marketers made the virtual-world decisions and computers reflected those decisions.

The game began with the world as it was—that is, with American truck and engine markets dominated by American companies, but with growing pressure on prices, the prospect of increasing foreign competition, and a sense of unease in the industry. Alliances seemed likely, but the players were wary of one another, behaving like boxers probing for an opponent's weaknesses. Change, if it came, would not come easily in this wargame.

As the game unfolded, everyone could see why change might arrive grudgingly.Fleet owners continued to insist on maximum flexibility: their right to buy the truck and engine of their choice even if the truck came from one company and the engine came from another. That seemed to paralyze the truck manufacturers. "Why should we take a chance on an alliance with an engine maker if it risks alienating a big fleet operator who might want someone else's engine?" asked one member of a truck team. Engine companies also worried about what an alliance with a truck manufacturer would mean: Would a truck OEM support its new engine "partner" or continue to outfit its trucks according to the dictates of its fleet customers? Breaking with that tradition, it seemed, would be very difficult.

At one point on the second day, the Caterpillar, Ford, and PAC-CAR teams announced that they had discussed a possible deal in which Cat would become the preferred engine supplier to the two truck companies. "The teams had been cautious, playing the game like it was real life," recalls Branstad, the Booz Allen partner who first suggested a wargame to Cat. There had been some minor maneuvering on the first day of the game, but nothing dramatic until the potential for a Cat-PACCAR-Ford deal went public the next morning.

That news came as a shock to the Cummins team and got its attention. For Cummins, a Caterpillar alliance with Ford and PAC-CAR, which manufactured trucks in the United States and overseas under the Peterbilt and Kenworth nameplates, could threaten its dominance in the big-truck engine business.

The Cummins folks—that is, the Caterpillar people playing the Cummins team—went into a team huddle and then requested a conference with Navistar. Navistar, the successor company to a stripped-down International Harvester, made heavy-duty trucks. However, the Cummins players, looking at this emerging new world objectively, had come up with an even bigger plan.

We had a Booz Allen facilitator with each team, and of course our partners and wargaming experts played the control team—the group that updated the financials and other data on the basis of what the manufacturing teams decided and the way the market team responded to those decisions.

Cummins and its Booz Allen facilitator came to control with a proposal: In cooperation with Navistar, Cummins wanted to establish an alliance with Daimler-Benz, the huge German automotive company. In addition to its famous Mercedes-Benz automobiles, Daimler manufactured big trucks with the Freightliner nameplate that sold worldwide. In short, its truck operation already was a big actor on the global stage.

The problem: We had not created a Daimler-Benz team in the first place. But Cummins was playing to win, and this creative step on its part was a fair representation of the way a new alignment might emerge in a changing business climate. We let it go forward.

It fell to Paul Branstad, a member of the control group, to make the official announcement when all the teams were assembled in a plenary session. "I walked in, went to the podium, and introduced myself as the new head of Daimler World Truck, the entity that Cummins and Navistar had come up with," said Branstad. "The room went dead silent." It was the classic "oh, my God" moment. Then all hell broke loose. The other teams felt emotionally crushed: They had been outmaneuvered not by the control team but by what they regarded as a plausible outcome in the virtual world all of them had helped create. Here was a proposal to combine the global reach of one of the great automotive names with an American truck manufacturer and the sales leader in big-truck engines, a company, not incidentally, with tremendous marketing and distribution skills. This was precisely the vertical integration Caterpillar feared.

Other deals quickly unfolded or were discussed, suggesting that a global market in truck engines was coming faster than many of the participants might have anticipated. That certainly was one the most significant takeaways for everyone involved.

Our commercial wargames do not promise outcomes. They do manage to create an imagined business environment in which unexpected change occurs as a consequence of the work done by the game's participants, who in almost all cases are employees of the corporate customer. Often, although not always, the real world mirrors the game, sometimes sooner than anyone might have imagined.

However, the wargame, or strategic simulation, also indicated that even with structural change, Caterpillar probably had time to respond to the actions of others. In a world of new alliances, there appeared to be a potential role for an independent engine builder that provided high-quality engines to truck manufacturers that chose to be independent, such as Ford and Mack. If a restructuring occurred in response to bold moves by a few major players, Caterpillar probably would be the first choice for the remaining players. Thus, another key learning for Cat was that it was not necessary to push proactively for a corporate dance partner. If vertical integration was inevitable, so be it. Marriage might be in its future, but Caterpillar, with its strengths and reputation in the marketplace, did not need to be the leader in pressing for such structural change.

Cat executives also learned that their company was investing in technologies no one really wanted, such as ceramic engines. Japanese companies were doing considerable research on ceramic engines, which offered the promise of significantly longer life compared with the era's typical engine. Cat had to build one of its own, it was thought. In the game, however, the Caterpillar people playing on the market team—that is, the customers—balked at the very idea of buying so-called cutting-edge engines. Truck owner-operators and fleet managers were investing significant money to acquire engines, and they expected those engines to last a very long time. They were not interested in being guinea pigs. What they wanted was proven technology under the hood. Innovation would come, no doubt about it, but on the issue of engines for 18-wheelers,

Cat learned, being a follower rather than a leader was just fine and certainly more cost-efficient.

Our commercial wargames do not promise outcomes. They do manage to create an imagined business environment in which unexpected change occurs as a consequence of the work done by the game's participants, who in almost all cases are employees of the corporate customer. Often, although not always, the real world mirrors the game, sometimes sooner than anyone might have imagined.

In the Caterpillar game, for example, our host company and other engine competitors were worried about Roger Penske, the automotive entrepreneur who had entered the engine business from his base in Ann Arbor, Michigan, with an 80 percent stake in the new Detroit Diesel. Penske was more than a famous name in auto racing: He was an automotive brand with growing interests in truck leasing and retail automobile sales, plainly a force to be reckoned with.

As the wargame proceeded in virtual time, Penske's truck engine operation competed aggressively and began to build market share: 20 percent, we projected, within four years. The Caterpillar people were downright disbelieving even though it was they—those on the market team—who made it happen. The thing was, they were right: In the real world, Detroit Diesel had secured more than 20 percent of the market by the first half of 1991, less than three years after we played the game.

Caterpillar played in Peoria, and so did Roger Penske.

○   ○   ○

Postscript: Today, Caterpillar and Cummins remain independent engine manufacturers that are listed on the New York Stock Exchange, with plants around the world. Detroit Diesel pushed its market share to more than 30 percent by 1993, when it became a publicly held company listed on the NYSE. In 2000, Detroit Diesel was acquired by DaimlerChrysler AG, which already was a major producer of heavy diesel engines. More recently, Daimler sold Chrysler to a private equity firm.

The three companies compete with one another at home and abroad and with manufacturers based in Japan and Western Europe and have established vertical alliances with suppliers and customers around the world.

CHAPTER 7

WHERE THERE'S A WILL, THERE'S A WAY

A commercial wargame can have an enormous impact on a company's short-term future, long-term strategy, product mix, and marketing plan. It is rare indeed when the takeaway from a business wargame does not lead to direct or indirect change even, paradoxically, if corporate decision makers choose to take no action at all. Corporations, by the way, usually respond faster to wargames than do military organizations because money is on the line. The military is more conservative; that is generally a good thing because lives are often on the line.

We advocate some basic truths as our corporate clients contemplate a wargame—or a strategic simulation for those a bit skittish about characterizing business as a game. We do not reject the past: It's a critical factor in any judgment about the future. But we also believe that straight-lining a successful past into the future can be treacherous in a world of dynamic change. Increasingly in business, someone or something—a competitor, a government, or an accelerating trend—renders the old rule book obsolete. Think about the huge regulatory shifts in the airline business starting in the 1980s in the United States and in the 1990s in Europe or the onrush of globalization today. Wargames provide an efficient way to fill the void by creating a world in which decisions can be made without risk. The objective of a game may be to refresh a business unit's strategy or address a regulatory change; it may be to examine a product launch, assess the competitive environment and merger options, review pricing tactics, or examine the resilience of financial services.

People say things in games that they could never say in a meeting at their company because it's against the corporate way of thinking or because telling the boss it's a dumb idea might be an unwise career option. But by playing the competition or the customer, for example, participants can gain new insights into what is going on in the marketplace. Games can provide a naked assessment of interests—the kind of self-interest that, surprisingly, big organizations do not always perceive. They also can be predictors of what is going to happen or should happen.

Timing can be important. Once we were in New York talking to a company about doing a game, and one of its senior officers said they were thinking about staging it just before a board meeting. Robb Kurz, one of the authors of this book, felt obligated to caution them about the potential consequences: If you have it just before the board meeting, the board members may make a decision incubated in the game that perhaps ought to be slept on for a couple of weeks. Those were wise words: Outcomes in wargames sometimes startle our clients and seem to send them to the barricades; that may be appropriate in some cases but certainly not in all.

Here, three wargames for major companies reveal a range of "learnings." The first demonstrates how a CEO's objectives for the game were realized and resulted in a call to arms. The second exposes the weaknesses in a corporate strategy and points to a better alternative. The third indicates how an industry is likely to change even though the client company chose not to act on the wargame's principal takeaways.

○   ○   ○

In September 1992, Phil Fletcher was named CEO of ConAgra, one of the largest American packaged food and food commodity companies, succeeding his boss and friend Charles M. "Mike" Harper. Harper, who had run ConAgra since 1974, was something of a legend; he had built ConAgra into a $21 billion company with a string of acquisitions, and he took great pride in a corporate structure that gave each of those so-called independent operating companies (IOCs) tremendous autonomy. "There's no way I'm going to be another Mike Harper," Fletcher was quoted as saying in late 1992. "He's a size 14; I'm a size 12."

We advocate some basic truths as our corporate clients contemplate a wargame—or a strategic simulation for those a bit skittish about characterizing business as a game. We do not reject the past: It's a critical factor in any judgment about the future. But we also believe that straightlining a successful past into the future can be treacherous in a world of dynamic change.

Fletcher got the idea for a wargame from Harper, who left ConAgra to become CEO at RJR Nabisco. Harper explained that "the tobacco guys" at his new company had just run a wargame we had designed and staged and that everyone was delighted with the outcome. Give Booz Allen a call, Harper suggested.

ConAgra's new CEO was receptive because he had plans of his own that he wanted to road test; one day, he called up one of our senior partners in Chicago and broached the idea of a wargame. As a result, in late January 1994, having spent four months preparing, testing, and retesting our design, we conducted a wargame for ConAgra at a hotel conference center outside Dallas. The game consisted of three moves played over three days—longer by a day or a day and half than most commercial wargames now—and included seven competitor teams, one market team, and a control team to adjudicate the decisions made by the others. It was designed to project forward 10 years, and it was especially complex because

Here, three wargames for major companies reveal a range of "learnings." The first demonstrates how a CEO's objectives for the game were realized and resulted in a call to arms. The second exposes the weaknesses in a corporate strategy and points to a better alternative. The third indicates how an industry is likely to change even though the client company chose not to act on the wargame's principal takeaways.

ConAgra was a so-called field-to-fork enterprise: It was everywhere in food, from raw commodities to packaged goods in supermarkets.

We had to simplify to make the game manageable. In the end, we narrowed it down to eight ConAgra product segments even though not all the other competitors were in each segment. For example, Kraft Foods, owned by Philip Morris, and Nestlé were across-the-board competitors, more or less. But Cargill was primarily in grains, and Tyson and IBP were principally meat companies; in other words, Cargill, Tyson, and IBP were "field" companies in the field-to-fork food chain. We also had a competitor team designated "other," which included a group of five companies, much smaller in the food business, that might prove to be opportunistic players in the game.

The game's stated objectives were to elevate the level of strategic thinking throughout the organization and get it to start thinking globally; enhance ConAgra's understanding of the industry, consumers, and competitors; and identify key strengths and highlight how they could be used more effectively. Officially, ConAgra wanted to identify cross-business opportunities among its IOCs and start tearing down the stovepipes that isolated them from the larger enterprise. Less formal and unstated but no less important, Fletcher wanted to determine whether ConAgra's 100-plus IOCs could continue to operate untethered from the mother ship. There certainly were reasons for concern. ConAgra's portfolio of IOCs now included companies that competed against one another—producing and selling microwave popcorn, for example—and that in some cases were sourcing commodities from competitors when a viable source existed within ConAgra.

The opening scenario for move 1 was the present day, but the players were to look out about three years in their discussions and decisions. The initial play turned out to be livelier and less tentative than it was in many other games. The big companies took steps to enhance their strength. Nestlé, for example, invested in product line expansion in developing countries, divested itself of marginal products, streamlined its distribution systems worldwide, and generally reinforced its claim to be the only player in the game with a genuine global reach. Tyson Foods and IBP, two giants in the protein business, bulked up their pork operations through acquisition and expanded plant capacity. Cargill worked to grow its grain operations and flour milling into global enterprises. What did ConAgra do? In move 1, the ConAgra team established a new regional business structure outside the United States to manage an expansion of its brands abroad. Critically, it expanded its investment in information technology systems to support initiatives across several IOCs.

In this game, we wanted to keep score. To keep it simple, each team was assigned a shareholder value of $1,000 at the start of the game, and control and the market team used a financial model we built to calculate an approximate appreciation or depreciation after each move. While we were doing the calculations, the Nestlé team got cute: It asked the hotel turndown service to place a Nestlé chocolate bar on the pillow of every market team member with a note expressing the Swiss giant's thanks for consideration of its products. The gesture got a laugh from market team members, but they proved immune to Nestlé's clumsy bribe: After we crunched the numbers, Nestlé and Cargill finished in the middle of the pack, with their shareholder value having increased to $1,300. The protein companies, Tyson and IBP, were the biggest winners at $1,700 and $1,450, respectively. What about ConAgra? ConAgra brought up the rear; its shareholder value had increased 10 percent over the three years to $1,100.

Move 2, out six years from the start, brought a tidal wave of activity aimed at strengthening strategic objectives. In a joint venture with Coca-Cola, Nestlé expanded its bottled-water business in Asia and Latin America. In Europe, it introduced high-quality entrees and dinners with a 60-day shelf life. Also, in a major move toward achieving its goal to become the premier branded food concern in the world, it acquired Campbell Soup Company. Tyson, through acquisitions, joint ventures, and supply agreements, underscored its objective to become the top protein supplier to the food service industry, and IBP, through acquisitions and new streamlined operations, strengthened its claim as the most cost-efficient, vertically integrated company in the red meat business. Cargill was making supply and marketing alliances with players such as Nestlé and Tyson, and Philip Morris was spinning off Kraft Foods' food-service distribution, reorganizing into three superregional entities (the Americas, Europe, Asia and Pacific Rim), and taking other measures to achieve its goal of becoming the leading worldwide producer of packaged goods.

ConAgra, the home team, was active too. Its objective in the game was to become the leading global food company working across the entire food chain. To move closer to that objective, ConAgra used move 2 to build its international presence through joint ventures and acquisitions abroad. In the United States, it was investing in the commodity end of the food business by building new slaughter plants to process beef and pork and in state-of-the-art distribution systems in an effort to rationalize its portfolio of IOCs and capture cross-company market opportunities. Those measures paid off: Control and the market team reckoned that shareholder value six years after the start of the game had increased to $1,580. Still, ConAgra was lagging its competitors in shareholder growth, which ranged from $2,100 (Tyson) to $1,600 (IBP and the team of smaller competitors designated "other").

In move 3, the teams took the steps they had taken in moves 1 and 2 and played them out another four years to see how shareholder value would be affected. Everyone improved. Tyson again topped the charts at $2,400, IBP came in last at $2,000, and ConAgra was dead center at $2,200.

What did ConAgra learn in the game? As the only team competing in both packaged goods and commodities, it faced pressure in regard to where to invest: in international infrastructure to broaden its sales of packaged goods and make runs at Nestlé and Kraft, for example, or in the commodity business to compete with focused producers such as Tyson and IBP. It would not be easy no matter what the company chose to do. ConAgra found in the game that moves by competitors, if they happened in the real world, would make life more difficult for its IOCs. A Nestlé-Campbell combination, for example, would further consolidate the branded grocery business and strengthen Nestlé's economies of scale. Actions in the game by Tyson and IBP would allow them to reduce costs and strengthen their share-of-market positions. Said one member of the ConAgra team: "If we aren't competitive, there is no defense."

Phil Fletcher, the new CEO, found the game a real eye-opener and used a concluding 20-minute address to his troops to sum up the principal takeaways for ConAgra's executives. Phil really got it.

THE BIG IDEA What Fletcher suddenly understood from a perch in early 1994 was that a marketplace going global at an accelerating pace would change the nature of competition and that his company had to do a better job of deciding where it chose to compete and invest and where it chose to retreat. Going global strategically is a matter of picking your battle.

Here are Phil Fletcher's words to his troops:

- **"We must be prepared for the unexpected.** We cannot forecast what's going to happen in the next 6 to 10 years.

- **"Don't underestimate your competition.** I think half of you had the daylights scared out of you when you got inside some of the competitor's strengths.

- **"We have a tendency . . . to ready, fire, aim.** Being preemptive includes a little more than firing at will. Firing at a target that we know strategically is extremely important to both us as well as potential competitors.

- **"We need to make choices.** We can't underspend on everything. We need to think strategically about how we aim our cash flows.

- **"We need to grow globally.** We must find the organizational structure to do that. We have not to date.

- **"We need to identify our core capabilities.** The entrepreneurial spirit of the IOC is extremely important to us. By the same token, I think you saw that we are fighting some very talented competition, where some of our IOCs don't stand a chance in hell. We need to figure out how to deal with that.

- **"We have got to figure out how to leverage one business to help another.** That means a number of things to us. That means that independence for independence's sake can't stand in the way.

- **"We will retreat in some businesses.** We cannot afford to pour capital into every business in this room. Some of you will not get a hell of a lot of capital. You better make damn certain that you are a viable competitor in your industry because you will not survive otherwise." Phil made it clear that investment capital would be considered "family money," that is, money from ConAgra corporate, which would decide on the merits of capital plans proposed by the IOCs.

"Any questions about going forward?" Fletcher asked at the end. "Because now we go back to the real world." In the real world, Fletcher's tough words resulted in the resignations of a handful of IOC presidents in the weeks after the wargame.

A footnote: Tyson acquired IBP a few years later. Nestlé did not buy Campbell Soup in the real world, but it was hardly inactive: In the late 1990s and throughout the first decade of the twenty-first century, it has acquired the San Pellegrino water company, Ralston

Purina, Dreyer's ice cream, Jenny Craig, and Gerber Baby Foods. What about ConAgra? It has navigated some difficult waters over the years. Phil Fletcher was succeeded as CEO in 1996 by Bruce Rohde, who also participated in the wargame; Rohde was followed by Gary Rodkin, the current CEO, in 2005. In the process, ConAgra has become a leaner company with $12 billion in sales and fewer IOCs. In the 2007 annual report, Rodkin wrote: "Going from 50 incentive plans based on each operating unit's results to one determined by ConAgra Foods' overall results has made a huge difference in how we think and act. Alignment creates momentum." Maybe Rodkin read the report on the 1994 wargame.

○ ○ ○

The end of the Cold War and the collapse of the Soviet Union meant many things to many people. To the head of the avionics unit of one aerospace and defense company, it signaled an opportunity to try something innovative—and, as it turned out, controversial—and make a killing in the commercial aircraft business.

His unit was not in the top tier of avionics makers; it was fourth or fifth among a half dozen companies, and he was under pressure from his corporate parent to improve that position. In fact, it was corporate's idea to do a wargame. We had conducted a wargame for another unit of this company, and corporate thought it had been successful. The implication, the avionics executive thought, was that his business unit might be shut down if the wargame did not show a profitable way forward.

The wargame, in the early 1990s, had several general objectives. Chief among them were to get a better understanding of changes in the civil avionics industry and to get a clearer perspective on strategies that might guide our client's future, including new and potentially unorthodox strategies. The so-called integrated cockpit— a flat-screen LCD digital display to summon flight information in one place instead of multiple boxes of individual gauges—was just making its way into commercial aviation. The leaders in avionics already had made breakthroughs in integrated-cockpit technology. Our client had not, but the head of the avionics unit had an idea he wanted to explore in the wargame. The Russians had made some strides in avionics; he thought his unit could partner with a Russian company and produce a first-class avionics offering that would appeal to the top-tier companies in air transportation: Boeing, Airbus, and other big original equipment manufacturers (OEMs) as well as the big airlines that bought their planes.

Five competitor teams, including our client, played the game. There were two market or customer teams, one representing the big OEMs and the major airlines and the other representing general aviation OEMs (Beech, Cessna, Gulfstream, and the like) and smaller regional airlines. Our control team represented regulatory authorities in the United States and overseas.

It was clear from the beginning of the game that there might be problems doing joint development work with Russian avionics concerns. There was still unrest in the former Soviet Union, suggesting potential delays in product development; there were questions about technological compatibility; and even with successful product development, there were credibility risks: Would Western OEMs really accept Russian avionics, American partner or not?

Early on, our client's managers playing the market team of big OEMs and big airlines settled the matter. In move 1, they said emphatically that they would not put Russian avionics in their aircraft. "We don't trust the stuff." "It hasn't gone through any test process according to U.S. standards." "Even if we went along, the FAA [Federal Aviation Administration] would put us through so many hoops that it wouldn't be worth it." Those are paraphrases of some of the comments by "customers" in the game during move 1.

However, something else happened in move 1: When our client's team bid on second-tier programs with smaller OEMs such as Fokker and smaller national or regional airlines, particularly in Europe, they were more than competitive on price; as a result, they got contracts from the other market team even with technology jointly developed with a Russian company. Crunching the numbers at the end of the move, the control team figured that the client's market penetration rose substantially in the midmarket commuter category out three to five years, providing a modest increase in its overall penetration of the avionics market.

When the game was over, many of the participants said the process itself was so valuable that it ought to be continued in some form as a tool to enhance understanding of the company's strategy among top managers.

In move 2, the client team again tried to penetrate the first-tier OEMs and again was rebuffed. The first-tier market team insisted that previous experience with integrated-cockpit technology for second-tier OEMs would have to be a prerequisite for doing business with the big boys. The client team did not have the long experience the first tier required. Still, one of the big lessons was that smaller players could pick their spots and succeed and that alliances, on balance, were valuable. Technological partnerships with other companies, foreign or domestic, could reduce costs and risks. They also might prevent gains in market share because of shared revenue. However, the crucial point was that the lack of an alliance or alliances may cause a decline in market share. That is the case because the game revealed that no single company had a full product line across all segments of the commercial avionics industry. Alliances could fill the gaps in a company's portfolio of avionics offerings and make it a more formidable competitor.

As the teams engaged to compete for OEM and airlines business, an unexpected takeway emerged. In-cabin entertainment already had become a fast-growing, intensely competitive factor in the airline wars. Now, as aircraft manufacturers and airlines began to move into a world of LCD displays in their cockpits, was it possible to think of LCD use elsewhere? Several teams came up with the logical next question: What about back-of-the-seat LCD displays?

When the game was over, many of the participants said the process itself was so valuable that it ought to be continued in some form as a tool to enhance understanding of the company's strategy among top managers. Several teams suggested that they retain their team identities to serve as a kind of red team sounding board for future company initiatives and meet periodically to assess competitive strategies and market conditions. Our client did not go quite that far, but it did use the lessons in the game to turn its avionics business into one of the corporation's most profitable units.

○   ○   ○

On January 1, 1984, perhaps the last great monopoly from a bygone era came to an end when AT&T, responding to orders from U.S. government trustbusters, split its vast network into seven regional phone companies. One of those "Baby Bells," as they came to be known, was U S West, or U S West Communications, Inc., after it consolidated all phone operations at its Denver headquarters a few years later. Back in the day, U S West was something of an innovator, but by the late 1980s and early 1990s, its world—indeed, the entire world of telecommunications—had begun to change. Some people, mainly corporate executives, upper-income types, and high-level government officials, had what passed for cell phones: crude devices that usually resembled small bricks. In 1989, however, Motorola introduced a personal cellular phone with a flip-lid mouthpiece. It was priced beyond the reach of most consumers, but the demand for wireless clearly was beginning to grow. By 1992, according to the CTIA (Cellular Telecommunications Industry Association), the trade group representing the wireless industry, 10 million cell phones were in service.

The Federal Communications Commission was doing its part by allocating more bandwidth for emerging technologies, including personal communications services (PCS), which is bureaucratese for cellular phones. In the spring of 1994, facing upcoming PCS auctions by the FCC, the wireless unit of U S West was trying to puzzle out whether to bid and, if so, exactly how. To provide perspective on the brave new world of cellular technology and its future, they asked us to conduct a wargame on the wireless marketplace.

Its objectives were threefold. U S West wanted to get a better handle on the competitive forces it would face as the market for cellular services broadened and deepened. The company also wanted to understand its competitors' strategies better. Finally, it wanted to see what strategic directions might give it a competitive advantage in the years ahead.

The game of three moves was to look forward three years in each move, with each team wrestling with several central questions: What is your company's wireless strategy? How would you carry it out? What are the three wireless products most critical to your strategy? How do you want the customer to perceive your company?

Six competitor teams composed of U S West executives and Booz Allen facilitators played the game: U S West; AT&T, which had been in the cellular business since 1983; MCI; Southwestern Bell; TCI, a telecommunications company that would be acquired by AT&T four years later; and "other," a grab bag of other real and potential cell phone competitors. A market team would compare the companies' offerings and react to what the companies did in the game, and the control team, acting as the companies' boards of directors, would exercise ultimate control over all team actions.

It is important to remember what the wireless business was all about less than two decades ago. Not all the telecommunications companies were in it then, and cell phones were used mostly in one city or region. There weren't really any national providers, at least reliable ones. And even with the small range and spare service, prices were sky-high. The phones could run hundreds of dollars or more, and monthly subscriber fees might be $80 or $100 or higher, which got you a very limited number of calls.

The game of three moves was to look forward three years in each move, with each team wrestling with several central questions: What is your company's wireless strategy? How would you carry it out? What are the three wireless products most critical to your strategy? How do you want the customer to perceive your company? Competitors could negotiate directly with one another or take any other actions their companies might take in the real world. We needed a market baseline to begin, and so before the wargame, each competitor team bid in a simplified auction for PCS licenses in five cities we chose for their population and geographical diversity: Phoenix, Portland, Seattle, Chicago, and Miami.

We worked extensively with the market team before the game began, not for a few hours or a day but in several full-day sessions. In the end, we designed a market model that tended to emulate the current thinking about wireless: that it was focused on high-end users, principally in business, and was essentially regional in nature. The fascinating thing about this wargame was also humbling and instructive: For once, we underestimated the power, capacity for creativity, and inevitable experiential learning of our work. During this pregame preparation period, the market team went off, contacted another company, and asked it to do a conjoint analysis. A conjoint analysis uses focus groups and other tools to ask potential customers what features they value most in a product relative to other offerings in the same product category and how they weigh each of those features or attributes in the purchasing decision. By scrambling the combination of product features and prices, you can come up with a mathematical model of what customers will pay for a product with a certain set of features.

Members of the market team, essentially acting as surrogates for wireless customers, thought they could use this conjoint model to make more accurate judgments about company offerings and purchasing decisions. They were wrong: As the game unfolded, the pace of change in product attributes and prices quickly overwhelmed the model. And that was in the first move, which usually is the sleepiest in a three-move wargame.

Several notional steps in the first move began to solidify in the second move and became established trends in the third. Indeed, those trends emerged as the principal findings in the game, all of them reflecting an essential truth of the emerging digital age in business.

> **THE BIG IDEA** Technology, moving in fits and starts, often advances at speeds far faster than even the experts antici-pate, driving faster change in the marketplace. Companies, as a consequence, need to be especially nimble.

Here are the key findings:

- **Prices were going to come down and come down sharply both for the wireless phone itself and for service.** At the end of the game, pay-as-you-go cell phones were selling for $15 or $20 a month. Southwestern Bell, for one, came up with a "McPhone" strategy for low-end customers. Bundled with minutes, the prices were higher, perhaps double, but still significantly below where they were at the time.

- **Bundling that included entertainment and other services, not just minutes, was going to arrive with a vengeance.** One team was talking about doing a joint venture with Disney to develop entertainment software for cell phones, and the US West team created an innovative alliance with Sega to offer games on hand-held wireless devices. Long-distance service, which was unheard of in cell phone use at the time, would be regarded as standard equipment in the new marketplace.

- **National networks would have to be the wave of the future.** It might require cooperative agreements with other companies at first, but teams in the wargame generally felt that the exploding growth of cell sites—there were 10,000 nationwide by 1992—meant that "islands" of one-city or one-region service would dis-appear. One-company national networks, they said, certainly fit within the nine-year time horizon of the game. As the market grew, scale and strong distribution capability for the consumer market, through a company's own stores and through other re-tailers, would be crucial.

- **Brand loyalty was going to be essential.** With the market team and its conjoint model besieged by the proliferating price changes and product offerings, "customers" became confused and tended to stick with their current providers, assuming they were satisfied with the service. The players concluded that as brands went national and as options for product and service continued to bewilder customers, branding would become especially important. Churn—that is, customer movement from one service provider to another—already was perceived as a problem; establishing brand loyalty would help reduce it.

- **Overcapacity would be an inevitable consequence of explosive growth.** The players thought it would take perhaps six years, around the year 2000, for excess capacity to begin to show up. There would be a shakeout, placing an even higher premium on brand loyalty and dependable national networks.

Remember, this wargame was played in September 1994. The findings were greeted with considerable skepticism by US West executives even though they had created those conditions in the imagined cell phone marketplace of 1997 and 2000 and beyond. Because of the state of wireless at the time, they simply did not believe that these developments could unfold as rapidly as the game seemed to predict. In fact, as we all know, they came even more rapidly in the real world. Within a few short years, the cost of cell phone service was a small fraction of what it had been. National networks quickly became a reality. As for bundling, we all are familiar with the expanding array of services bundled in today's cell phones. Churn, estimated at roughly 25 percent at the time of the game, began to sink into single digits as brand loyalty took hold.

One finding in the game was widely accepted by the players: Wireless could not succeed as a stand-alone business. To be successful, it had to be integrated with a broad range of telecommunications offerings. In the game, that proposition was driven principally by the AT&T team, which sought to meld its cell phone and long-distance services. AT&T's idea was that wireless could be subsidized by wireline service, which was still expensive then compared with today's long-distance costs. US West, however, was running its wireless as a separate business, and that meant the company had to integrate the two or countenance losses in its cell phone unit. Today, most major wireless service providers do have a wireline affiliate, with the exception of Sprint Nextel.

Because of the state of wireless at the time, they simply did not believe that these developments could unfold as rapidly as the game seemed to predict. In fact, as we all know, they came even more rapidly in the real world.

Postscript: US West never became much of a player in the burgeoning wireless world. It was acquired in 2000 by Qwest Communications, a company originally built on high-speed data transmission for businesses. Among other telecommunication offerings, the company now sells wireline and wireless services, the latter through Sprint's national wireless network.

8

THE GOOD, THE BAD, AND THE UGLY

L aunching a new product or service is almost always an exercise in calculated risk juxtaposed to perceived opportunity and leavened in equal measure by hope and fear. A big company usually has spent tens of millions of dollars, perhaps hundreds of millions, in product or service development, and those sunk costs may prove to be minor compared with advertising, promotion, regulation, and other expenses associated with the launch itself. Today's marketplace, and by that we mean the competitive and dynamic global market that has grown up over the last couple of decades, has raised the bar for new-product introductions. The stakes and potential payoffs can be much higher if a launch is successful; conversely, the price of failure can prove catastrophic for companies and, on occasion, for executive careers.

We have conducted many wargames for companies eager to test a new product or new service, ranging from products and services well along in the development process to those still in the earliest stages. The point is the same at any stage of the product-development chain: A wargame can put a new product or service

Today's marketplace, and by that we mean the competitive and dynamic global market that has grown up over the last couple of decades, has raised the bar for new-product introductions. The stakes and potential payoffs can be much higher if a launch is successful; conversely, the price of failure can prove catastrophic for companies and, on occasion, for executive careers.

into a plausible imagined market of competitors, sometimes hostile regulators, stubborn customers, and more. Risk and opportunity serve as active partners of the participants in those wargames, providing valuable lessons without the tough schooling the real world can exact. Here are three new-product wargames that illustrate what we mean.

○　○　○

It was the fall of 1995, and Biogen, one of the innovative biotechnology companies founded over the previous couple of decades, was finally ready to launch its first product. Until then, the company, based in Cambridge, Massachusetts, had survived mainly on royalty payments from research. Now it had a new drug, called Avonex, that was used to treat relapsing multiple sclerosis. There already was competition in the marketplace. Schering AG, through its Berlex Laboratories division, had a drug called Betaseron in use in the United States and Europe, and a clutch of other companies, including Ares-Serono, a Swiss firm, and Teva Pharmaceuticals, based in Israel, had potential competitors in clinical trials.

Biogen was expecting the U.S. Food and Drug Administration to approve Avonex for consumer use very soon. What's more, its scientists felt that their product had superior qualities and offered patients more convenient and user-friendly administration: a single intramuscular injection once a week compared with multiple injections every week for the others. What troubled Biogen was that it was up against some formidable competition, including the much larger Schering, and had no previous experience with commercial prescription drugs. The company had to shift from familiar ground—its core strength of research and development—to terra incognita: the unfamiliar and challenging world of market competition.

The main objective of our wargame, then, was to test pricing and marketing strategies in the United States and Western Europe. We wanted to take Biogen's small team of executives, fewer than 20 of them; put them in the shoes of their competitors; and encourage them to take on their own company with everything they could muster. That way, we hoped, the entire management group at Biogen would come away with a better understanding of what it faced in the marketplace for MS drugs.

Four competitor teams—Biogen, Schering/Berlex, Teva, and Serono—played the game in a simulation of three moves projecting forward four years. A market team assessed the proposals of the competitor teams and adjusted market shares accordingly, and the control team of our people took market-team decisions and translated them into financial statements and stock market performance, since all the companies were publicly held (see Figure 8.1).

For the Biogen team, the issue on the table in move 1 was the central question: How should the company price its drug? Betaseron, the Schering/Berlex drug, cost about $8,500 per year per patient. Avonex was the superior drug, the Biogen scientists believed, but would a lower price aimed at grabbing market share undercut that claim among doctors and their patients? What were the potential pitfalls of a higher price?

The Biogen teammates decided to find out. In move 1, they priced Avonex in the U.S. market well above Betaseron at $11,000 per patient per year, compared with a Betaseron price that rose somewhat under the price umbrella set by Avonex. However, the Biogen team had another wrinkle up its sleeve: To underscore the quality of its product vis-à-vis the competition, it offered what it called the Biogen Outcome Guarantee. Specifically, the guarantee relied on a measure of MS impairment called the Kurtzke expanded disability status scale. The EDSS quantifies disability in eight functional systems: cerebellar, brainstem, sensory, visual, bowel and bladder, and

FIGURE 8.1

Testing, pricing, and marketing strategies for
Biogen's new drug. Four competitor teams
and a market team interacted within five regions to
simulate responses to a variety of initiatives.

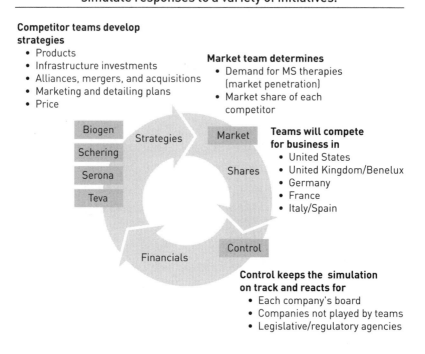

Competitor teams develop strategies
- Products
- Infrastructure investments
- Alliances, mergers, and acquisitions
- Marketing and detailing plans
- Price

Market team determines
- Demand for MS therapies (market penetration)
- Market share of each competitor

Biogen
Schering
Serona
Teva

Strategies

Market

Shares

Teams will compete for business in
- United States
- United Kingdom/Benelux
- Germany
- France
- Italy/Spain

Financials

Control

Control keeps the simulation on track and reacts for
- Each company's board
- Companies not played by teams
- Legislative/regulatory agencies

so forth. Neurologists assign a score to each one. On the EDSS scale, 0.0 equals a normal neurological examination and 10.0 indicates death from MS. The scale includes half-point gradations. Up to 4.5 on the EDSS refers to people who are fully ambulatory, and from 5.0 to 9.5 indicates people who are defined by their degree of ambulatory impairment.

What Biogen promised in its guarantee was strong stuff: If a patient's condition deteriorated by increasing one full point on the EDSS in a 12-month period, the company would refund the full cost of the drug.

Teva, meanwhile, was saying to potential customers: "Wait for us; we've got the best MS drug coming to market"—that is, as soon as its trials were complete. Serono, still in clinical trials in the United

States, began to market in Europe, matching Schering/Berlex's price.

The market, which essentially ignored Teva's "wait-for-us" promise, responded favorably to Biogen. Avonex, with its superior product profile and convenient dosing, secured 60 percent of all new patients. Even so, Schering/Berlex managed to retain 80 percent of its existing patients and capture 40 percent of new patients, giving it an overall market share of 66 percent. Also, Biogen's outcome guarantee ran into problems as competitor teams raised questions that Biogen had not addressed.

There was confusion about patient eligibility and the need for more physician training in EDSS, for example, and there was a paperwork burden that Biogen had not anticipated. Other teams, with the agreement of control, demanded what probably would have been required in the real world: a reserve fund as an offset against future product refunds. Since the product had not been tested in the consumer marketplace, the fund was set by control at 25 percent of Avonex revenues. That clobbered Biogen's stock price when control did the financials after the first move. Before the move, the price was $60 a share; after the move, $34 a share. Meantime, Schering nudged up a bit, from $70 to $74 a share.

In move 2, with some necessary adjustments to its outcome guarantee, Biogen started discounting in the United States, but Schering/Berlex was discounting too. Both companies were offering guaranteed discounts based on volume in arrangements with pharmacy benefits managers. (Prices remained reasonably firm in Europe because of the widespread use of single-payer government health care.) Schering/Berlex also invested in product improvement, principally an improved delivery system for Betaseron, in an effort to improve market share, and Biogen began to advertise heavily to both physicians and patients. To the doctors it said: We're the most convenient and best-tolerated drug for your MS patients. To the patients: Remember, we're the once-a-week drug that "manages your disease with minimal intrusion." This was 1997 in the game, and Teva had yet to receive FDA approval for its drug. Still, its team accelerated its efforts to get the word out to potential customers, both physicians and patients, and committed to doubling Biogen's sales efforts to counter its tardiness in getting to market. Serono, having launched in the United States, undercut Avonex's price by 20 percent in an effort to gain market share. Its real success, however, was in Europe, where it was entrenched and where it matched Betaseron's price.

When move 2 was over, Biogen was still the highest-priced competitor, according to the market team, though not by much. Betaseron's request for approval for its new autoinjector was rejected. Biogen's share of new patients in the United States dipped a bit to 40 percent, with Schering/Berlex and Teva splitting the rest, assuming that Teva got FDA approval before the year was out. Serono, winning big in Europe, was not a factor in the U.S. market.

Move 3 was in most respects a straight-line extension of move 2, with Schering/Berlex and Biogen holding their prices steady in the U.S. market and Teva following suit. All three companies, in fact, had largely aligned their prices. What Biogen learned was an emerging strategic fact of life in the international marketplace:

> **THE BIG IDEA** It may pay big dividends to be bold in marketing a new product. It may pay bigger dividends to exercise caution, especially when the product must pass regulatory muster.

Indeed, a pricing strategy was one of the takeaways for Biogen:

- A price significantly higher than that of the competition might pose problems for patients trying to get reimbursement from Medicare and private insurers. Biogen would have to convince Medicare of Avonex's clear superiority, which might prove onerous, lengthy, and expensive. The exercise simply was not worth it. Biogen could price Avonex at rough parity with Betaseron, promote its qualities, and retain a healthy share of the market.

- Biogen had to be aware of the "noise level." Schering/Berlex, the larger company, was advertising heavily in advance of the Avonex introduction, and so Biogen had to respond in kind. The result, in the game and in the real world, was that the company was overwhelmed with calls and letters from MS patients seeking more information and advice. Biogen, having no experience fielding mass inquiries, had not expected the deluge and was temporarily flummoxed, but it turned to some bigger pharmaceutical companies for guidance. The bigger companies were helpful. As a result, Biogen hired nurses and pharmacists to answer queries from the public.

In the real world, Avonex came to market priced roughly equal to Betaseron. Both products remain leaders in today's market for drugs to treat MS, with Biogen claiming that its product still is the market leader in the United States. In 2003, Biogen merged with IDEC Pharmaceuticals, a San Francisco biotech firm founded in 1985, to form Biogen Idec. In 2006, Schering was acquired by the German pharmaceutical giant Bayer AG.

○   ○   ○

International road warriors, listen up: Does Qualiflyer ring a distant bell? No? Qualiflyer was born in 1992 as the frequent-flier program of Swissair, then the national airline of Switzerland. The 1990s was a heady time for Europe's airlines. Deregulation, which began in the United States in the late 1970s, finally had arrived in Western Europe. The new freedom allowed hookups between and among airlines in Europe, North America, and Asia, resulting in a scramble to join emerging alliances. Alliance membership meant cooperation in frequent-flier programs, some coordination in flight schedules, generally lower prices on long hauls requiring transfers between airlines, and much more.

Swissair had another idea. It almost certainly would join one of the big alliances, which were OneWorld, anchored by British

Airways (BA); Star Alliance, anchored by Lufthansa; and Wings, anchored by KLM. (Wings now is known as SkyTeam.) But first, Swissair just might try to form a minialliance of its own. The airline began to invest in other European airlines, taking a minority interest in the airlines of several other countries—TAP Air Portugal, Turkish Airlines, and Sabena (Belgium), for example—and even a few private-sector carriers. In 1998, it formed the Qualiflyer Group, with the smaller airlines as members sharing frequent-flier programs and other services.

By 1999, the company was trying to sort out how to proceed. Swissair's CEO did have a strategy. Part of it was to take the Qualiflyer group and brand it bigger by getting into logistical services for other carriers: services such as food preparation and airport lounges, scheduling, and operations. Big carriers such as BA and Lufthansa did this kind of work for others. Why not Swissair? The idea was to turn these logistical services into profit centers, handling the work for airlines in the Qualiflyer group and perhaps others as well.

Now it was time to move forward. To that end, Swissair wanted us to conduct a strategic simulation—a kinder and gentler euphemism for a wargame—designed to address several related objectives. The corporate leadership wanted to establish how Qualiflyer could succeed in Europe, identifying and linking up with the best intercontinental partners. It wanted a better understanding of the factors for success for both Qualiflyer and alliance affiliation. Finally, it wanted to begin to attune its managers, through the simulation, to the increasingly competitive world of less regulation and airline alliances.

We set it up with 40 Swissair executives playing six competitor teams: Air France, Delta, BA/OneWorld, Swissair/Qualiflyer, Lufthansa/Star, and KLM/Wings. The four alliances, including Swissair's miniversion, were charged primarily with the interests of the lead airline but also were directed to take account of the interests of other alliance members. The game was to play out in three moves, each representing a three-year period: 1999–2002, 2002–2005, and 2005–2008. The players could take any action or negotiate any deal they could in the real world, but a control team would represent regulators and the airlines' boards of directors as an offset to irresponsible behavior. A market team would assess customer reaction to competitors' actions, adjusting market share accordingly. There was one additional curveball: At the beginning of move 3, the rules would change. Antitrust immunity would be eliminated, cross-border mergers would be allowed, and United Airlines and Delta would be assumed to have merged. (There was much talk about such a corporate marriage in those days.) The idea was to see how the airline industry behaved in a deregulated environment.

The opening scenario for move 1, in mid-1999, had Qualiflyer in talks with American Airlines on codeshares. Air France, which had not affiliated with an alliance yet, was in talks with Continental Airlines, Delta, and the Wings alliance. In the move, there was some jockeying among the players that seemed inconsequential at the time but would have greater meaning by the game's end. For example, Delta accepted Air France's proposal for a wide-ranging alliance between them; Air France also proposed—and control accepted—to raise capital to underwrite an expansion of its fleet. Qualiflyer approached American Airlines about a possible transatlantic partnership separate and apart from American's long-standing relationship with British Airways and its membership in the OneWorld alliance. It got nowhere: Instead, OneWorld offered Qualiflyer a cooperative agreement, which Qualiflyer spurned because it still had not decided how it wanted to play the alliance game.

By the end of the move, then, not much had happened. Again, tentative behavior in the first move of a wargame is not unusual. For most players, especially in business simulations, this is their first experience with wargames; they're trying to understand the team they're playing, and since most of them are Type A personalities, they do not want to make an early mistake that might jeopardize their chances of winning. We tell them to compete aggressively, and they take us at our word, but often not until the second move.

Move 2 did heat up, in part because control had adjusted the scenario on the basis of what happened in move 1. It was now 2002 in the game, and airline prices had slipped 6 percent since 1999—the start of the game—because of increased competition and some softening in the global economy. Asian markets, which had been slumping a bit at the start of move 1, were recovering at the start of move 2, control said. Asian carriers, which had resisted overtures to join the big alliances, finally might sign on.

Move 2 was the moment Swissair/Qualiflyer chose to announce the formation of three new companies: Qualiflyer Revenue and Management, Qualiflyer Planning and Scheduling, and Qualiflyer Operations Center. In the game, those companies, which were approved by control, were the realization of the CEO's plan to create new profit centers that would be based on services delivered to other carriers. Swissair/Qualiflyer also did a bunch of deals, mainly with smaller players in the airline business.

Once again, it was approached by OneWorld to join and partner with the BA-anchored alliance. The OneWorld/BA team made Qualiflyer an attractive offer: It could keep its current network and hub structure and grow through new relationships with American Airlines, an alliance member, and any incoming Asian partners. It also would keep its airline brands. However, it had to lose its Qualiflyer branding. The OneWorld/BA team and the other competitors regarded Qualiflyer as simply a loose federation of carriers, not a single entity; in short, they thought the brand itself had little value in an alliance configuration.

The Swissair/Qualiflyer team was not getting the message, however; it still had what seemed to others as delusions of grandeur. In a counter to OneWorld's offer, it proposed to join OneWorld with voting rights equal to those of British Airways, the alliance anchor and a carrier many times its size. The two sides agreed to continue discussions, but the outlook for an agreement did not seem promising.

In move 3, some new rules were applied, as we suggested earlier. With mergers allowed, the majors acted to shore up their positions. BA proposed a full merger with American Airlines and U.S.

Airways, which was approved by control, making the OneWorld alliance even stronger. Delta and United had merged before move 3—remember, we're now in 2005, pointing ahead three years—and that strengthened the Lufthansa-anchored Star Alliance. The Wings alliance went wild, too: Its proposed merger of KLM, Alitalia, Northwest Airlines, and Continental also was approved by control, along with the group's bid to acquire Southwest Airlines.

What should happen next? When we asked, those managers answered almost as one. In a paraphrase, they said: "Our CEO ought to be on a plane to London first thing Monday morning." Translation: He ought to be sitting down with the bosses at British Airways as soon as possible to work out the details of Swissair's membership in the OneWorld alliance.

Air France, its bid for a closer relationship with Delta frustrated by the Delta-United merger, was left without an alliance membership until OneWorld, during move 3, asked the French carrier to be its preferred continental carrier. Because of its size, the deal gave Air France a significant minority stake in the alliance. What about Qualiflyer? In the end, in the game, it became part of the Star Alliance.

Our client thought the game was a huge success, ratifying the CEO's strategy. Although there was an acknowledgment that the Qualiflyer "brand" needed to be strengthened to deliver "a consistent, common face to the customer," according to one summary of the game, the Swissair/Qualiflyer leadership felt there was no compelling reason to act immediately to join one of the big alliances.

In contrast, many of the Swissair managers who played the game saw the outcome differently. What should happen next? When we asked, those managers answered almost as one. In a paraphrase, they said: "Our CEO ought to be on a plane to London first thing Monday morning." Translation: He ought to be sitting down with the bosses at British Airways as soon as possible to work out the details of Swissair's membership in the OneWorld alliance. If a requirement of the deal was an end to the Qualiflyer brand name, they said, so be it.

Swissair never did join one of the major alliances. Within two years, the Qualiflyer Group was history; a year later, so was Swissair, which went bankrupt. A new national airline, Swiss International Air Lines—SWISS for short—was formed out of the wreckage. It has been a member of the Star Alliance since 2006. This adds some emphasis to what were the real lessons of our Swissair wargame.

THE BIG IDEA Strategic plans, particularly in global industries, must take special account of the largest players in the field. Their competitive advantages are not absolute, but they may be large enough to frustrate or even crush the plans of smaller fry.

Of the many takeaways in our Swissair game, three stood out:

- Strengthened international alliances and perhaps even transnational mergers in the airline industry were coming in an age of deregulation and price pressure. It would be important for smaller players to emphasize their strong suits and sign up with one of the major alliances sooner rather than later.

- It would be difficult to counter those alliances unless a competitor had what amounted to a unique selling proposition. In other words, not everyone can be a Southwest Airlines.

- If the game outcome is at serious odds with your corporate strategy, it's worth examining the game's play in even greater detail than you otherwise would. The fact that the home team often loses in business wargames is not a signal that the strategy is wrong. As we say early and often, our games must be plausible, not predictive. But just because we call it a game does not mean its outcomes are capricious. Sometimes they tell a very disturbing story.

In the post-9/11 era, as we already have learned, asymmetric—or irregular—warfare has become a much-studied field in American war colleges and regional commands. It also has occupied more and more of our wargamers' time and creative talents as one of our clients, the U.S. Department of Defense, tests the most productive ways to counter a new range of threats against the United States and its allies around the world.

Every so often, we find ourselves engaged in building a business wargame that in the playing seems to resemble asymmetric conflict. Consider the European insurance executive who had been working with one of our firm's commercial partners about a prospective new service he had in mind. He headed a new business unit at his company and was having trouble convincing his masters at corporate that his inspiration, fully realized throughout the Continent, would be a huge financial success. Our partner suggested that perhaps a wargamed simulation of the issue would prove convincing, although he also cautioned his client that there are no guarantees and that wargames sometimes reveal truths that their sponsors find difficult to swallow. The client said he understood and wanted to proceed.

His brainstorm sounded intriguing at first blush. Incomes in Europe were growing, and the prosperous cohorts at the top had no trouble securing good financial advisers to handle their investments. Those at the bottom—that is, people who tended to live from paycheck to paycheck—sadly had no need for guidance on buying stocks and bonds and other investments. But what about the huge group in the middle? What about people with modest discretionary income that was not being put to work? Even in the welfare states of Western Europe, where pensions were lucrative, an additional investment in retirement could produce a fat nest egg if handled wisely over time. Why not tap that market?

In the post-9/11 era, asymmetric—or irregular—warfare has become a much-studied field in American war colleges and regional commands. It also has occupied more and more of our wargamers' time and creative talents as one of our clients, the U.S. Department of Defense, tests the most productive ways to counter a new range of threats against the United States and its allies around the world.

What this executive wanted to do was establish a chain of offices amid the retail stores that line streets throughout cities in Western Europe. Those storefront offices would be staffed by financial consultants who would provide advice on the purchase of relatively safe securities; they also would execute transactions that customers wanted to make on the basis of the guidance they were getting. People could stop in on their way to work in the morning, during lunch, or on the way home at the end of the day. The executive envisioned a kind of one-stop shopping for financial management—stocks, bonds, and perhaps insurance too: Come in, spend 15 or 20 minutes chatting with a counselor and making adjustments to your portfolio, and then off you go. Insurers were prohibited from offering commercial banking services, but the executive did not see that as a problem. People could have their checking accounts at banks; what he wanted was a shot at the money they otherwise might keep in simple savings accounts.

In our discussions with this executive and his top people, the objective of the game was abundantly clear. In effect, they wanted to stress test the product launch. How could their value proposition be refined and made even more attractive? How would competitors respond? What are we missing? How many stores do we need, and in what cities? And how are we going to communicate this to our constituencies: potential customers, of course, but also inside our parent company? The company was huge, the executive's business group was small, and he anticipated further resistance even though his concept was innovative and a likely gold mine.

We constructed the game with the home team, our client, and

several competitor teams staffed by managers from the insurance company. The competitors included two other insurers, a couple of banks, and even a huge retail grocery chain because such organizations were beginning to offer some financial services. A market team served as the customer, and a control team played everyone else: regulators, financial adjudicators, and the like. We asked each competitor team the following questions: What is your product proposition? Why should a customer buy it? What is your strategy, and how do you plan to implement it in terms of advertising, personnel, management, and information technology? We wanted to play the game in three moves, going out two years in each move.

We constructed the game with the home team, our client, and several competitor teams staffed by managers from the insurance company. The competitors included two other insurers, a couple of banks, and even a huge retail grocery chain because such organizations were beginning to offer some financial services.

In fact, the game did not last that long. In business games, the home team often loses because the executives playing competitors know all the home team's weaknesses and move quickly to exploit them. That is exactly what happened here. The first move was anything but sleepy. Banks could not sell insurance, but they could offer retail investing services through their branches, and in the game they did that almost immediately. Their value proposition was significantly greater, since the banks could provide genuine one-stop shopping through a vast network of branches that included checking, regular savings, and the new financial-planning services.

Of course, their net investment was small, since the new financial planning offering would be placed in an existing facility using existing information technology and other services. Our client's network of outlets had to be built from scratch, from real estate acquisition on up.

We played it out for two moves, and there was blood on the

floor. "This is just too easy to counter," said one member of a banking team, essentially speaking for all the other competitors in the game. We played a desultory third move, with the executive suggesting modest adjustments in the home team's approach, but the game was over. Even the supermarket chain had gotten into the act, allowing small bank branches to open up in its stores and offer more than just checking and saving services.

> **THE BIG IDEA**   The best chief executives drive innovation, but they must be strategic about it. A dumb idea is a dumb idea, and no amount of cheerleading can make it smarter. Every good idea should support the goals of the organization and contribute to its differentiation in the marketplace.

- Talk about asymmetric warfare: The big learning in this one was that the banks could and probably would provide considerably more services at many more outlets and at lower cost.

Our client's business unit, we understand, was closed down in a matter of weeks. He had wanted to use the game to convince a skeptical corporate parent of his idea's efficacy, but sometimes Father and Mother know best.

CHAPTER 9

ENERGY PLAYS

I f you had to name a single industry that has been central to the American economy, domestic politics, and national security over the last four decades, it would be hard to come up with one that surpasses energy in importance. The electronics revolution has spawned a new age of advancing productivity and stunning invention, helping to make the United States a technological powerhouse, and the health-care industrial complex has grown like topsy, for better and for worse, to meet the demands of an aging population. However, nothing is quite at the center of things the way Big Energy is. Transportation, plastics, agriculture, electric power, the environment, drilling and mining, the Middle East and the Persian Gulf, Russia and Venezuela and Mexico—almost everything you see, almost everything you touch, almost everything that touches you rubs up against the oil and gas industry in some way.

It was hardly surprising, then, that the energy sector emerged as an important part of our work after we started to apply military wargaming principles to strategic simulations for major corporations. That work, which began in the late 1980s, has increased in recent years as climate change, dependence on foreign oil, and a nascent emphasis on alternative energy sources have captured greater public attention. The three wargames described below

One of those companies came to us in mid-1994 with a problem. It had been test-marketing compressed natural gas (CNG) since 1990 and had formed an alternative transportation fuels business unit. By 1994, it had invested tens of millions of dollars a year and had 26 CNG refueling sites in operation, mainly at airports, with expansion plans under way.

intersect with some of the pressing issues of our time and reveal why it sometimes seems so difficult to move forward and deal with them.

○   ○   ○

The 1990s was a reasonably quiescent time in international oil markets. Having briefly soared to almost $35 a barrel after Iraq invaded Kuwait in August 1990, the price of crude oil fluctuated between $15 and $20 during the middle of the decade, and supply and demand seemed in rough balance. Still, the combination of environmental consciousness and a gathering concern about dependence on oil from the Middle East had prompted some experimentation with alternatives. The federal government was interested in alternative fuel vehicles (AFVs) and had provided incentives to private-sector actors to market them, mainly to Washington's automotive fleets. Some states also had dipped their toes in those waters. Of course, a few large oil companies—those with vision, a keen sense of the potential payoff, or both—had begun to fund their own programs.

One of those companies came to us in mid-1994 with a problem. It had been test-marketing compressed natural gas (CNG) since 1990 and had formed an alternative transportation fuels business unit. By 1994, it had invested tens of millions of dollars a year and had 26 CNG refueling sites in operation, mainly at airports, with expansion plans under way. CNG was a fuel of the future, the unit's officials thought. Even though it was not renewable like solar or wind, it was an abundant resource in the United States, and that meant it could help cut dependence on foreign oil. CNG also was clean-burning, it was far more environmentally friendly than oil refined into gasoline, and the price seemed right: less costly than gasoline. Getting in early and putting down a marker made a great deal of sense.

However, the business unit was struggling: There was no clear strategy for AFVs as a real ongoing business, and the parent company was raising questions about priorities, resources, and feasibility. Now the business unit was under some pressure because the company's management wanted a study of the prospects for CNG-powered vehicles. The unit was eager to get outside help to challenge its own analysis, develop and analyze strategic alternatives, and pick a way forward. We thought a wargame could be a powerful supplement because it would push beyond the limits of traditional analysis and perhaps provide valuable guidance about upcoming investment decisions.

The timing was critical: We had to finish our work for this unit so that its results could be incorporated into the company-mandated study and presented to management in early 1995, presumably before the company's next quarterly board meeting.

After several months of consultation and research, we conducted the wargame in January 1995. It was designed to have three moves, with each move simulating three years in time, and its objectives spoke to many of the issues that puzzle public policymakers and large energy companies to this day: Is there a market for alternative transportation fuels, and if so, how big is it? Are there barriers to entry? Is there a "first mover" advantage? What is the strategic value of a domestic alternative transportation fuels business? What are the regulatory, environmental, and technological factors?

The game included a half dozen competitor teams consisting of other oil companies, a market team, and the control team. The competitors were asked to come up with product offerings, technology and infrastructure investment, marketing plans, and even strategic lobbying efforts in Washington. The market team, which included a kind of automotive subsidiary to represent General Motors, Ford, and Chrysler, would make decisions about the type and volume of AFVs produced and allocate market share to alternative

Today, nearly a decade and a half past that wargame, compressed natural gas is still a fuel in search of automotive products in search of a market.

transportation fuel providers. Control, as usual, would play everyone else: each company's board of directors, other private-sector corporations, and government regulatory agencies.

This is one game in which it is not necessary to go through all the moves. The teams competed, to be sure, and came up with a variety of approaches to CNG-powered vehicles. However, every strategy bumped up against related obstacles involving technology, convenience, and infrastructure. In the third move, one player summed up what had become the unanimous conclusion: Making a successful business out of CNG, one that could stand alone as a profit-making enterprise, depended largely on "three engineering miracles."

First, the cylinders or tanks holding compressed natural gas had to come down in size. At that time, the mid-1990s, they essentially filled the entire trunk of an automobile; that was why the vast majority of CNG-powered vehicles were vans, trucks, buses, and other large vehicles. The problem was one of physics: Natural gas could be compressed only so much, so how was it possible to shrink the tank enough to fit into a passenger vehicle? There were no easy answers.

The second engineering miracle was to lessen the time it takes to refill the tank. Because of the tank size and the speed of the pump, filling up generally required 20 minutes or so. As one player said: "Right now, I pull into the station, put the pump into my car, walk inside, get my cup of coffee, come back, and the pump's already clicked off. Five minutes max. And now you're telling me I have to wait 20 minutes?" His point, universally shared, was that most impatient Americans would balk at such lengthy pit stops.

The third engineering miracle came down to this: You mean if I live 30 or 40 or 50 miles away, I've still got to drive to the airport to fill up? Despite modest expansion plans, there was no national infrastructure for CNG and no real plan to develop one.

Today, nearly a decade and a half past that wargame, compressed natural gas is still a fuel in search of automotive products in search of a market. Gas-electric hybrids have gained a tenuous foothold in the marketplace, and demand for ethanol-gasoline blends has increased, driving up corn production and corn prices. But CNG still powers government and private fleets for the most part, with few prospects for a major breakthrough any time soon.

Given that history, the overriding lesson from our 1995 wargame was simple and, it turned out, prescient.

THE BIG IDEA A good or even noble technology is no guarantee of decent returns on investment, especially when that technology attempts to challenge an entrenched product such as gasoline refined from crude oil.

- There would be no payback on investment in CNG for 5 years or even 10 years—in fact, as far out as the eye, observing public policy, could see.

The oil company business unit reflected the outcome of our wargame in its report to top management. As a result, the company essentially folded up its CNG experiment as the centerpiece of its work in alternative transportation fuels. The savings: tens of millions of dollars.

○　○　○

Naming conventional sources of crude oil amounts by now to a rounding up of the usual suspects: Russia, Saudi Arabia and other Persian Gulf states, North Africa, Mexico, and Venezuela, not to mention Canada, Britain and Norway (the North Sea), and the United States (in Alaska and on- and offshore in the lower 48). But what about *un*conventional oil? What exactly is it, where do we find it, and is it economically viable now that conventional crude oil prices have reached record levels?

One place to find the unconventional stuff is the Canadian province of Alberta, where a viscous heavy oil called bitumen mixes with sand, clay, and water to form what are commonly known as tar sands. Bitumen can be mined, with the oil separated from the sand and clay after it is brought to the surface, but it isn't easy. Even so, the potential reserves—perhaps as much as 2 trillion barrels—have attracted big oil companies, which have targeted the tar sands region of Canada and have begun to exploit its oily bounty.

Another place to find unconventional oil is the state of Colorado, which sits atop something called the Green River Formation. A couple thousand feet below the surface rests a vast sea of oil, perhaps as much as 1.8 trillion barrels of it. There's only one problem: All that oil is locked into hard rock known as shale. Technologies for extracting the oil from the rock exist but remain unproven or at least untested under real-world conditions, and all of them raise significant environmental, logistical, regulatory, and economic issues. As a result, although several major oil companies covet the oil shale of Colorado, none has cleared all the hurdles required to begin development and exploitation.

Not long ago, one of those oil companies asked us to wargame the possibilities and impediments to oil shale development in Colorado. With such formidable obstacles, did it make sense? Was it better to be a leader or a follower in oil shale? What were the elements that could derail even the best projects? What were the competitive challenges?

The game we built included our client and two other large oil companies as competitor teams; a market team to represent capital markets and oil industry transactions in global markets; a team representing local communities and nongovernmental environmental organizations such as the Sierra Club and Western Resource Advocates; a team playing federal, state, and local agencies; and, of course, a control team to act as referee, play the media when necessary, and introduce external shocks. It was an exceptionally big game, with five moves over two and a half days and, because of the huge lead times for such unprecedented exploration, stretching out a decade. One other thing: The game assumed that the technologies of the competing companies would work even though they still would be faced with environmental, public relations, and regulatory challenges.

Remember, these were people from our client company playing the locals. Some of those communities had been through boom-bust energy cycles before, and they feared another one.

We began the game with our client filing with the state and launching a research and development effort in Colorado. Its goal was to establish a leadership position in oil shale exploitation, and this filing was its letter of intent to go big and go first, in effect, to make oil shale a game changer in the world of energy. But going big and going first also meant that the company would be leading the way in every facet of the project: requests for permits from local, state, and federal regulators; relations with communities affected by the project; the concerns of environmental groups; and, not least, the reaction of its competitors. As one player put it, "They'll be leading with their chin."

As the game unfolded, it quickly became clear that competitor A was positioning itself to follow close behind our client. It hired away from the client company a vice president who was an oil shale expert, and it began to urge the Colorado communities on land above the Green River Formation to endorse joint planning for oil shale development. That way, competitor A figured, it might get the best of both worlds: The client company would take most of the flak from environmental groups and the locals; if the locals prevailed on a joint planning arrangement, a consortium approach among oil companies also might be required, and that probably would give the competitor a piece of the action down the road.

Competitor B was no slouch either. Publicly, it stressed its broad-based oil portfolio, barely mentioning oil shale. Meanwhile, in the game, it started to buy up global oil shale properties not controlled by our client.

Not surprisingly, environmental groups were up in arms. Any project to extract oil from shale would involve huge power requirements, perhaps even a huge and dedicated power plant, probably coal-burning, either onsite or in a nearby state; that meant greenhouse gases, raising the global climate issue.

The project also would involve water-use and land-use issues. It would involve social issues in the many affected communities. What really galvanized the environmentalists, however, was the gap between what our client had described in its earlier statements on the project and what the filing with the state of Colorado actually revealed. The first statements talked about a relatively benign and contained program; the filing pictured something vastly more ambitious and threatening to many environmentalists. They felt blindsided by the scope of the project and remained unappeased through most of the game. In fact, as the environmental groups' tactics escalated and as they refused efforts by our client to negotiate a peace, control had to step in and rein in the groups by saying no to some of their proposed actions.

As the game played out, local communities, grasping the import of what was being proposed, reacted with a sense of panic. Remember, these were people from our client company playing the locals. Some of those communities had been through boom-bust energy cycles before, and they feared another one. "Hey, look, wait a minute," said one participant on the team representing the communities. "You're going to bring in thousands and thousands of workers for a number of years, then leave. How are we going to pay for schools, the additional cops, and all the rest? And what do we do when you leave?"

The agency and regulator team, predictably, was squarely in the middle. Its goal was to balance the needs of U.S. energy security with the need for a good measure of environmental protection. On the one hand, the team granted our client the right to draw water from various river basins in Colorado; on the other hand, it warned our client of groundwater contamination and the price to be paid—financial and regulatory—if such contamination was discovered by its monitors.

Under heavy pressure from environmentalists and politicians, the agency-regulator team supported legislation limiting CO_2 emissions on the project and requiring a program for carbon sequestration, that is, long-term underground storage of carbon.

Later in the game, the control team changed the scenario with injects that elevated the energy crisis and jeopardized the security of oil supplies. For example, an imagined *Washington Post* story quoting "former and current U.S. intelligence officials" was invoked. It said that Hezbollah's substantial presence among the Lebanese Shia in the Foz Di Iguazu triborder area of South America was enabling joint training there of Venezuelan and Iranian commandoes. Iran's chief of strategy, one Hassan Abassi, was quoted: "Once we destroy 29 sites in America," he said, "we will destroy Anglo-Saxon civilization." The commandoes were training with handheld electromagnetic pulse devices to destroy electronic circuitry.

Then move 3 opened with Venezuela's and Nigeria's expropriation of oil and Iran's commitment to a nuclear weapons program that would force a U.S. embargo.

The injects in turn sparked a policy debate within the agency-regulator team that engaged other teams as well. The result in the game was the introduction of comprehensive energy legislation at the federal level that included a combination of conservation, greater diesel fuel and ethanol use, incentives for shale development, and a strong nudge toward consortia, sometimes with government involvement, to deal with huge projects.

Consortia would not necessarily be limited to oil companies either. In the game, our client's team resisted partnering with the other oil company teams and preferred to fly solo. But competitors A and B got our client's attention when both identified General Electric as a natural partner to build power generation and distribution equipment. GE, with its long history and expertise in such businesses, figured to be involved in any plan to extract oil from shale. If a competitor took GE out of the equation through a preemptive partnership, it might pose difficulties down the road for our client. GE might prove so crucial that some players declared it the real winner of the wargame.

The market team's reaction to all this was fascinating. Again, these were our client's executives playing the role of capital-market decision makers. Their focus, similar to what most investors and analysts do in the real world, was on near-term and midterm performance by these publicly held oil companies. They gave the home team a hard time, downgrading its stock relative to the other two because of its leadership on shale, all the unwanted attention it had engendered, and the uncertainty about the eventual prospects.

The game ended inconclusively, as it should have, but it generated a bunch of lessons for anyone contemplating the development and exploitation of unconventional oil in politically sensitive areas.

THE BIG IDEA Even in an era of high demand, constrained supply, and rising prices, global giants in extractive industries face a new set of strategic decisions about where they invest because the number and variety of stakeholders they must satisfy has increased significantly. This idea also applies to any organization or industry that has a high impact on the environment, security, or finances of the community in which it functions.

The players in the game identified a half-dozen principal takeaways:

- **Leading the way may prove financially beneficial in the long run, but you'd better be prepared for the pushback.** You'll be in the crosshairs of skeptical environmentalists, regulators, and local townspeople. In those circumstances, more transparency early on probably will pay dividends later.

- **Going it alone certainly is feasible, but there would be many benefits to partnering.** It would spread the financial risks, of course, and diffuse some of the incoming artillery from critics of the project.

- **Carbon sequestration is a sine qua non of such massive projects.** Being proactive on the matter should be an essential part of strategy. It's the right thing to do, and you'll get big points with environmentalists for acting without being ordered to act.

- **You need a coherent strategy to deal with key suppliers.** Even giant companies sometimes cannot do everything by themselves. It makes sense to line up suppliers, even provisionally, early in the planning phase.

- **You need a coherent strategy for infrastructure investment.** Small communities may welcome the jobs you bring, assuming you do not environmentally degrade everything in sight, but they have a right to expect significant help from you to cope with the burden your presence places on the size and cost of essential services.

- **Be prepared to encounter even more uncertainties than you imagined.** We always tell our clients that they will be forced to operate with imperfect or incomplete information in a wargame. Especially in an enterprise that involves so many politically charged issues, it's best to take a page out of Desert Crossing (see Chapter 3): Hope for the best, plan for the worst.

When we did this wargame, the price of crude oil was running in the range of $80 to $90 per barrel. As we write this, it's about $110 a barrel, having reached almost $150 a barrel a couple months earlier. If prices remain at such levels or go higher, oil reserves that previously were judged uneconomical to exploit will become more attractive. Right now, work in the Canadian tar sands is running around the clock. The Green River Formation in Colorado may not be far behind.

○　○　○

Politicians continue to debate the science of climate change, but the scientists themselves—with a relatively small minority taking exception—have coalesced around a set of causal findings: Human beings, by continuing to burn more and more fossil fuels, have caused greater and greater quantities of CO_2 and other so-called greenhouse gases to be released into the atmosphere. That has led to a gradual warming of the earth's surface; if this trend is not arrested and reversed within the next several decades, the earth could be in existential peril.

Finding ways to deal with global warming is certainly at the center of energy policy discussions in the United States, Europe, Japan, and, increasingly, China and India, two vast and populous countries with rapidly developing economies that face huge environmental challenges. There is no shortage of proposed solutions for the carbon problem. One idea, much discussed in the United States, is to impose a so-called cap-and-trade system on carbon emissions. Some entity, perhaps an independent body appointed by Congress, would establish a total cap for carbon. Groups that burn fossil fuels—big companies and especially big utility companies—would receive a certain number of allowances for carbon emissions consistent with the cap. A market would be established to buy and sell allowances. If utility A reduced its emissions, it would have a surplus of allowances and could sell them to utility B, which was having trouble getting under the cap. In each subsequent year, the cap would be lowered, forcing a steady decline in carbon emissions. In theory, good things would flow from a cap-and-trade system: more fuel-efficient automobiles, greener manufacturing processes, cleaner air, and, farther out, an end to melting polar ice caps.

This isn't pie-in-the-sky stuff. A cap-and-trade system for carbon is in place in Western Europe. In the United States, a cap-and-trade program for sulfur dioxide—the cause of acid rain—was enacted in 1990 and proved enormously successful in cutting emissions and rehabilitating lakes and forests in the eastern United States. The SO_2 program "completely transformed the paradigm that had historically pitted environmentalism against economic growth," wrote Fred Krupp, president of the Environmental Defense Fund, and his associate Miriam Horn in their provocative book *Earth: The Sequel*.

In 2007, we were asked by a major international oil company to wargame a cap-and-trade system for an annual conference it was holding. The main objective of the game would be to explore how utilities and power generators might respond in a national cap-and-trade regime for carbon. What would be the impact, depending on one's strategic choices, on carbon emissions, power use, public attitudes, and shareholder value? In short, how does a company go "green" and make money at the same time?

The game was to consist of three moves, beginning in 2009 and extending to 2030. Normally, we bring all the players together after each move to tell them what they did during that move. This time, we dispensed with the plenary sessions and captured the play and data in two other ways. Instead of asking players to digest fat briefing books of graphics and data, we created huge wall posters that reflected each team's power portfolio.

The company, with a packed agenda for its conference, could not devote as much time to the game as we normally require. Fortunately, we had conducted a cap-and-trade game for executives from a half dozen utility companies a few months earlier. We borrowed from it, using the same concept of four competing utility teams, but we added two additional competitor teams, each representing the sponsoring oil company. A control team oversaw the exercise, as usual, and a subset of control—a regulator team, in effect—reacted for state and federal regulatory interests and customers.

We made some other adjustments to accommodate our client's

time limitations. The game was to consist of three moves, beginning in 2009 and extending to 2030. Normally, we bring all the players together after each move to tell them what they did during that move. This time, we dispensed with the plenary sessions and captured the play and data in two other ways. Instead of asking players to digest fat briefing books of graphics and data, we created huge wall posters, four feet by six feet, that reflected each team's power portfolio. In a two-page fictional newspaper, we conveyed what had happened in the teams' virtual world—in effect, our injects that changed the scenario—and summed up the steps taken by each team in the previous move.

The opening scenario assumed a cap-and-trade system that would cap carbon emissions at 2006 levels in the year 2014. After that, carbon allowances would be reduced by 2 percent per year for the next 15 years. For the simulation, we divided the country into two distinct regions: Coal Land and Gas Land. In Coal Land, the market price of power was set mainly by coal-fired plants; in Gas Land, mainly by gas-fired plants. The competitor teams, all considered for game purposes to be publicly held companies, were the following:

Two client teams, A and B. Each team was an integrated oil and gas company with gas-fired power plants and significant interests in wind and solar power, and each sought to be a leading provider of low-carbon power in the future.

Heartland. This was a large, vertically integrated utility with a large power-generation portfolio and a substantial retail business. It also owned profitable transmission and distribution assets. It had a small renewable energy portfolio and was under pressure from independent power producers such as Renew and other integrated utilities such as Miners and NuVolt. Its management was struggling with a strategy: Should Heartland cut its losses and close its least profitable power plants or fight to regain market share? Heartland also was under fire in the media for its absence of a renewable power strategy.

Miners. Its profile was similar to Heartland's: It had relied on coal-fired power stations but had diversified over the last two decades to include gas-fired, nuclear, and hydroelectric power stations as well. Now a new CEO had ordered a strategic review that presented executive leadership with three options to address the company's goals of expanding its generation asset base and reducing its environment footprint. The options were to build renewable power stations instead of coal, build clean-coal plants, and build a mix of gas and nuclear, which would reduce emission levels.

NuVolt. Another vertically integrated coal-and-gas utility, NuVolt had worked to shift its assets from regulated markets to unregulated markets, mainly by building merchant power plants in Coal Land and Gas Land. It had reduced its old-coal profile, which improved its chances of doing well in a new carbon-constrained world. It moved into nuclear and began to build a strong renewable portfolio. The CEO wanted to expand the company's generation assets, but some senior managers worried about a price collapse if too much supply flooded the market.

Renew. This company was an independent power producer, that is, a firm that produced electricity and sold it to utilities for resale or to end users directly. Only two decades old, it had built a large portfolio of new power stations with significant diversity, from coal, gas, and nuclear to hydro and geothermal. Tightening emission standards could prove a boon to the company, management believed, as older coal plants were retired.

Perhaps it was the subject matter or perhaps it was the time limits or the poster-filled walls of information, but the players engaged in this game much more quickly than players normally do

Perhaps it was the subject matter or perhaps it was the time limits or the poster-filled walls of information, but the players engaged in this game much more quickly than players nor-mally do in the first move of a wargame. There was a big rush to nuclear.

in the first move of a wargame. There was a big rush to nuclear, which meant pleas to the regulators; the regulators turned down some companies because they had not proposed retiring older coal plants fast enough. Meanwhile, a few teams got serious about renewables early on; that was a good thing in light of an opening scenario that had Congress setting a federally mandated renewable portfolio standard (RPS) for electric utilities. The RPS was 25 percent by the year 2020 and 35 percent by 2030.

Both client teams, A and B, began to comply with the cap-and-trade emission requirements by investing in relatively cleaner gas turbine technology for new power plants. Team B also started to lobby for carbon taxes and promote itself with the public as a Mister Clean wannabe. "We care deeply about our customers and look forward to joining forces with the public to champion reduced emissions," its chairman said.

The Heartland team recognized from the start that a new world was coming. Its CEO asserted that the company wanted to extend its history of operating excellence into "our new clean offerings." It began to phase out its older coal plants in Coal Land; in their place, Heartland invested in geothermal energy and made plans to build a new nuclear plant and a wind-turbine facility, each capable of generating 1,000 megawatts of power, or enough to service roughly 1 million homes. It chose investments in both regulated and un-regulated markets, spreading its risks.

Miners, another traditional utility, also stepped briskly away from its past, making plans to retire the bulk of its old coal plants. It recently had invested in nuclear power and in renewables: solar and wind farms onshore and offshore. "Miners' legacy of dirty coal is history," its CEO said. "We're now beyond dirty."

NuVolt announced a two-part strategy to reduce its CO_2 footprint and expand its base in Coal Land with regulated nuclear power and unregulated wind power. However, the regulators rejected a request for a nuclear building permit because of the long lead time involved; instead, they ordered that the utility retrofit an old coal plant to keep it operational. Long term, it wanted to replace reliance on coal with a shift to gas turbine power, renewables, and eventually nuclear.

Renew continued to diversify its portfolio, adding nuclear, clean coal, geothermal, and wind facilities in Coal Land and similar plants in Gas Land. It stressed that it was a "key deregulated utility," in the words of its CEO, that could offer "great opportunity for low-carbon power generation to our valued customers in Coal and Gas Lands."

At the end of move 1, it was the year 2016, and changes had occurred. A backlash against stringent carbon policies had begun. Subsidies for clean coal technologies were enacted by a Congress concerned about job losses in coal country. Congress had relaxed its RPS; electric utilities now were required to have 20 percent of their portfolios in renewables instead of 25 percent, and the time frame was pushed out five years to 2025. State regulators, meanwhile, had taken steps to ease the financial burden on utilities building nuclear plants. Instead of waiting until a plant was operating to allow a utility to reflect the cost in its rate base, the regulators permitted the companies to put costs into the rate bases as the investments were being made as part of a program called CWIP, or construction work in progress. Cap-and-trade was still controversial, in part because of its complexity and price volatility.

In move 2, most teams stayed on course, but some stepped up the pace. Client team B, for example, chose to accelerate its renewable production platform, including a huge investment in solar energy. Renew made significant new additions to its portfolio in wind, solar, and geothermal and retired an old Coal Land plant in 2018.

According to our fictional newspaper, over the seven years of move 2, from 2016 to 2023, the marketplace has begun to respond. The cost of electricity has risen sharply as utilities have reflected the cost of their new investments in their rate bases, with predictable complaints from consumer groups. But electricity bills also have included exhortations to conserve, and customers have been paying attention. Many utilities have begun to offer demand-side management programs for customers: financial incentives for efficient insulation and retrofitting, lower rates in off-peak hours, and more. Demand, especially during off-peak hours, actually has been increasing at a slower rate and in some case actually shrinking.

A control team inject after move 2 tried to focus minds on why attacking greenhouse gases was so important: In the fictional newspaper, it was reported that the worst drought in U.S. history had been blamed on climate change—a sharp increase in temperatures worldwide. Global warming had pushed the water levels of the Colorado and Tennessee rivers to record lows, imperiling hydroelectric supplies, hampering firefighting efforts, and posing a threat to the economies of states in the American West and the Tennessee Valley.

Move 3 gave the teams an opportunity to refine what they had done in moves 1 and 2. Most continued to play out the strategies they had established in those moves. There was one big merger: Heartland acquired client team A in a combination that made good sense because of their like-minded plans. If there was a big winner, it was Renew; it began the game with a renewable portfolio and built it up from there, reducing its emissions footprint and delivering solid shareholder value in the process. It was much the same with client team B. The others did less well when it came to shareholder value.

In fact, although we certainly stressed competition in this game, it was not really about winners and losers. The larger point was to explore what happens in a new world of mandated change. The lessons were bracing:

THE BIG IDEA The green revolution will impose costs on all players: government, utilities, regulators, environmentalists. The public companies that generate electric power need strategies that in effect embrace their traditional opponents— environmentalists and public-interest groups—as the price of getting the approvals they need from regulators. An effective carbon policy may require private-public partnership commensurate with its scope. Oh, yes, transparency might be a wise adjunct to policy development.

The critical takeaways:

- **Everybody wants to go green, but all of us had better get ready to pay for doing so.** Major changes in the profile of power generation aimed at a sharp reduction in carbon emissions probably will have profound price effects. There is no free lunch; in fact, this lunch could prove very expensive indeed. It's no accident that California, probably the greenest state, has some of the highest utility rates in the country.

- **If there is no rush to clean-coal technology, the government may have to subsidize its development.** Otherwise, it may take too long for traditional utilities to jettison aging and polluting plants. Renewables also may require subsidies.

- **The nation's electric utilities cannot solve this problem on their own, even with a cap-and-trade program that works.** Government will have to be involved, essentially driving the industry toward the solution it wants.

DON'T FIGHT
THE SCENARIO:
THE PLUS SIDE

The outcome of a wargame sometimes can reveal a lot by revealing very little; that is, the outcome serves as a mirror held up to reflect the real marketplace. Of course, wargames for or about corporations can expose a company's self-interest in ways that were obscure before the game because institutional forces or BAU—business as usual—inadvertently or sometimes advertently bottles it up. Then there are the wargames that go prescient on us. We insist with the passion of zealots that wargames do not predict the future. They pose plausible scenarios; players take those scenarios, discuss how to proceed and work through the issues, and then, sometimes, it is the players who point to an actionable outcome. Sometimes that outcome in a game winds up predicting a corporate decision in the future even if the decision in the real world is not to act. The two merger-related wargames that follow each make that point: the first on a merger that went right and the second on a merger that did not happen.

○   ○   ○

We insist with the passion of zealots that wargames do not predict the future. They pose plausible scenarios; players take those scenarios, discuss how to proceed and work through the issues, and then, sometimes, it is the players who point to an actionable outcome. Sometimes that outcome in a game winds up predicting a corporate decision in the future even if the decision in the real world is not to act.

In August 1991, communist plotters tried to seize power from Soviet party boss Mikhail Gorbachev. They failed miserably but still secured their place in history as ham-fisted exemplars of the law of unintended consequences. In less than a month, Russian President Boris Yeltsin became an unlikely political rock star, the old Soviet Union collapsed, and the end of the Cold War was in plain sight.

About the same time, we were putting the finishing touches on a wargame designed for FMC Corporation. Bear with us for a few moments and we'll answer your question, which probably is: What in blazes is the connection between this particular wargame and the demise of the Soviet empire and the end of the Cold War?

FMC began life as the Food Machinery Corporation, an apt name for an early twentieth-century manufacturer of equipment that washed, dried, sorted, and packed citrus products. By World War II, however, the company was making military vehicles as well as specialty chemicals, and it flourished over the next four decades as the Cold War fattened U.S. defense budgets. Among its Defense Systems Group's best-known products were the M113 Armored Personnel Carrier and the Bradley Fighting Vehicle. But orders for tracked combat vehicles began to plateau in the mid-1980s and fell sharply later in the decade when Poland and other Soviet satellites broke free, dooming the empire.

Our firm began working with FMC a couple of years before the game, in part because its top management believed the decline in defense markets would continue and perhaps even accelerate with a post–Cold War peace dividend. FMC's leaders thought the answer to their problems was a merger, and by the time they asked us to wargame their strategy, they already had settled on a prospective marriage partner: General Dynamics' Land Systems division, which made the M1 Abrams Main Battle Tank. They had run the numbers and figured a combination with their Defense Systems Group made financial sense; there were economies of scale in a merger even in a troubled market for tracked combat vehicles. Now it was time to test the proposition in a wargame.

In designing the game, we had a marketing team and four competitor teams: FMC and General Dynamics, of course, but we also included two others, including the BMY Division of Harsco Corporation. BMY was also in the defense business, producing tank-recovery vehicles and artillery pieces.

We began to play the game, and the FMC and General Dynamics teams just couldn't strike a deal. The GD team members did not see why General Dynamics needed FMC; they recognized that the two companies had separate military systems and that GD was on the threshold of selling its tanks all over the world to countries in need of upgrading their ground forces. Remember, these were FMC executives playing on both teams, and both teams were saying that a deal did not make sense on the basis of the numbers they were crunching.

In fact, in the second move, an FMC manager playing on the FMC team piped up with another proposal. "Look, what we ought to do is get together with BMY because they built all those howitzers that are all over the world," the FMC executive said. "All the NATO countries have them, and most of our other allies have versions of them." All those artillery pieces—or most of them, anyway—would need to be rebuilt, he added. "We could help them do that. And we could combine our manufacturing assets to achieve cost savings." At the end of move 2, FMC ended up partnering with BMY to create a new company (a newco), which seemed quite successful when the impartial marketing team did projections out five years.

The head of FMC's Defense Systems Group was Thomas W. Rabaut, and he was having none of it. At least twice in the course of the game, he stood up and told his people—principally the FMC and BMY teams but by extension everyone in the room—to rethink the problem. That outcome, he said, was plain nuts. FMC has been talking about the need to do a deal with General Dynamics for two years, and now this wargame says we should combine with BMY? He and others insisted the problem had to be the market model we were using. It was getting very testy.

Instead of going to the next move, we told everyone to take a break while we revisited the market model. Afterward, with different assumptions, we quickly replayed the game and came to the same conclusion: BMY was the merger partner that seemed ideal. Still Rabaut and his associates were not convinced. The entire game was starting to come unstuck. But Mark Frost, one of the co-authors of this book, had an idea. At the end of that day, we grabbed one representative from each competitor team and brought them into a room with the market team. All right, we said, what if the market model looked out 10 years instead of 5? Would you do anything differently? The team reps went back to their teammates, the teams huddled, and we played the game again—and got the same result.

In all, we played the game four times under different marketing assumptions and got the same answer all four times: A deal with BMY was not only the best merger choice, it would produce a terrific outcome. Still FMC resisted. At that point, everyone was kind of exhausted. We were scheduled to meet the next morning, but the FMC people went back to their offices late in the day and ran the numbers using their own spreadsheets. Suddenly the light dawned.

The next morning, Rabaut took ownership of the wargame by acknowledging that BMY was the superior merger partner. The reasons seemed obvious in retrospect, but it took the wargame to reveal them. FMC's Bradley Fighting Vehicle was made using a special process to sheath it in laminated aluminum armor. General

Dynamics' M1 battle tank was also an armored combat vehicle, but it hardly resembled the Bradley in its manufacture. Its armor was made of layers of steel, ceramics, plastics, and Kevlar. The production lines were completely different, and retooling to accommodate both vehicles would be wildly expensive if it was possible at all.

BMY, in contrast, armored its vehicles with aluminum laminate, and its manufacturing facility used the same tools FMC's defense group did, except that BMY did its work in a much more modern plant in York, Pennsylvania. FMC's defense group could move to York, use the relatively new BMY facility, and keep retooling costs to a minimum. It was a perfect fit.

Tom Rabaut was a West Point graduate who spent five years in the Army before moving into the private sector. He also had a Harvard MBA—all in all, a very impressive guy. In the final session of the game, everyone had loosened up a bit, and Tom wasn't fighting the outcome of the game anymore. But there was one other matter on his mind. His group also had a pending acquisition of a small aerospace company—not the entire aerospace company but a division that made military communications equipment. Now, in light of what had transpired, adding another defense component completely unrelated to FMC's redefined core mission—that is, the strategic merger with BMY—seemed a wrongheaded notion to every single person in the room. "This one's really stupid," he said. "Why didn't anybody tell me this was such a dumb idea?" Tom Rabaut was a powerful personality, and his operating style did not exactly encourage pushback among his senior managers. But one FMC guy pushed himself away from a wall, stood tall, and answered Tom's question: "Because it was your idea, boss." The room went quiet.

We have always told our clients that wargames should play out in a no-fault, no-blame environment; otherwise, middle managers or junior officers in the military might be tempted to censor themselves to please their bosses. In this case, and to Rabaut's credit, he got the message loud and clear. He had been ready to spend several hundred million dollars to buy a company that was essentially

It's fine to have a strategy going into a wargame. Our job is to test that strategy as rigorously as we can. The participants can fight the scenario, even though we always caution them against it, and can question the outcome of team deliberations, the assumptions made in market models, and even our motives.

worthless to him. Now, in that moment of recognition, the deal with the aerospace company died an appropriate death.

It's fine to have a strategy going into a wargame. Our job is to test that strategy as rigorously as we can. The participants can fight the scenario, even though we always caution them against it, and can question the outcome of team deliberations, the assumptions made in market models, and even our motives. But we do not have a dog in the fight. Sometimes a wargame ratifies a strategy, sometimes it suggests nudging it in a slightly different direction, and sometimes it leads to an outcome no one could have anticipated. It's the impossibility theorem at work again: The power of the game is in the experiential learning of the real experts, in this case, the people in FMC's defense group. It was their collective minds that startled the room.

In January 1994, when Tom Rabaut was vice president and general manager of his company's Defense Systems Group, FMC and Harsco came to terms and formed a new company, United Defense LP. United Defense, headquartered in York, Pennsylvania, combined the defense businesses of the two companies. Three years later, the Carlyle Group, one of the premier U.S. private equity investors (and the majority owner of Booz Allen Hamilton since July 2008), bought United Defense, which Rabaut was running as president and CEO, for $880 million. Rabaut continued to run United Defense with great success. Carlyle took the renamed United Defense Industries public in late 2001. Less than four years later, BAE Systems, a major defense contractor, bought UDI. The sale price was almost $4.2 billion.

The wargame's recommended course of action turned out to prescient and profitable.

THE BIG IDEA When one is contemplating mergers, open-mindedness is critical. The seemingly no-brainer pairings may not withstand scrutiny. True synergies—the kind that produce economies of scale and lead to better performance over the long haul—are often not obvious. Leaders must be willing to keep their eyes on the greater goal, even if that means jettisoning cherished merger targets, to create combinations that make sense for both parties.

A few years ago, a big player in the human nutrition business—part of a large transnational company—asked us to design and conduct a wargame on a potential acquisition. The head of that division, which made vitamins and other supplements and marketed them to food manufacturers, was considering an acquisition that would represent in effect a step toward vertical integration. The potential target was a so-called flavors house.

When a food company cooks up a new product or wants to alter an existing one, it contracts with a firm that specializes in creating the taste, or flavor, of the product, as well as its aroma. The food company may put its request out for competitive bidding to, say, five preferred flavor houses; it then picks the one it likes best and either manufactures the flavoring itself or outsources it. These flavors outfits often design the scents for perfumes too, and despite their size, they tend to have an aura of artisanship about them. The division head reckoned that putting a flavors house together with his human nutrition group could provide one-stop shopping for food companies, giving him some leverage on price and perhaps a larger share of the market.

The three-move game, with each move representing two years in time, began with the assumption that our client company had acquired the flavors house, spun off its perfume business, and integrated the rest into its human nutrition unit. In the first move, the idea was to develop a strategy moving forward. The second move was to be a test of that strategy, and the third move was to examine whether the strategy could be sustained. In the wargame, the competing teams included our client; another flavors house, which was a traditional competitor of the target acquisition; a company that competed in health ingredients with our client before the acquisition; and a major cash-rich commodities company with in-house health ingredients and some recent acquisitions in the flavors business. A market team would represent existing and potential customers and provide feedback on strategies and market trends. As usual, a control team would represent everyone else—board members, other competitors, and regulators—and provide overall guidance. The competing teams would take strategic actions in three market segments: flavors, traditional nutrition or health ingredients such as vitamins and minerals, and new health ingredients such as omega-3 fatty acids and soy proteins.

From the very start, in move 1 and in the subsequent moves as well, the home team—our client—was rebuffed at almost every turn. A food company, represented by the market team, would say: "Look, we want to introduce a new sparkling beverage that tastes fruity and contains healthy ingredients." Our client would bid on the business, packaging its flavors component with health ingredients, but it turned out the food companies were not interested. They wanted to buy a flavor design and then shop for ingredients among many potential suppliers. The competing flavors house was more attractive to the food companies because it was not tied to one health ingredients company; it could leverage multiple ingredients suppliers—including the Chinese, who had become big players in the ingredients game—and knock down costs to the food company. In short, the synergy our client anticipated from bringing a flavors house and nutritional ingredients together in one enterprise turned out to be evanescent. When the acquired flavors house was branded with new corporate colors, it lost its luster in the eyes of food-company customers.

> **THE BIG IDEA**   Corporate culture is an elusive thing, much
> discussed and little understood. But any merger or acquisi-
> tion ought to be analyzed for potential culture shock before
> papers are signed. Clashes are all too common and can have
> negative impacts that go directly to the bottom line.

That big idea spoke directly to the one of the two key lessons of the wargame:

- **This merger *was* a corporate culture mismatch.** The flavors house was artsy-craftsy, with a strong individual identity; the parent of the human nutrition division was a huge company with dozens of business units and a corporate culture that stressed assimilation. It was just a bad fit.

- **The pure segment players had a competitive edge compared with a combined new business unit.** By sticking to their current business models, with some slight adjustments, these segment leaders could remain highly competitive and increase their business. The acquisition might work if the flavors house continued to operate independently. But as part of a merged business unit? No way, and that led to the second major insight.

Our client got that message loud and clear: In short order, the potential acquisition went up in smoke.

CHAPTER 11

ALL HAZARDS, ALL THE TIME

Here's a small, telling story. Not too long ago we were conducting a wargame for a financial services organization that, among other scenarios, postulated a terrorist attack on a data facility; this processing center was built and configured to handle a particularly crucial category of financial transactions. In the game, the company's chief operating officer, playing on the company team, seemed to take the blow in stride: "Let's just roll over that function to the backup site," he said. The company had spent several hundred million dollars on the backup site, which looked as imposing as NASA's launch facility in Florida. "Just roll it over," he repeated.

"We can't do that, sir." a tentative voice said from the back of the room.

The COO was taking umbrage: "Well, why not? I bought that function for all the other backup sites; why can't I roll this one over?"

"I don't know, sir, but you didn't buy it for this site," said the little voice.

The COO looked down, seeming to examine his expensive shoes for several painful seconds, then looked up and said: "Could you buy it now, please."

The capacity of a system, community, or society potentially exposed to hazards to adapt by resisting or changing in order to reach and maintain an acceptable level of functioning and structure.

That's the definition of "resilience" according to the United Nations International Strategy for Disaster Reduction. In the post-9/11 world, resilience has become a critical imperative for democratic governments and private-sector organizations.

Our wargames group has been asked to conduct many wargames designed to test the resilience of financial institutions. In the process, we and the financial institutions have learned a great deal, not least that the men and women in charge of these megabillion-dollar or even trillion-dollar pots of money frequently underestimate how vulnerable their enterprises are. This is not so much false bravado as it is a condition of the world they know: When you run an organization that is participating in a vibrant global marketplace, losses in the hundreds of millions or a billion dollars—perhaps even in a single day—are, if not commonplace, at least to be expected now and again. These men and women live with a familiar uncertainty every day. They are what Robb Kurz calls the "Galactic Capitalists," the new masters of the universe. Is it any surprise they feel invincible?

But they are not invincible. Threats to large institutions can start small, posing no immediate danger to the organism, but then grow and metastasize and become quite large—big enough and fast enough to challenge an organization's ability to manage the threat effectively. Just think about the speed with which the subprime mortgage crisis swept through financial institutions in 2007 and 2008.

The vast majority of large, complex companies do some form of business continuity planning (BCP), but a subtle conflict exists in most enterprises between the people who run major lines of business and the people in charge of BCP. How can this be? The line-of-business executives seek the most efficient and productive organization possible, all the better to maximize revenue and minimize costs. Business continuity planning is a cost. It costs money to build backup centers and purchase other forms of redundancy. In other words, to support resilience, you need to allocate resources to contingencies that you hope and in fact believe will never occur. Because that money represents a diversion from investment in what otherwise would be profit-generating assets, profit and resilience are in dynamic tension with each other. Too often, resilience suffers until a companywide crisis makes it clear that the senior executives really do not walk on water.

In the post-9/11 world, "diversity" has become one of the new buzzwords in resilience planning, that is, diversity in delivered services such as electric power and communications.

That is why the CEO and his or her top people would benefit by testing themselves and their organization against an imagined crisis in a wargame. In the post-9/11 world, "diversity" has become one of the new buzzwords in resilience planning, that is, diversity in delivered services such as electric power and communications. We did one game for a financial institution that wanted to test the resilience of an information technologies site. In our pregame interview with company executives, they were quite proud of their diversity in telecommunications for the site: They had three lines from three different providers coming into the building. However, it turned out that those three lines met at a single switch in a telecom facility about a mile from their site. If that telecom facility went down for some reason, their IT operation would be rendered deaf, mute, and blind.

We want to take you through two wargames, each one for a major financial institution with offices, operations, and branches in the United States and dozens of other countries around the world. (We have fictionalized the names of the institutions for reasons of confidentiality.) We call these all-hazards wargames, or simulations, because financial organizations of this size, scope, and visibility seem particularly exposed to multiple threats that could hit them one at a time, all at once, or anywhere in between. The idea behind these all-hazards games is to pose plausible scenarios, some of them arguably hostile, that reveal weaknesses an organization can offset with smarter strategic planning that does not discount worst-case possibilities.

○   ○   ○

Pan-Europa Bank International is a global giant, a huge and prosperous institution with operations in every facet of banking, brokerage, money management, and more. The time in the real world was spring 2006, but the opening scenario in the wargamed world of Pan-Europa Bank was a year in the future: the spring of 2007. We designed a game to be played by three teams: two made up of the bank's senior managers and the third representing corporate functions such as specific lines of business, communications, governmental relations, and marketing. We intended to do the equivalent of what we have done in certain military games; that is, we planned to stress the client. In this case, the specific objective was to test how the bank performed in a series of disrupted environments.

The start of move 1 set the tone. We began with an opening scenario of international tensions that cause ripple effects in key financial markets. Tensions between Sunni and Shiite Muslims continue to plague the Middle East, placing greater strain on governments throughout the region and in South Asia as well. Anti-Western, especially anti-American, sentiment is growing. Pan-Europa Bank has highly visible ties in some of these Muslim countries, and so it is singled out for criticism and protests. Chaos erupts in Pakistan when terrorists attack its political leaders: Pervez Musharraf is assassinated. India takes advantage of the tumult, moving troops into Kashmir, and Pakistan's military responds in kind. There are rumors that the U.S. government is considering a noncombatant evacuation for both countries. Meanwhile, a developing country where Pan-Europa Bank has significant operations is talking about greater government control of its banking industry, possibly even nationalization of foreign interests. Oil prices and interest rates rise sharply, stock prices fall, and signs of trouble at major hedge funds are beginning to surface.

A point we stress before, during, and even after a wargame is that however incredible these scenarios may seem, incredible things happen in the real world all the time. Do not argue about plausibility; accept what you see and hear as a simulation of what could happen and make decisions that are based on it. Not enough information? Sorry, but you make decisions every day with incomplete information.

This was a fairly tough opening scenario, but not unduly so. We were not in the business of playing "gotcha." Instead, we wanted to challenge bank executives and make them feel reasonably comfortable with the simulation; in other words, we wanted them to think that this scenario could be plausible in their world.

The company reacts to the scenario with confidence, even when our control group ratchets up the pressure with "injects": changes in the scenario reflecting changes in the simulated environment. The injects include intelligence indicating possible terrorist attacks on key financial institutions. A recovered laptop computer contains details of Pan-Europa Bank's infrastructure and IT networks as well as the bank's air and ground transportation assets. Meanwhile, the new president in the developing country cited in the opening scenario has demanded all documents related to Pan-Europa Bank's purchase of a local bank five years earlier. Pan-Europa shares begin to fall sharply after rumors that large foreign investors in the Middle East and elsewhere may be shedding stock. Hedge fund woes worsen, and the bank's private-wealth clients suffer some big losses. The Federal Reserve wants an update on the bank's problems. Then CNN breaks a story: The Department of Homeland Security, a correspondent says, is evaluating an intelligence report that terrorists have targeted key facilities of Pan-Europa Bank in the United States. The authorities believe, according to CNN, that attacks may be imminent. Suddenly, one of Pan-Europa Bank's problems is glaringly public.

These injects are not exactly beanbag, and they come at participants while they discuss the opening scenario, complicating their deliberations. A point we stress before, during, and even after a wargame is that however incredible these scenarios may seem, incredible things happen in the real world all the time. Do not argue about plausibility; accept what you see and hear as a simulation of what could happen and make decisions that are based on it. Not enough information? Sorry, but you make decisions every day with incomplete information. It's no different here.

We told the teams that after move 1, we would ask them to assess the situation, gauge its impact across the organization and its operations, and tell the other participants and the control team what actions they needed to take and what message they needed to convey to customers, shareholders, employees, and regulators.

The two teams of senior managers did not see any systemic crisis, although they conceded that one was possible and that individual difficulties could worsen very quickly. For the most part, the bank's regional crisis-response mechanisms were operating. The developing country threatening Pan-Europa Bank's subsidiary? "It's noise," one top executive said. If the country's leader nationalizes, let it happen. We can take the financial hit.

As for the hedge funds, more information was needed to make a clear assessment, although exposures should be reduced. Physical threats in Pakistan and India should be a higher priority than rumored threats in the United States, at least until senior managers have better information. Meanwhile, new activity by the bank in the Middle East should be curtailed.

The safety of employees, they said, should take precedence, contingency plans should be tuned up, and risk-management scenarios should be reviewed. Corporate communications should produce press releases that address the situation as well as internal memos for all employees. New York is among the top priorities. Management has begun to recognize that operations in the U.S. financial center are critical. But thus far, the situation is not out of control. Difficult but discrete events can be managed, even if it means significant financial loss. In other words, it's largely BAU.

But business as usual becomes inoperative in move 2, when the scenario evolves and the damage to the company becomes apparent. In the scenario, U.S. intelligence authorities have a source who has provided detailed information about potential terrorist activities against the bank, information that came out of Pakistan and is linked to Al-Qaida. The information includes details about key IT facilities, evidence of forged badges to provide access to the bank's headquarters, and data identifying the bank's airplanes, helicopters, trucks, and vans. At one point, responding to a surge in intelligence that suggests possible attacks, antiterrorism authorities recommend an evacuation of the bank's headquarters building.

Press reports in the *New York Times* and on the BBC point to bank customer data—names, account numbers and balances, Social Security numbers—appearing on a Web site linked to the bank's main Web site. The bank denies involvement, takes down the Web site, and promises to investigate. But the Web site may have been up for more than 24 hours, and there are reports that customer accounts have been penetrated. Financial analysts worry that consumer confidence in the bank could erode. It doesn't help that the bank's main provider of business process outsourcing, in South Asia, is under investigation for links to organized crime.

As the teams begin to wrestle with the move 2 scenario, fresh injects squeeze the bank even more tightly. That developing country has placed senior bank officials under house arrest for failure

Now the Wall Street Journal *is on the case: A major piece to run tomorrow raises questions about the security breaches, the bank's hedge-fund vulnerabilities, and its flagging reputation— indeed, its very future.*

to provide the documents it has been seeking. As tensions between Pakistan and India escalate, the United States orders all nonessential government personnel to leave those two countries; meanwhile, the Pentagon, according to the *Washington Post*, has begun expedited planning for a possible noncombat evacuation order.

And that's the least of it. Bank customers begin to close accounts because of the security breaches. Lines begin to form at branch offices, and withdrawals at bank ATM machines spike. But it is not money the cyberattackers are after. Government and bank investigators soon learn that the goal is identity theft, which sets off an even bigger panic among many bank customers. Within days, more than 10 percent of the bank's customers close their accounts. That means tens of billions of dollars and euros in motion. Bank regulators intensify their review of bank operations, and angry members of Congress, besieged by frantic constituents, call senior bank executives to Washington to testify before the appropriate committees. Now the *Wall Street Journal* is on the case: A major piece to run tomorrow raises questions about the security breaches, the bank's hedge-fund vulnerabilities, and its flagging reputation—indeed, its very future.

The teams took steps during move 2 to meet the multiple threats. They asked for government help because they recognized that they were under attack and perhaps at existential risk. They invoked the bank's continuity plans across the organization. They evacuated the bank's New York facilities as recommended. They activated a Computer Emergency Readiness Team, or CERT, a joint venture of the public and private sectors, to counter the cyberthreats. They tried to determine what the organization would need to cover a genuine run on the bank, and they began to communicate better with customers and employees.

> **THE BIG IDEA** In a new world that has globalized finance, commerce, and, sadly, terrorism, contingency planning for multinational enterprises is a strategic imperative. But planning cannot be successful if it is designed in isolation from the greater community or is aimed only at a single threat or if the organization is vulnerable to a single point of failure. Nor is contingency planning a one-time initiative. Rather, it must evolve as threats evolve, and all the organization's stakeholders must know what to expect if there is a breach.

The players from Pan-Europa Bank boiled down the many takeaways to a precious few:

- Bank officials thought they could solve the problems on their own, but they should have reached out to the government earlier. Large banking institutions tend to regard government the way the rest of us, at least in America, regard water: It's there, readily available, and all you need to do is turn on the faucet when you need it. But government does not respond instantaneously in all cases. Getting the government involved earlier would have helped.

- The bank's contingency planning hadn't caught up to ever more sophisticated threats. The bank executives underestimated how skilled the bad guys have become. Multiple events have the potential to defeat single-threat contingency planning. Returning to precrisis business as usual is not an option. The bank needs new security strategies.

- Top executives don't know how robust the bank's communications plan is. Internal and external communications—with employees, customers, regulators, all constituencies, and stakeholders—is critical early and often because if you do not respond immediately to manage the risk to your reputation and brand, you

Single points of failure can cripple decision making in a companywide crisis.

could face the perfect storm. Moreover, communications plans and business continuity plans need to be joined at the hip.

The most significant takeaway, however, was that single points of failure can cripple decision making in a companywide crisis. This is an organization that counts among its strengths the empowerment of local and regional staffs to make daily decisions. But in a crisis that amounted to an existential threat to the organization, key individuals in senior management needed to make critical decisions. And in this case, those managers—in particular the key crisis managers—became the single points of failure. Why? Because in the exercise, the bank's headquarters were evacuated. Normal and cell-phone communication was suspect, and no one had a satellite phone. Security tried to get the bosses to a secure backup site more than a hundred miles away. However, security was unable to use the bank's fleet of aircraft or ground transportation because of the potential terrorist threat; as a result, security had to scramble, and the executives were effectively out of the pocket for several hours.

Single points of failure in a disrupted environment: The potential consequences could be catastrophic.

◇   ◇   ◇

A disrupted environment—more accurately, the possibility of it—was very much on the mind of another major bank. HerculesBanc had combined a series of smart acquisitions with internal growth to become one of the world's largest and strongest banking institutions, but its crisis-response structure had not evolved as the bank expanded in size and complexity. Hercules-Banc had established a new enterprisewide group called Crisis Management and Mitigation, or CM2, to develop an all-hazards plan. However, the plan was still very much a work in progress, and

CM2 team members wanted to assess what they had produced thus far before presenting it to the senior levels of management at the bank. They asked us to stage a wargame that would field-test the CM2 framework, pinpoint its strengths and weaknesses, probe for additional solutions, and identify opportunities for the bank to demonstrate its corporate citizenship in a crisis atmosphere.

Four teams played the three-move game over two days in summer 2006. An enterprise leadership team represented the bank's senior executives, who were critical to decision making during a crisis. A crisis communications team was responsible for internal and external communications. A wholesale line-of-business team and a consumer line-of-business team rounded out the bank players. As usual, our folks played the control team, introducing external shocks, reacting for customers and regulators, and assessing the impact of actions taken by the teams playing the game. The CM2 members told us they did not want these teams playing the equivalent of Terrorism 101; instead, CM2 challenged us to develop unfamiliar and even shocking scenarios. We took them at their word.

In the game, it is September 1, 2007. HerculesBanc's leadership gets word from the FBI that a raid on a suspected terrorist safe house contained details about the bank's headquarters in the United States and several offices in the United States and abroad, several fake bank visitor badges, information about the bank's data centers, and the tail numbers of bank planes and helicopters used to move people and data. We concede that this part of the opening scenario of move 1 echoes the previous wargame. But what happens over the next few days advances the opening scenario as injects are added and then two distinct scenarios in the next two moves are added. It all comes together as a collection of huge hits HerculesBanc must confront in an imagined world of plausible—not predictive—disasters.

The troubles come at the bankers quickly. In this first week of September 2007, several bank customers and bank employees are shot entering or leaving the bank offices in three Midwestern cities,

The discussion and the decision making in move 1 of wargames tend to be tentative. In this one, the internal debates were lively, and the teams made some sound decisions.

in Seattle, in Boston, and in cities in the mid-Atlantic states. On September 7, a senior executive in charge of global investment banking is shot to death in his car at a stoplight in the bank's headquarters city. The FBI is on the case and has confirmed that all the shootings took place at some distance—probably skilled snipers at work. The bureau believes it may be the work of a disgruntled employee or an angry customer. Absentee rates at bank offices and branches begin to rise, and customers are closing accounts at a rate of $1 billion a month; ATMs, where some of the shootings have occurred, have become lonely symbols of a bank under siege, which is more or less what the *New York Times* and the *Wall Street Journal* report on September 9 in stories that suggest the bank may have been targeted by terrorists. The "HerculesBanc Sniper" crisis is America's top news story.

The gathering attention sparks other woes. The bank's vendors, from cleaning crews and caterers to IT technicians and private security firms, begin to back away, worried about putting their employees in harm's way. Vendors contracted to refill and service ATMs are balking, and around the country, machines are out of cash. Customers want to close out accounts, but they are frightened to visit their local branches; meanwhile, soaring traffic swamps the bank's main Web site and call centers. HerculesBanc shares sink by about 10 percent and then stabilize, but analysts on Wall Street contemplate downgrading the stock. The violence continues: Two traders are shot and killed at 6:30 a.m. as they enter the bank's Manhattan office.

Control has instructed each team in the wargame to respond to a set of questions. The enterprise leadership and line-of-business teams, for example, were asked to describe what actions they took, identify their main concerns and priorities, and indicate how they interacted with one another. The crisis communications team had to worry about how it got its information and how it "talked" to customers, the public sector, bank employees, clients, external vendors, and regulators. Such questions, with some variations because of the evolving scenarios and the enterprise team's unique leadership role, serve as the template to trigger discussion by the teams and their communication—by e-mail—with the other players throughout the game.

The team performance was much improved in move 2. The enterprise leadership team, for instance, was communicating with the lines-of-business teams and coordinating both internal and external messaging with the crisis communications team.

The discussion and the decision making in move 1 of wargames tend to be tentative. In this one, the internal debates were lively, and the teams made some sound decisions. CM2 members communicated with the bank CEO, whose top people in turn reached out to the Federal Reserve and sought and received reassuring statements that might help mitigate the impact. Security was beefed up, and employees were told that their safety was paramount as HerculesBanc moved forward. But for the most part, the teams left much undone. Lines of authority in the crisis were still unclear, and the teams were operating largely in independent silos. Everyone was reacting to the unfolding scenario, but no one was thinking proactively about the long term; for example, there was no strategic planning, no actions to protect the brand, no real solution to growing absenteeism.

Move 2: It is six weeks after the first alert from the FBI about documents suggesting that HerculesBanc might be a target of terrorists. Acting on an anonymous tip, the bureau arrests six sniper suspects across the United States. The connection among them and their motives remain unclear, but one suspect is found with a notebook detailing plans for every attack. Mercifully, the shootings have stopped, and bank operations are starting to return to BAU— business as usual.

But not for long. Five days after the arrests, rolling earthquakes rock California, where the bank has many branches and other operations, and early reports indicate massive damage to infrastructure throughout the state, especially in the major metropolitan areas. Bridges and roads have been destroyed, power lines are down, and communication networks are paralyzed up and down the West Coast. People are trapped in collapsed buildings and houses, and thousands are feared dead.

Experts say that the quake and its aftershocks have left 6,000 dead and 20,000 seriously injured; millions, with their apartments or single-family homes destroyed, have become refugees, with no money and no place to go. It is simply a massive humanitarian disaster, worse than 9/11 and Katrina combined.

For the bank, it's a catastrophe. Several office buildings are devastated, data centers suffer severe damage with flooding and loss of power, and internal communications networks are slow or crippled. ATMs in the state are not working, a major call center is inoperable, other centers are overwhelmed, and wire transfer operations are in chaos. Customers outside California are beginning to complain about botched handling of their accounts. In human terms, many bank employees cannot return home; fires in their neighborhoods make matters even worse.

The team performance was much improved in move 2. The enterprise leadership team, for instance, was communicating with the lines-of-business teams and coordinating both internal and external messaging with the crisis communications team. The leadership team secured hundreds of housing units for displaced employees and committed tens of millions of dollars in immediate aid to help employees and customers. Even though the earthquake was the top priority, the team continued to monitor the terrorist threat situation, especially around critical operational sites.

Other teams were improving as well. The crisis communications team made sure the word was out that the bank was focused on its employees and their families, had launched a customer-support program, was working with the governor of California and the national leadership, was coordinating with the Red Cross and the National Guard to dispense aid, and was working with other financial institutions to ensure financial continuity in the United States and worldwide. The lines-of-business teams were looking after their employees and focusing on communicating with their customers and clients. Still, the bottom line after move 2 was continuing confusion about roles and responsibilities.

Move 3 may have seemed like piling on, but unprecedented things happen in the real world as well as the one conjured by creative wargamers. A month after the California earthquake, a large bomb explodes in the lobby of the bank's main office building in New York. Damage is extensive. The building is evacuated as quickly as possible, but early estimates of casualties have reached 700 or more. The blast also has crippled data and trading operations in an adjacent building. Bank communications and Web support slow down, and even the best of the bank's institutional clients prove difficult to reach.

Minutes after the explosion in New York, a smaller bomb goes off at HerculesBanc's London office. As the building is being slowly evacuated, first responders at the scene detect radioactivity in the immediate blast zone. British authorities confirm the initial readings and establish a quarantine area around the building.

The two bombs have created a ripple effect, and bank employees are evacuating bank offices at locations across the United States and in selected offices abroad. HerculesBanc is global news once again as financial analysts and banking experts wonder aloud about the potential impact on the global financial system. Then, late the same day, the final insult: Al Jazeera airs an Al-Qaida video featuring Osama bin Laden, who claims the attacks are the work of Islamic warriors, a warning against anyone who "might financially help subjugate Islam."

The teams responded to another set of questions after move 3, suggesting that they finally understood the holes in their crisis planning and what was needed to repair them. In fact, the final takeaways demonstrated that HerculesBanc's participants had used the process of experiential learning to reveal their problems and provide solutions to them.

Move 3 may have seemed like piling on, but unprecedented things happen in the real world as well as the one conjured by creative wargamers. A month after the California earthquake, a large bomb explodes in the lobby of the bank's main office building in New York. Damage is extensive.

Consider the 80-20 rule. One learning from the game was that preplanning is an essential part of an effective all-hazards plan. In the game's third move, we introduced participants to an example of crisis planning employed by a U.S. Army Ranger unit. The unit's mission in this drill is to assemble 120 soldiers and their materiel and equipment and be "wheels up" within 18 hours so that they can construct a staging area within 24 hours of landing. The staging area, or "city," must be capable of providing shelter, medical triage facilities, weapons ranges, an ammunition depot, mock buildings for final assault practice, and general supplies. Here's the catch: They must be prepared to deploy to four different environments: arctic, desert, jungle, and mountains. How? To be successful, they determine that 80 percent of what they need is core to the mission wherever it is, which means that only 20 percent needs to be done at the last minute. Example: You need tents in all four environments but leave the potbelly stove at home unless you're heading for the North Pole.

"ALL HAZARDS" CRISIS PLANNING

Mission: assemble120 soldiers, materiel, and equipment, be "wheels up" in 18 hours, and build a staging area within 24 hours of landing to provide shelter, medical, and dental triage facilities, weapon calibration ranges, ammunition depot, mock buildings, and general supplies.

Challenge: Must be prepared to deploy in four very different regions: Arctic, desert, jungle, and mountains.

In bank terms, the 80-20 rule can and should inform behavior at every level of the institution. Employees must ask themselves: What do I need in my grab-and-go packet? Preplanning and pre-packaging have to be tested on a regular basis, and leadership must convey its commitment and a sense of urgency to the exercise or it will fail. Business as usual is now a nonstarter.

> **THE BIG IDEA** A plan for crisis management and mitigation —a must for transnational companies—should be made clear and transparent to all employees. It should be simple, with clear lines of authority, and it should be drilled often enough that responses are confident and automatic.

The list of additional takeaways is a long one. The following six are key:

- **Roles and responsibilities in a CM2 plan must be clear and understood at every level of the organization.** Decisions in the first hours and days of a crisis are key, and confusion may lead to chaos, slowing or even crippling the bank's response and potentially endangering the bank's human, physical, and financial assets. Decision rights are critical: Every manager cannot be in charge; in a crisis, egos must be checked at the door.

- **Lines of succession must be transparent so that a bank leader who is not available during a crisis can be replaced by someone with fully vested authority.** In the game, the California quake provided a vivid example of why this is absolutely necessary. The CM2 planning had designated someone to run California operations in the event of a natural disaster. But as the scenario unfolded, a participant on the enterprise leadership team who was playing the designee demurred. In a paraphrase of his remarks: "You people don't understand. I'll be dead. And if I'm not dead, I'll be looking for my family or trying to find food and a place to sleep, or all of the above. Look, I'm not going to be able to run this." Everyone else said, No, no, you're in charge. It was an organizational disconnect: He was the designated guy in theory but not in fact.

- **Unless people are trained in exactly what they are supposed to do in a crisis, they will fall back on what they know.** In HerculesBanc and other global financial institutions, this idea is countercultural. Such banks thrive on local entrepreneurial action that benefits from—forgive the oxymoron—creative repetition, which is another way of saying business as usual. A clear command-and-control structure is a sine qua non in a crisis. That said, wargame participants noted how well the bank had assimilated new acquisitions by using transition teams to cut across business lines. The suggestion—a good one—was to adapt what works well in the bank's culture to the new age of crisis management and mitigation, or CM2.

- **CM2 can and should minimize the confusion and differences among existing crisis-response plans.** As a global enterprise with offices in hundreds of cities and countries and a tradition of ceding authority to its local and regional entrepreneurs, HerculesBanc has more than 2,000 independent business continuity plans. Their sheer number, limited integration, and variability mean an inevitably slowed response in a crisis. The CM2 plan would replace this hodgepodge with one basic crisis management and mitigation framework that is adaptable to address details in a specific crisis.

- **The CM2 plan, in its construction and explanation to employees, should employ KISS principles: Keep it simple, stupid.** Without a clear understanding of how the plan is supposed to function, rank-and-file employees and even bank leaders may find themselves flummoxed in a crisis. When the plan goes live, it should be communicated to one and all in brief summary form—no more than two pages—and scrubbed to remove any and all jargon.

- **Communication, internal and external, is of paramount importance.** Transparency, information sharing, explanations of decisions, clear guidance—all these things and much more should be part of a communications process that is disciplined, timely, and concise; serves to calm the bank's constituents without deceiving them; and supports the brand as the bank responds to the crisis.

There is more, of course. It was especially heartening that the participants thought the bank in a crisis could serve purposes beyond its own successful responses. Indeed, it could even distinguish itself. How? If the bank could use CM2 to protect and stabilize itself, there might be opportunities to reach out beyond its own universe of employees and customers to assist the broader community or a troubled competitor. In other words, even in adversity, corporate citizenship need not be sacrificed, indeed, *should* not be sacrificed.

PART III

GLOBAL CRISIS WARGAMES

CHAPTER 12

THE IMPACT OF 9/11

B efore the attacks of September 11, 2001, we had not done wargames that brought together private-sector people and public officials to address issues of our choosing. However, 9/11 upset the traditional patterns and introduced a significant discontinuity: a sharp break from the past. It used to be, for instance, that law enforcement was what happened onshore and national security was what happened offshore. No more: The two have melded in many ways as those in the public and private sectors struggle to figure out how to deal with their altered worlds.

These are people who often are in the business of managing risk; the problem is finding a way to manage risk when you cannot understand it. In such circumstances, the best option may be to reinvent risk in a new environment. Wargames have become an important mechanism for doing that, allowing participants to begin to discover the new world.

Our firm lost three people at the Pentagon on 9/11. They were our colleagues and our friends, and we felt the loss deeply. We feel it to this day. In that emotional early autumn of 2001, however, there also was a huge sense of resolve: At every level, people at the firm said we had to do something. We already had a large group of people focused on homeland security and defense, and so we decided to expand our wargames practice to include public-private partnerships, that is, conceive games on national-security issues that we would cosponsor with a nonprofit organization. We never had given away wargames before, but we planned to do these games for free and make the findings available to anyone who wanted access to them.

These wargames have differed in important respects from our military and business wargames, although they bear some resemblance to the games described in Chapter 11, which focused on the resilience of large financial institutions under siege. We call these global crisis wargames because the issues can and often do transcend national boundaries. They are designed to test systems and probe for weaknesses that reveal, as successful wargames often do, a set of lessons and next steps. They rarely include the kind of competition central to most military and business wargames. Instead, the emphasis is on leadership and cooperation, bringing groups of stakeholders together to work toward a common objective.

The subject matter varies widely: We have conducted wargames on HIV/AIDS in China and India, disaster relief, political and economic stability in western Africa, and a simulation for the New York Fire Department in advance of the Republican National Convention in that city in 2004. The scenarios we pose in these games are not predictive; we hope such crises, with the loss of human life they imply, never occur. However, we live in an age when potential threats seem to be proliferating, and asymmetric or unconventional warfare is gaining greater purchase. Raising awareness and assessing preparedness for such calamities can help, we believe, if the real thing happens sometime in the future.

The first of these wargames, and the focus of this chapter, is on bioterrorism, a reaction in part to the series of anthrax attacks and related incidents that began the third week in September 2001 and continued through the fall. The objective of the game, conducted over two days in mid-December 2001, was to mobilize the participants to improve U.S. preparedness for and response to an act of bioterrorism. The game, which was cosponsored by the

Council for Excellence in Government, brought together top people from the federal government, including the Department of Health and Human Services (HHS) and the Department of Defense (DOD) as well as the Federal Emergency Management Agency (FEMA). In addition, our 75 attendees included state and local government officials, corporate CEOs and other executives, and representatives of companies throughout the health-care industries, from pharmaceuticals and hospitals to insurers and health-industry associations.

We call these global crisis wargames because the issues can and often do transcend national boundaries. They are designed to test systems and probe for weaknesses that reveal, as successful wargames often do, a set of lessons and next steps. They rarely include the kind of competition central to most military and business wargames. Instead, the emphasis is on leadership and cooperation.

For this wargame, we organized the participants into three business stakeholder teams (health insurers, medical products, and medical providers) and three government stakeholder teams: HHS/FEMA, DOD/VA (Veterans Affairs), and state and local. A Booz Allen control team structured the game, introduced external shocks, and monitored and arbitrated play.

The opening scenario was right out of a horror novel: In what seemed to be a coordinated attack, unidentified persons simultaneously released aerosolized pneumonic plague bacteria in two American cities: Detroit, Michigan, and Norfolk, Virginia.

Pneumonic plague is very serious business. It is highly contagious and can be spread easily through the air. The initial symptoms of this plague resemble the flu: aches and pains, fever, headache, and muscle weakness. Then, according to the U.S. Centers for Disease Control and Prevention, pneumonia rapidly develops, bringing with it shortness of breath, chest pain, cough, and sometimes bloody or watery sputum. "The pneumonia progresses for two to four days," according to CDC, "and may cause respiratory failure and shock." There is no plague vaccine available in the

The first of these wargames is on bioterrorism, a reaction in part to the series of anthrax attacks and related incidents that began the third week in September 2001 and continued through the fall. The objective of the game, conducted over two days in mid-December 2001, was to mobilize the participants to improve U.S. preparedness for and response to an act of bioterrorism.

United States; without early treatment, the disease is almost always fatal. However, the disease *can* be treated. If strong, fairly common antibiotics such as streptomycin, doxycyline, and tetracycline are administered within the first 24 hours of treatment and continued for a week, the victims survive what would otherwise be a killer.

Our instructions to the teams at the beginning of the first move were both general and specific. We asked them to develop their objectives and the immediate steps they had to take. Were there impediments, risks, and economic consequences to taking those steps? If you are the government, what do you need from health-care companies? If you are in the health-care business, what do you need from the government? What's your message to the public, and how do you communicate it?

The players were to assume that the first move began three days after the attack. We built a computer model to simulate a pneumonic plague epidemic that was based on the virulence of the disease and how quickly antibiotics were administered to sick patients and to potential victims as prophylaxis. Three days after the attack, of course, the true measure of this assault with biological agents was not evident: There were confirmed cases of plague in New York, Illinois, and Windsor, Ontario, as well as Michigan and Virginia and suspected cases in six other states, but the numbers were not huge. Our model projected 108 dead and 447 sick after three days. However, the infection clearly was spreading. The numbers would get a lot worse.

As we have said before, players in wargames often seem tentative in the first move, and this one was no exception. In fact, they were worse than tentative. All the teams were paralyzed, looking elsewhere for guidance. Pharmaceutical companies— the medical products team—was saying in effect: "Who's in charge? What do you want from us? Look, we've got the antibiotics. Where do we send them?" The medical products folks could not get a straight answer from any of the government players, and neither could the other business teams. At the time, only three months after September 11, the U.S. Department of Homeland Secu-

The players were to assume that the first move began three days after the attack. We built a computer model to simulate a pneumonic plague epidemic that was based on the virulence of the disease and how quickly antibiotics were administered to sick patients and to potential victims as prophylaxis.

rity did not exist. A national response plan was in place, but it did not really address the details of decision rights in this kind of crisis. As a result, all the teams struggled to define their roles and understand where to go for information, direction, and resources.

The indecision was so alarming that we did something that we've done only on very rare occasions in military and business games: We stopped the game, rewound the clock, and told the teams to replay the first move from the beginning. The problem was not the setup for the game. The problem was institutional caution— no one wanted to make a bad choice that might make matters worse—combined with an unwillingness to suspend disbelief. It was obviously important to use this teachable moment to reiterate what we always preach to participants in wargames: Remember, the real world always surprises you with astonishing things you could not have imagined. What's more, you never have all the answers to your questions when you make decisions in your day job. In a crisis, we do the best we can with the imperfect information in our possession. You can do no less here. It is better to make mistakes in the imagined world of our wargame, where you can

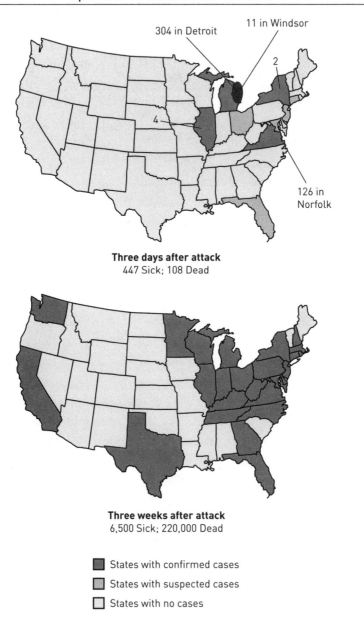

FIGURE 12.1

In the epidemic simulation, the disease struck first in Detroit/Windsor and in Norfolk and then spread to 15 states in three weeks.

304 in Detroit

11 in Windsor

2

4

126 in Norfolk

Three days after attack
447 Sick; 108 Dead

Three weeks after attack
6,500 Sick; 220,000 Dead

■ States with confirmed cases
▨ States with suspected cases
☐ States with no cases

acknowledge errors and learn from them, than to make them when the real crisis arrives and the stakes of decision making are life and death. Dithering in such circumstances can cost millions of lives.

In a crisis, we do the best we can with the imperfect information in our possession. You can do no less here. It is better to make mistakes in the imagined world of our wargame, where you can acknowledge errors and learn from them, than to make them when the real crisis arrives and the stakes of decision making are life and death.

We also combined the replay of the first move with the second move, which assumed a time frame three weeks after the attack. At that point, the full dimensions of the crisis were coming into focus. The Rocky Mountain and Great Plains states remained free of infection, but the West Coast and the eastern half of the United States had tens of thousands of confirmed cases. It actually was worse than that: An estimated 220,000 people already had died (see Figure 12.1). "If we knew how many people might die," said one participant, "we'd have been out there handing out drugs ourselves."

With the harsh numbers front and center, the teams finally engaged. In briefing teams for the second move, we had asked the participants to explore how their priorities had changed now that the disease clearly was spreading. What additional steps did they need to take in this move? Are there points of stress that threaten to collapse key elements in efficient treatment? In other words, what "breaks" and how soon? How do government and business coordinate? Is there a model? Are there risks to being more aggressive?

The teams began to understand that no mechanisms were in place for fast coordination across government agencies and businesses to mobilize needed resources. Mass prophylaxis and protective isolation—quarantine in some cases—were needed within the first few days of the epidemic to prevent the unchecked spread of the disease, but such steps were not taken until the big push three weeks into the time line. They also came to recognize that government and business need each other desperately in such crises. "We had become a vital part of national security," said one businessman after government and business finally began to cooperate.

The timidity in the first play of move 1 evaporated as the players came to realize the enormity of the crisis before them. In the first move, some people on the medical provider and insurer teams worried about the potential consequences of too much prophylactic treatment, particularly for well people who seemed at relatively low risk. The government was initially hesitant to push out too many drugs too quickly, but there was no need to be hesitant. A national pharmaceutical stockpile program was created in 1999 to help cities and states after terrorist acts and in natural disasters. In theory, so-called push packs of pharmaceuticals and other medical gear, strategically positioned around the country, could be delivered to localities in need within 12 hours. In short, there were plenty of drugs out there, and there was no good reason to wait. "We thought we should save for a rainy day," said one participant on the DOD/VA team, "but we realized that this *was* the rainy day."

What was problematic, the players learned, was the distribution of prophylactic drugs to the "worried well"—those who had not been infected but might be. At first, the participants thought the National Guard was the natural choice for distribution, but jurisdictional problems made that impractical. It was not legal for the Guard to cross state lines on official business, and antibiotic drug distribution could not function with stop signs at the border between, say, Michigan and Indiana or Virginia and Maryland. Therefore, a decision was made to flood an area or region with antibiotics, but how could we deliver the goods?

One participant in the game was the CEO of one of the nation's largest insurance companies. He also was a doctor. As it turned out, he had a quirky and entirely plausible solution to the problem: "What about using the U.S. Postal Service?" He reasoned that the Post Office delivered the mail every day but Sunday. What other entity in American life visited homes and apartments six days a week?

He was on the insurer team, and his suggestion was communicated by e-mail to the other teams. The medical products and medical providers teams blanched at the idea. Absolutely not, they said. What if people try to steal the drugs? Well, send a National Guard soldier or a police officer with the mail carrier. What if someone pilfers the box after they leave? If you do not receive your drugs on day 1, put up a red flag or its equivalent and we'll return the next day.

One participant in the game was the CEO of one of the nation's largest insurance companies. He also was a doctor. As it turned out, he had a quirky and entirely plausible solution to the problem: "What about using the U.S. Postal Service?"

The push packs, which can weigh 50 tons each and can include scores of containers, are assembled and stored on bulky pallets that have to be opened and broken down. Once they were disassembled, however, how would the drugs get packaged for delivery by mail carriers? A participant on the medical products team had an answer to that one: Someone in authority would need to go to a Wal-Mart or a large supermarket and purchase Baggies. The drugs, to be taken orally, would go into the Baggies, the Baggies would go to the letter carrier, and, well, you get the idea.

Would it work? It might. But even if it was flawed, the insurance man's idea demonstrated that examining possible solutions, however unconventional, before a crisis can provide valuable input when the people in charge wrestle with the details of a plan. As one participant put it: "It's better to innovate around a plan than to invent a plan on the fly."

Using our computer model for projections, we drilled down for the impact of the pneumonic plague crisis on Detroit under various scenarios. In the game itself, team actions, especially in the second move, significantly constrained the disease's progression. Containment and quarantine lowered the infection rate by 75 percent seven days into the crisis. Prophylactic drugs were brought in from multiple sources—push packs and other government and

Using our computer model for projections, we drilled down for the impact of the pneumonic plague crisis on Detroit under various scenarios. In the game itself, team actions, especially in the second move, significantly constrained the disease's progression.

industry stockpiles—and pharmaceutical companies said they could provide an additional surge in 30 days if stockpiles became depleted. National Guard personnel helped with distribution, and that jacked up the delivery of drugs to 340,000 doses per day at the peak.

In the worst-case scenario, only 50 percent of the Detroit population would have received prophylaxis within three weeks of the attack. The number of deaths in the city, in Michigan, and in other states in the Upper Midwest and Ontario could reach 1.8 million. In the best-case scenario, with 100 percent of the city's population treated with prophylaxis within the first three weeks, mortality would be about 16,000. The realistic scenario, based on the actions of teams in the game, was that around 70 percent would be treated in the first three weeks, followed by an antibiotic production surge at 34 days; that would raise the total of treated people to 90 percent within two additional weeks. In other words, it would not quite be perfection but would be a reasonably prompt and effective response to the crisis. Still, the bottom line was sobering: Even in this scenario, the death toll might rise to as many as 380,000 people.

There also was a serious economic impact on the health-care sector in the Detroit area because under any scenario, many patients might continue to be symptomatic for several months. This is what we meant when we asked our wargamers to address the issue of "what breaks?" What collapses under pressure? Given the huge claim on their resources, we calculated that the minimal cash reserves of Detroit's hospitals might be depleted within 60 to 75 days because of the gap between surging labor costs, which must be paid during the crisis, and inevitable delays in insurance payments due to the sheer volume of claims. By the end of the epidemic, Detroit's hospitals might lose as much as $250 million as a result of costs associated with treatment of the uninsured and patients exceeding their insurance limits. For their part, the insurers in the area might lose as much as $300 million during the course of the crisis; the hit would not exhaust their reserves, but it might lead to changes in coverage—that is, result in less of it. Clearly, some extraordinary measures needed to be taken to shore up hospital finances during the crisis.

We did not model the economic impact on health-care businesses outside Detroit or on other business sectors, but one has to conclude that the ripple effects would be significant. How much? The participants in the wargame guesstimated losses approaching $200 billion.

The lessons of this wargame were clear and painfully paradoxical:

- **To react quickly, industry needs a single point of contact with the government.** That's easier said than done because statutes, policies, and programs for dealing with terrorism create multiple points of entry on a horizontal level—that is, among federal, state, and local governments—and on a vertical level: among agencies at every level of those governments. It's a tough dilemma. Government is both a regulator and a first responder in a crisis, and there is an implicit conflict between the two roles. In essence, industry says it wants somebody to work with across the board. Government says sorry, we don't work that way.

- **Aggressive containment and prophylaxis can limit the spread of the disease.** Right, except that moving too quickly can consume reserve capacity needed later in the crisis or for future contingencies. In a sense, this is why we replayed the first move. The players' initial hesitancy would have caused millions of deaths. That was unacceptable. They had to push out as much antibiotic treatment and prophylaxis as they could, and they had to do it even in the unlikely event of a vulnerable drug supply chain down the road.

- **Response plans normally focus their efforts at the local level.** Yes, but bioterrorism, as we saw in our wargame, quickly becomes a national problem, requiring coordination across federal, state, and local governments and among all sectors of the health-care industry: hospitals, drug makers, insurers, and more. In this wargame, business took the lead: It said in effect, "This isn't so hard to fix; let's just do it."

- **Suspending legal, regulatory, and procedural restrictions may be necessary to meet immediate needs.** Remember, huge pharmaceutical companies such as Pfizer and Merck compete against one another, but a bioterrorism incident of the scope posited in our wargame would require a level of cooperation that might bump up against the antitrust laws. On the financial front, government funds or loan guarantees might be needed to ensure that hospitals could pay their employees. What about the civil liberties implications if the government ordered the quarantine of large portions of the population to contain the disease's spread? Immediate communication with the public would be absolutely necessary.

In our postmortem on the wargame, we asked the teams to reflect on what had transpired and give us their key observations, internal priorities, and requests to and from other entities. There were dozens, and they ranged from the specific—for example, the CDC establishing triage criteria and educating the public through television on its role in the crisis and the benefits of protective isolation—to the more general. But only one key observation coming out of the timid start in move 1 made the list of every team in the game, and it always came first: "A leadership void in the beginning led to delays in action, with catastrophic results." That void, in a crisis of national proportions, must be filled at the national level. What's more, the identity of that leadership cannot be a mystery: In fact, it needs to be communicated throughout government at every level and to the private sector as well.

CHAPTER 13

THE NEXT PORT
IN THE STORM

After 9/11, when 19 terrorists exploited security gaps at the border and at airports, commandeered four commercial jetliners, flew three of them into buildings, and killed nearly 3,000 people, it was understandable and long overdue that official Washington began to ask fresh questions about potential breaches in homeland security. The House Permanent Select Committee on Intelligence was examining the nation's port system and trying to determine a set of priorities for its security in the new age of asymmetric warfare. U.S. Representative Jane Harman of California, then the ranking Democrat on the committee, was especially concerned: She represented a district that included the Port of Long Beach, a gigantic seaport that handled $140 billion in cargo in 2007.

Harman and other key members of the committee recognized that the United States had a fundamental problem in thinking about the ports, not least because of their link to a vast spiderweb of transportation networks that also were vulnerable. The nation's shipping infrastructure begins with its 85 deepwater ports, 46 of them equipped to handle containers: the huge rectangular boxes on tractor-trailers that can be detached from a truck's chassis for loading into a vessel or onto a railcar. Hundreds of commercial vessels call at these ports every day, carrying up to 32,000 containers imported from abroad. Beyond the ports, however, lies the length and breadth of the United States, laced with more than 185,000 miles of railroad tracks that snake across the continent from points east, west, north, and south. This system, with its 8,000 locomotives and 1.6 million freight cars, carries 6 million containers a year. Meanwhile, trucks transport containers to points closer to ports, say, within 500 miles.

You get the idea: If a bad guy did slip a weapon of mass destruction through a port, it could end up anywhere in the shipping system within hours or days. It could end up in a big city or a small town, near a nuclear power plant or a U.S. military base, outside a football stadium or close to a large public gathering on a sunny summer day. In short, security at the nation's ports needed considerable attention, but simply throwing money at the problem did not make much sense. Harman and the others on the intelligence committee wanted as much input as they could get.

We wanted to help if we could. A group of us met with some members of the committee and their staff to discuss their concerns. We said we were interested in wargaming port security on a pro bono basis, and they were plainly keen on the idea; they worked with us, which helped shape our thinking on the design of the game, and even pointed us to people in the government who could both contribute to the play and benefit from the simulation. In the Conference Board, the prestigious research group in New York, we found an enthusiastic partner to cosponsor the project.

On October 2, 2002, less than 10 months after our bioterrorism wargame, we brought together nearly 100 people to participate in a two-day, three-move wargame on port security and the implications for U.S. supply chains. The participants included officials from 14 federal, regional, and state agencies that ranged from the CIA, FBI, and U.S. Department of Defense to the Port Authority of

New York and New Jersey and the Georgia Port Authority. The private sector was represented by managers from companies such as AT&T and Maersk, the big shipping concern, as well as Toyota, Motorola, and several customs, freight, and logistical firms; other participants included trade groups representing port authorities, railroads, engineering, shipping, and advanced manufacturing. We also had some experts from a private-sector alliance that, among other things, sponsors programs to combat chemical, biological, and radiological threats. The ports at the center of the game were Los Angeles and Savannah. Sadly, the Los Angeles dockworkers were on strike the week of the game, and that meant the Los Angeles representatives had to scrap their participation. As we always say in the wargaming business, unexpected things happen all the time in the real world.

In this game, we divided the participants into five teams. One represented the ports of Los Angeles and Savannah; the others represented ocean, rail, and highway freight carriers; automotive, consumer food, and retail supply chains; border operations (customs, immigration, commercial airport security, and the U.S. Coast Guard); and federal policy (the alphabet soup of DOD, CIA, FBI, DOT, and DOJ, plus the U.S. Treasury). As always, a control team that structured the game and introduced external shocks or injects reacted for everyone else: the White House, state governors, foreign governments, and the general public.

The game was designed to nudge players to address four key objectives. First, we wanted to push them to identify critical, systemic threats to port infrastructure. Second, we sought to uncover ways to ensure port security even as the system maintained an open and efficient flow of goods through U.S. supply chains. The third objective was to assess the ripple effects of a major port closure on key industry supply chains and their logistics providers. Fourth, we were eager to get a better understanding of the roles of public and private actors in the context of port security.

In our research into and discussions about port security, the biggest fear was the prospect of some sort of explosive device smuggled into the United States by container, transported to a big city, and then somehow detonated, triggering a chemical, biological, or radiological disaster. It had not happened yet, but only 5 percent of the imported containers unloaded from ships at American ports were inspected closely enough to observe visually or detect electronically suspect cargo. In fact, the vast majority of containers were not opened for the first time until they arrived at their final destinations. In those circumstances, even the optimists in the intelligence community figured it was only a matter of time—when, not if.

We wanted to get their attention with an opening scenario that shocked them and seemed plausible in light of what we knew about the degree of cargo inspections. A radiological "dirty" bomb was found in a shipping container just inside the gate at the Yang Ming Terminal of the Port of Los Angeles. It was found quite literally by accident: The truck carrying the container had suffered a minor mishap and overturned, drawing a crowd of port officials. The Los Angeles Fire Department's bomb squad was summoned to the scene. It defused the bomb, which was removed from the area by the Nuclear Emergency Search Team (NEST), a kind of first responder group of public and private nuclear experts under the U.S. Department of Energy. Officials cleared the area where the bomb was discovered within three hours, and no radiological materials were dispersed. Even so, those in the area of the accident were dispatched to local hospitals as a precaution.

But the day was not over. In our opener, the same morning as the incident in Los Angeles, three men were arrested by the Georgia Port Authority (GPA) police on suspicion of attempted cargo theft in the Port of Savannah's Garden City Terminal. When the authorities ran the suspects' names through the computers, one popped up on the FBI watch list of suspected terrorists. The GPA police turned over the suspects to the FBI for further questioning.

In the scenario, the two incidents came at a time when intelligence analysts had noticed a heightened level of chatter—e-mail traffic, intercepted phone calls, wiretaps—referring to upcoming "deliveries" in the United States. The intel had not been actionable: It had been too vague to identify a specific threat. However, with the events in Los Angeles and Savannah in mind, the analysts were trying to determine whether the dirty bomb on the West Coast was linked to the electronic intercepts referring to deliveries.

Now what? The challenge for the war-game players was to react to the threat of an unknown number of dirty bombs entering the United States. The teams going into their individual discussion groups for move 1 were asked to examine their immediate concerns, priorities, and objectives. What steps must you take now? How prepared are you? What are the near-term consequences of your actions? What is your message, how do you communicate it, and to whom?

We wanted to get their attention with an opening scenario that shocked them and seemed plausible. A radiological "dirty" bomb was found in a shipping container just inside the gate at the Yang Ming Terminal of the Port of Los Angeles. It was found quite literally by accident: The truck carrying the container had suffered a minor mishap and overturned.

Three fundamental points of tension emerged as team play began. First, it was clear that security and efficiency tended to tug in opposite directions; that was not unlike what we learned in Chapter 11 when we saw how two global financial institutions facing threatening scenarios had to come to grips with the same phenomenon. Second, short-term solutions and long-term solutions seemed at odds; the former were not sustainable, for the most part, and the latter were difficult to implement on a spot basis. Third, the imperatives of domestic policy and foreign trade were in conflict. These three tensions would influence the steps taken by the players and the lessons they took away after the two-day game.

Almost immediately in move 1, which was designed to simulate the first five days of what would become a crisis, the government teams were largely unresponsive to the requests from other players, particularly the teams playing the ports and the ocean, rail,

Three fundamental points of tension emerged as team play began. First, it was clear that security and efficiency tended to tug in opposite directions. Second, short-term solutions and long-term solutions seemed at odds; the former were not sustainable, for the most part, and the latter were difficult to implement on a spot basis.

and highway carriers. The ports and the carriers were looking for guidance at a minimum; even better, they wanted some decisive action about what they ought to do. But the two government teams, one representing border operations and the other representing federal policy, were paralyzed: They simply did not know what to do in these circumstances. The ports and carriers essentially said: "If you guys can't figure out what to do, we'll do it ourselves," and they did. The port team shut down the Los Angeles and Savannah operations, and the carrier team issued an order to stand down for 24 hours. The order halted the unloading and loading of ships and essentially grounded all surface transportation into and out of the ports while the authorities at both ports began to inspect as many cargo containers as possible.

At that point, the control team communicated an inject to all the teams: The day after the initial events, political pressure was building in Los Angeles as the public started to panic despite reassurances by the port's management, the mayor of the city, and the governor of California. Both the ports and the carriers continued to ask the government teams, particularly the one made up of key federal policy bodies, for more information and intelligence. What they got in return was the equivalent of uplifted palms and shrugs.

At day 3 in the simulation, the ports had reopened, and control was busy again. According to a fresh inject, U.S. intelligence officials reported that one of the suspects arrested in Savannah apparently had links to Al-Qaida. His mission was to locate a particular container at the port, get inside, and pick up supplies—supplies that could be used to deadly effect, it was thought—and link up with the other members of a team. He also revealed to his interrogators that other teams with similar instructions may have been assigned to other ports. That was enough to get the big trucking companies to conduct voluntary inspections of containers on their 18-wheelers within the continental United States. Meantime, security at the ports was being beefed up.

Day 4 turned nasty with another inject from control: A second dirty bomb, identical to the one found in Los Angeles, was discovered while a container was being unpacked at a distribution center near Minneapolis; the container had been transported by ship from Thailand to the Port of Halifax along the Canadian East Coast and then trucked to Minneapolis. It was defused, and there was no indication that any radiological materials had been released. But the incident, coming as it did within days of the events in Los Angeles and Savannah, was the tipping point for the government. The customs team ordered all ports and border crossings nationwide to be closed indefinitely. The next day, with the state's major ports closed, the governor of California activated the National Guard for possible deployment to back up container inspections and help make sure there were no violations of the edict issued by what is now known as U.S. Customs and Border Protection (CBP). Meanwhile, the port shutdown was beginning to ripple through the economy and was reflected on Wall Street and, by extension, Main Street when the Dow Jones Industrial Average plummeted 500 points in a single day. (Note: At the time the wargame was played, the Dow was around 8,000.)

Going into move 2, which was designed to simulate the next couple of weeks in the evolving scenario, the teams were eager to restore normal operations as soon as possible. Our guidance to them: Address how your priorities have changed. What actions do you need to take now to get operations back on track? What risks do those steps entail? And what are the long-range consequences of your actions?

With the ports still closed across the nation, control added an inject at day 8 in the simulation: Gas prices were skyrocketing because the port closures had prevented oil tankers from docking and

When faced with the threat of multiple radiological weapons entering the United States in containers, business and government wound up halting all foreign trade as the authorities looked for other bombs.

delivering crude oil. At the same time, the team representing automobile, consumer food, and retail companies reported that supply chains had been interrupted, resulting in inventory shortages and even temporary plant closings. Indeed, the shutdown was whacking thousands of companies across the nation that depend on intricate logistics to make their supply chains run smoothly. Many had long ago adopted just-in-time management, the system made famous by Toyota that reduced the costs associated with large inventories of parts and supplies. The port closing threw a wrench into those carefully fashioned programs.

The next day, the Port of Los Angeles requested that backlogged ships not targeted for inspection be sent to Canada and Mexico. The Canadian government, with the control team as its voice in the game, agreed to open its ports to ships unable to reach their U.S. destinations. Finally, the industry teams and the government teams were communicating. Ten days after the first bombs were discovered, a joint industry-government task force agreed on rules to prioritize containers for inspection.

Two days later, all U.S. ports were reopened and operated on a 24/7 basis in an effort to reduce the growing backlogs. With the help of the National Guard, the Port of Los Angeles was inspecting 20 percent of its containers, four times the proportion it had inspected before the crisis. The port also did what came naturally: It asked that ships dispatched to Canadian ports return to Southern California. In short, it was eager to return to business as usual as quickly as possible.

But business as usual was not to be. On day 18 of the simulation, control injected more trouble: This time, radiation had been detected on two ships that had docked at the Port of Savannah. The U.S. Coast Guard immediately ordered them back to sea, where they would be inspected. The news sent a shudder through American ports, which called for a 24-hour stand-down. On day 19, they returned to *normal* operations, that is, a pace that did not run 24/7. One day later, according to control's inject, a railcar carrying a container of wine imported from France exploded in downtown Chicago. The container had entered the United States through the Port of New York and New Jersey. Carriers called for another 24-hour stand-down, but it seemed likely to last longer. That pessimism was reflected in control's last inject of the second move: More than half of the Fortune 500 companies, dependent in part on container shipments from overseas, issued earnings warnings. Production slowdowns were spreading with the continued disruption in supply chains. As the major stock indexes headed south with a vengeance, trading was halted on the New York Stock Exchange, the NASDAQ electronic market, and other exchanges.

When faced with the threat of multiple radiological weapons entering the United States in containers, business and government wound up halting all foreign trade as the authorities looked for other bombs. Logistics networks imploded under the stress as small effects multiplied and led to dramatically larger consequences. In the first few days of the crisis on the West Coast, for example, the economic loss was calculated to be running at $1 billion per day. However, inventories were being depleted quickly; alternative sourcing was difficult even when it could be arranged with suppliers in the Americas. Some companies mitigated their problems by stocking up early, but they faced higher inventory carrying costs; others switched to air carriers to get what they needed at costs that ran 10 times what they normally paid for ocean transport.

As a result, the economic loss essentially doubled on a per-day basis: Through 10 days, the total approached $20 billion; by day 20, total losses had accumulated to nearly $50 billion, or an average of $2.5 billion per day. Our calculations assumed that the Port of Los Angeles would return to normal schedules and inspection rates about 26 days after the opening scenario. In that event, it still would require another four weeks to clear the backlog of ships. Nationwide, it might take a full three months for the shipping industry to stabilize. If the ports had been closed longer, the impact would have snowballed, probably leading to a global recession.

Move 3 was the place to address new questions raised by the events, the responses, and the consequences of decisions made in the first two moves. This had been a learning experience for these stakeholders, a brave new world they probably had not contemplated. We wanted them to reflect on what they had gone through. How do we change the way we do business to accommodate the need for improved security? How can the team you played on help ensure port security and also maintain an open and efficient flow of goods through U.S. supply chains? What are the next steps? If you are the government, what do you need from business or other governments? If you are business, what do you need from the government or from other businesses?

It won't surprise you that every team, including the two representing the U.S. government, stressed the need for strong, *unified* federal leadership, ideally with decision rights vested in a single agency. "I was puzzled," said one business participant. "What is the lead government agency? Who should we communicate with regarding potential threats and/or actions that we're taking?"

Collaboration between business and government also was a common theme in the reflections of the players. Information and intelligence sharing was considered crucial, and cooperation with other countries was deemed essential: American authorities cannot operate in a vacuum of their own making. "What business needs," said one participant, "is a single integrated international container security system based on a clear vision and strategy." Business also may have to make some adjustments in its practices, some participants thought. Asked one: "Should just-in-time inventory control become 'just-enough' inventory to ensure a bit of margin?" Carrying costs inevitably would increase under normal conditions, but in a crisis that disrupted supply chains for more than a few days, having that extra cushion in the warehouse might pay big dividends.

Living in and reacting to the imagined world of peril posed by our scenarios and injects, these participants identified weaknesses in existing protocols and reached a set of conclusions that in many ways form the bedrock of port security policy today. Among the lessons learned were the following:

- **A single government focal point is needed to ensure the security and resilience of global trade.** In the wargame, government essentially was paralyzed on three different questions: Do we close the ports? How do we prioritize cargo? When do we reopen the ports? Imagine an absence of responses to such questions in a real crisis. Without decision-making authority concentrated in one place, fragmentation, ineffectiveness, and perhaps inaction are all but guaranteed.

- **Single-point solutions simply don't work.** Global trade resilience requires a layered, end-to-end approach to security that begins at the point of origin—the original manufacturer of the product—and ends at the cargo's destination, with equal or perhaps even greater attention to the loading port and the discharge port. "The border is a point of capture," said one wargame player, "but the capture process should begin elsewhere." In addition, improved container design can make it easier to inspect and track shipments. We also need to develop international standards for end-to-end shipping.

- **Security cannot be bolted on.** It's an economic cost, and it needs to be embedded in whatever business model a company or industry develops. It cannot be an afterthought. We are in a new age of unconventional threats, and security must be an integral part of business planning, something, in fact, that should be regarded as productivity enhancer because of its objective of maintaining efficient operations even in adverse situations.

- **Public-private partnerships are crucial.** It will not be easy, but finding effective solutions to asymmetric threats will require a shared burden by all stakeholders. Business and government response and recovery plans ought to be integrated locally and nationally. "The government needs to involve industry in designing their port security solution," said one player. Otherwise, he feared, government could do more harm than good.

- **It's not just about the ports.** The international economy is a dynamic and vital force with global supply chains that are central to the well-being of billions of people all over the planet. The United States and other trading nations need to come up with solutions that strike an appropriate balance between security and economic efficiency.

Postscript: This wargame was designed and conducted during the debate over the creation of a new Department of Homeland Security, which was formally born on March 1, 2003. DHS has had its share of coming-of-age organizational problems, but it has enthusiastically embraced the so-called Container Security Initiative created by the old U.S. Customs Service immediately after the 9/11 attacks. The CSI counts among its signatories 58 foreign ports. Now under the authority of U.S. Customs and Border Protection (CBP), the program continues to expand. According to the CBP's Web site, fully "86 percent of all maritime containerized cargo imported into the United States is subjected to prescreening." CBP has added inspectors, placing some of them in foreign ports that are cooperating in the Container Security Initiative. Does this cause delays in the flow of goods through such ports? No, CBP insists. "Cargo typically sits on the pier for several days waiting to be exported. CSI targets containers and screens them before they depart." That way, CBP uses the waiting time at the port of export to do its work so that the inspected container can be released immediately after it arrives at a U.S. port.

○   ○   ○

A s we've said, this section of the book is devoted to global crisis wargames in which we partner with a nonprofit organization and work on a pro bono basis. Still, it's worth noting briefly that we have designed and conducted wargames to stress test supply-chain resilience for several large corporations, including international automobile companies. The scenarios in these games differ from our port security game, of course, but they all begin with external events—for example, the closing of key bridges between the United States and Canada— that disrupt or threaten to disrupt carefully constructed supply chains. Perhaps not surprisingly, the players in these wargames come away with "learnings" not unlike those in the port security simulation. For example, they believe that it is important to consult with governments at every level *before* a crisis and include public officials in the planning process. Public-private partnerships have become a mantra.

We have designed and conducted wargames to stress test supply-chain resilience for several large corporations, including international automobile companies. Perhaps not surprisingly, the players in these wargames come away with "learnings" not unlike those in the port security simulation.

In such games, there was recognition that security is essential to economic well-being even though it's an added cost and that planning for the worst-case scenario—much discussed but rarely done—has to be implemented. Without such planning, it would be even more difficult to achieve a controlled and orderly shutdown of the company's logistics network when a real crisis arrives and even harder to ensure a smooth resumption of normal activities once the crisis has passed. Decision rights in such matters are critical. In the port security wargame, the players all agreed in the end that a single point of contact in government was needed. In these private-sector wargames testing supply-chain resilience, a single point of contact within a company's logistics high command must be designated and given the authority to make key decisions.

CHAPTER 14

THE ONCE AND FUTURE BIRD FLU

O ver the last century, planet Earth has experienced three influenza pandemics from different strains and with varying severity. Fortunately, each successive battle with global flu has proved less painful and traumatic. The big one, of course, was the flu pandemic of 1918—the so-called Spanish flu—that broke out several months before the end of World War I and lasted more than two years. As a killer, it was indiscriminate and efficient: In the United States, 500,000 people died in a total population of 103 million, and it was bad enough that 1918 was the only year in the twentieth century when the nation's population actually declined (by 60,000). Nearly half the victims were between the ages of 20 and 40, defying the conventional wisdom that influenza visits its harshest judgment on children and the elderly.

Worldwide, the death toll was estimated at 50 million to 100 million, doubtless made worse in the United States and other countries by an absence of preparation, poor if any communication by government, and grossly inadequate responses by public health officials.

It takes an outbreak of human-to-human flu before scientists can identify the culprit and fashion a vaccine to take it on, a process that is thought to take three to six months at a minimum. What's more, in the 40 years since the last pandemic, the population in country after country has become more urbanized, with densely packed cities creating conditions that almost certainly would accelerate the spread of highly contagious influenza.

Subsequent flu pandemics were of a different order of magnitude. The 1957 version was considered moderate. Even so, it killed 70,000 people in the United States and 2 million worldwide. The mild flu pandemic of 1968 killed 34,000 people in the United States and 1 million worldwide.

It would be comforting to believe that the next flu pandemic will be milder still because of advances in medical research and technology, better communications, and, one hopes, a more knowledgeable public. However, there are no guarantees, and some factors suggest that the next one could be very nasty indeed. For one thing, making a vaccine to combat a specific strain of flu requires a sample from the suspect: In short, it takes an outbreak of human-to-human flu before scientists can identify the culprit and fashion a vaccine to take it on, a process that is thought to take three to six months at a minimum.

What's more, in the 40 years since the last pandemic, the population in country after country has become more urbanized, with densely packed cities creating conditions that almost certainly would accelerate the spread of highly contagious influenza. The boom in international travel also would contribute to the spread of a flu virus. It took four or five months for the pandemic flu of 1957, first detected in China, to reach the United States. The 1968 flu originated in Hong Kong and reached the United States in two or three months. Now that scores of jumbo jets crisscross vast oceans in a matter of a few hours every day, it's hard to imagine a pandemic in Asia or anywhere else kept at bay for more than a few weeks at most. Think about a married couple boarding a jetliner in

Hong Kong bound for Los Angeles; neither husband or wife is symptomatic yet, but both have been infected by the H5N1 flu virus, and by the time they land at LAX 13 hours later, they have spread the disease to just about everyone else on the aircraft.

So what are we to make of H5N1, the strain of avian influenza monitored and studied by international health organizations for the last decade? The virus, which originates in birds, has caused the largest and most severe outbreak among poultry on record. It has caused deaths, principally in Asia, among people who have handled sick birds. It has yet to mutate to a form that can result in human-to-human transmission. Still, at the United Nations, at the U.S. Department of Health and Human Services (HHS), at research institutes, and in scientific laboratories in countless countries, a consensus view has emerged that it is probably only a matter of time before we have another flu pandemic on our hands and that if it is H5N1, the virus could be extremely aggressive. By some estimates, a pandemic flu in the United States might sicken 30 percent of the population, strain hospital capacity, overtax medical technology, and cause as many as 2 million deaths.

In 2006, several of us thought the subject of pandemic influenza, which was very top of mind at the time, could be a prime candidate for a wargame. It was not of a piece with bioterrorism and port security, which were wargames designed to address human-made threats to national security, public health, and the nation's economy, but its potential consequences in the event of genuine pandemic would be huge: It would disrupt major segments of American society, imperil public health, hurt the economy, and even fairly be called a matter of national security. We needed a cosponsor in the nonprofit sector and found a perfect partner in the Center for Health Transformation. The CHT was started in 2003 by Newt Gingrich, the former speaker of the house. Securing Newt's help meant that we could tap into the ideas of one of Washington's most creative and unconventional thinkers on big public-policy issues. We jumped at the chance.

For a three-move game played over two days in late March 2006,

In 2006, several of us thought the subject of pandemic influenza, which was very top of mind at the time, could be a prime candidate for a wargame. It was not of a piece with bioterrorism and port security, which were wargames designed to address human-made threats to national security, public health, and the nation's economy, but its potential consequences in the event of genuine pandemic would be huge.

we brought together 100 people from key government agencies, including HHS, the Centers for Disease Control and Prevention (CDC), and the Food and Drug Administration (FDA); representatives from state and local governments; executives from major companies in banking, telecommunications, health-care and consumer products, transportation, and heavy manufacturing; public-affairs experts; and more. The objective of the wargame was to assess the impact of pandemic flu on government and business, including supply chains and the workforce. We also wanted to test and evaluate different approaches to responding to the crisis and identify additional ways government and business could improve and coordinate their preparedness.

It was a big game that included seven teams: the U.S. federal government, state and local agencies, health care, financial services and telecommunications, heavy industry, the consumer products and services sector, and transportation and logistics. Each team would have a mix of people, including those playing in someone else's shoes—for example, a banker playing on the federal government team, a Washington bureaucrat playing on the consumer products team, or a state official playing on the health-care team. The control team would oversee the simulation, update the scenario, inject additional events, and supply information as needed. Crucially, control also represented the media and the general public, which would play an active role in this game.

We designed an opening scenario that we hoped would get everyone's attention. It was November 28, 2006. Twelve days earlier, an outbreak of suspected bird flu had occurred in Hong Kong, with nine reported cases. A few days later, the World Health Organization (WHO) confirmed that a new strain of the H5N1 virus had mutated to a form that was transmissible from human to human. WHO traced the origin of the strain to an outbreak in China. In Hong Kong, there already were five deaths and 17 new cases. The outbreak in China turned out to be more severe than first reported, causing WHO to raise its six-stage pandemic alert level from 3 to 5, indicating "significant human-to-human transmission" (see Figure 14.1). In the United States, CDC issued a health warning, putting U.S. hospitals on alert for new flu cases. November 24, the day after Thanksgiving, gave new meaning to Black Friday, named for the color of ink on corporate books because of the Christmas sales crush. This Friday, in contrast, was a sales bomb written in red ink.

The flu had advanced to Vietnam by Saturday; in the United States, hospitals reported more cases of seasonal flu patients seeking care, principally because people were spooked by WHO's confirmation of the new virus. With the beginning of the workweek, parts of Europe, including Paris and southern Germany, confirmed a dozen cases of the new strain.

On Tuesday, November 28, the last day of the opening scenario, the virus was continuing to spread in southern rural China and Hong Kong. The flu also was moving north toward Beijing, where residents with memories of the outbreak of severe acute respiratory syndrome (SARS) were beginning to wear protective masks. In the United States, seven deaths—four in Atlanta and three in Philadelphia—were traced to the new strain. None of the victims had traveled to East Asia recently, but three of them had visited the West Coast, flying to Los Angeles International Airport for the long holiday weekend. The authorities believed H5N1 had made the big leap across the Pacific Ocean, and with the seasonal flu off to a strong start, hospitals and doctors' offices across the country were swamped with patients worried about the new strain. So were the people at the World Health Organization: With a confirmed death

FIGURE 14.1
Pandemic flu timeline

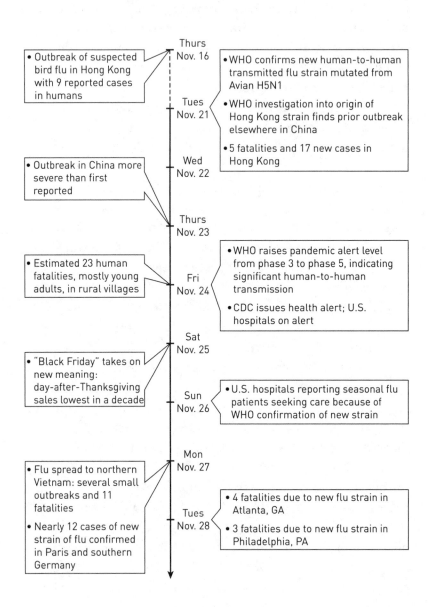

Source: Booz Allen Hamilton, CHT pandemic influenza simulation.

toll of 36 in China, 13 in Hong Kong, 7 in the United States, 3 in Germany, and 2 in France, WHO raised its Pandemic Alert System to level 6, its highest, indicating a pandemic with efficient and sustained human-to-human transmission.

The first move was supposed to cover the first 30 days of the pandemic—that is, through late December—and concentrate on containment. On the basis of the opening scenario, the teams were given a set of questions to focus their discussions. The federal and the state/local government teams were asked: What is your role in the pandemic response, and what are your priorities? What steps are you taking to contain the pandemic? How will you ensure continuity of government and essential services? How will you keep the population informed? What is your message?

The health-care team got different queries, tailored to what figured to be a serious challenge to the entire health-care sector: hospitals and their personnel, manufacturers of hospital equipment and supplies, and drug makers. How will you contain the pandemic and protect your workforce? What are your priorities for the care and treatment of flu victims? Given the impact of the virus on your workforce, facilities, and supply chains, how will you sustain operations? What and how will you communicate to the public?

We wanted the business teams to address the potential impact on their operations. How will you identify essential operations and employees? What actions will you take to protect employees and sustain operations? How will you keep employees, vendors, and customers informed? What actionable steps should they take?

Teams in wargames often act very deliberately in the first move, in part because the experience is new for most players, who want to get a sense of the simulation's dynamics before they make firm decisions that could backfire on them later. This pandemic flu game fit that pattern in the first move, but only up to a point. The federal team, following the script we had written, dutifully addressed the setup questions point by point. The team declared a public health emergency and began to coordinate with the states based on existing disaster plans. It activated the federal government's Continuity

We wanted the business teams to address the potential impact on their operations. How will you identify essential operations and employees? What actions will you take to protect employees and sustain operations? How will you keep employees, vendors, and customers informed?

of Operations Plans (COOP) and said it would provide support and guidance to the private sector as needed to identify essential personnel in especially critical areas such as utilities, telecommunications, and transportation. It pledged to keep the public informed, providing a daily briefing. Its principal messages to the public were: "Your government is working to support the health-care infrastructure. We are secure, and our economy is strong. The country will weather this crisis."

Those words sounded a bit like a cheerleading State of the Union speech, with more expressed confidence than underlying conviction. In fact, the federal team had acknowledged privately in its discussions that the outbreak of H5N1 in mutated form was no longer containable and that the only strategic course was to try to minimize its impact. One of our control team observers asked two members of the team about their first-move deliberations afterward. "I'm not sure we fully appreciated the dimensions of the problem," one of them said. The subset of the control team playing the public was plainly underwhelmed by the federal government's initial response to the crisis. Its members staged a press conference late in the first move, essentially asking two big questions that Washington had not addressed to their satisfaction: What are you doing to help us? Who's in charge; where should our attention be focused?

The state and local team, in contrast, got out of the blocks very quickly. Its priorities were to activate actionable crisis-management plans that already were in place, minimize morbidity and fatalities, and maintain public order. It moved to protect health-care assets at the local level by telling hospitals, among other things, to defer elective surgeries, maximize home care, and beef up security. It ordered personal protective equipment (PPE) such as masks and latex gloves for high-priority workers, especially in health care and law enforcement. Also, it immediately took on the delicate problem of home quarantine for those who were ill or had been exposed to people who were symptomatic: Otherwise healthy people were urged to stay home if they got the flu and try to use antiviral drugs.

State and cities also began to implement social-distancing policies. In one of the first affected cities, officials ordered the Metropolitan Atlanta Rapid Transit Authority to close, halting MARTA's buses and rail lines, which normally carry close to 200,000 passengers each day. Part of the state and local team's media strategy, disseminated to the public through newspapers, television, Internet Web sites, and toll-free phone numbers, was to stress the small stuff that can make a huge difference: Wash your hands frequently. Remember respiratory etiquette: no uncovered sneezing or coughing. If you are in a high-contact situation, use a mask. We have a long-term problem here, this team made clear, and cooperation in these matters is not really optional in these circumstances. It is everyone's civic duty to follow official guidelines. Some of these steps and recommendations resonated with the public team, which sought information about what individuals could do and what the impact of the pandemic might be on their communities.

The participants on our health-care team felt overwhelmed from the start, and for good reason. The numbers plainly were stacked against them. The health-care infrastructure in the United States includes 5,800 hospitals, the vast majority of them community facilities, and nearly a million staffed hospital beds; 700,000 doctors who practice patient care; 2.9 million nurses; 6,000 noncardiac intensive care units; and 105,000 mechanical ventilators, which are an important part of respiratory treatment for those particularly hard hit by the flu.

Those figures may sound impressive, but not when juxtaposed against the potential gravity of a flu pandemic. A million staffed beds? If a pandemic sickened an estimated 90 million people, or

30 percent of the U.S. population, the number of hospital beds would prove inadequate even though the majority of victims would not need hospital care. As for ventilators, demand even in a normal flu season runs around 100,000. Estimates of additional demand in a flu pandemic range from 65,000 to 740,000, depending on the severity of the crisis.

Drug availability reflects the same situation. With no vaccine in the early months of a pandemic, the best treatment for sick people probably would be antiviral drugs such as Tamiflu and Relenza. Worldwide annual production of Tamiflu is 400 million treatment courses; for Relenza, it is 150 million. That would not come close to covering the billion or more people around the world who would get sick. In the United States, the CDC's Strategic National Stockpile, which has significant quantities of drugs and medical supplies to help in a human-made or natural disaster, contains roughly 20 million treatment courses of Tamiflu, compared with the estimated 90 million people in the United States who might get sick.

Clearly an underdog in the fight against pandemic flu, the health-care team focused on steps to protect hospital workers and other frontline responders: measures such as personal protective equipment, containment of any disease within each health-care facility, transportation for essential workers, and Tamiflu for perhaps half its workers. More broadly, it also made a plea for guidance when it came to treatment. With likely shortages of drugs, beds, ventilators, and other medical supplies, triage planning was sure to come and hospitals would need a legal and ethnical framework. What about critically ill patients with a poor prognosis? In a triage situation, could care for those patients be suspended? Should health-care providers maximize their limited resources by focusing on those with a good chance for survival?

These were not easy questions, and there would be no easy answers. The public was not satisfied: Its members wanted basic information: Jane and John Q. Public worried about what drugs would help and where and when they would be available. Would there be enough for everyone? And what, they wanted to know, would this pandemic flu mean for our health-care bill if we and the kids got the virus?

The four business teams seemed to assimilate the scope of this evolving crisis into their thinking faster than the others did. They understood that a pandemic would hammer their supply chains and, in an echo of the port security wargame, that serious planning for such catastrophic events might include adjustments in just-in-time inventory management. Teams knew that communicating to employees, vendors, and customers was crucial, that reassurances from top management were important, and that their security needs would increase. Telecommuting was on everyone's short list of how to cope with the pandemic, but absenteeism—people getting sick at work or getting sick at home while they were telecommuting—was bound to clobber productivity. Some talked about providing critical supplies—food, water, masks, gloves—and elder care and child care at the workplace.

The financial services and telecommunications team broke with the scripted questions for the first move, which was fine with us, and came up with a list of "judgments" that were based on the opening scenario. Its list in part went like this: Expect a significant reduction in our ability to service financial customers. We'll have limited cash, and we expect long lines at branches because demand will rise and supply will fall as a result of the flu's toll on our tellers and other service employees. Our capital ratios will be affected un-less we receive relief from the Federal Reserve. Small banks will close temporarily; others will disappear for good. We need to make aggressive use of trade groups such as the Securities Industries and Financial Markets Association to share information across the industry. For telecom, we would rely on the National Coordinating Center for Telecommunications, a joint industry-government en-terprise under the U.S. Department of Homeland Security.

This team identified a set of actions to be put in place in ad-vance of a flu pandemic or another global crisis. Those preplans would include rules for telecommuting; the purchase of medical products such as drugs, masks, and gloves; prescribed absenteeism

The four business teams seemed to assimilate the scope of this evolving crisis into their thinking faster than the others did. They understood that a pandemic would hammer their supply chains and, in an echo of the port security wargame, that serious planning for such catastrophic events might include adjustments in just-in-time inventory management.

policies during the crisis; training and awareness in matters of hygiene and personal behavior; and communication with clients and employees.

During the course of the first move, the public team either was peppering the business teams with questions or was raising its issues in press conferences. Jane and John Q. Public's concerns here went to the heart of American anxiety in the face of a flu pandemic. What would be considered essential travel? Would non-essential employees in big manufacturing companies—people told to go home and wait it out—continue to receive their standard pay and benefits? Hey, consumer products companies: Will your stores maintain stocks of food and drugs, or will you be forced to ration?

Finally, everyone was talking about greater use of electronic networks within companies and institutions and through the Internet to communicate with key constituencies, telecommute, and transact business as a substitute for face-to-face contact. There was a supply-demand question on networking: Would the supply side hold up, or would an anticipated surge in demand overtax server capacity and cause entire systems to seize up or collapse under the strain?

The answer came in the updated scenario for the second move, roughly five weeks into the pandemic. There was not as much telecommuting as the optimists on various teams had hoped because workers had fallen ill or taken time off to care for their families. Still, network servers and switches buckled under a substantial surge in demand, dramatically slowing communications. The flu had spread across the United States, hitting the East Coast especially hard; in Atlanta and Philadelphia, where the virus first was reported, alternative care sites had been established to relieve the burden on hospitals. Many small companies had closed down or failed. Most private universities had closed indefinitely, sending their students home. The pandemic continued to sweep across Asia and was spreading to Africa. In Europe, as in the United States, some companies had shut down nonessential operations.

Move 1 was all about containment. The second move was about dealing with the pandemic in the middle of the first wave, basically the first three or four months of the crisis, and focusing stakeholder teams on finding ways to maintain essential government functions, health and business operations, and public order. How were they communicating with the public and with each other? What collaborations should be undertaken? What about issues of financial liability? Of antitrust?

The federal team was ratcheting up its engagement in move 2. It responded to requests for help by augmenting local law enforcement with federal law enforcement officers. It eased certain regulations to keep industries functioning and got the Federal Reserve to relax capital ratios for banks and ease interest rates to increase liquidity in the economy. Meanwhile, it was engaging state and local leaders, corporate CEOs, and religious leaders, sometimes individually and often through associations and other groups. Its message, through a public information campaign conveyed by the media and various government Internet sites, was succinct: The pandemic was Washington's primary concern, and the country, for all the strains and stresses, remained secure.

Perhaps, but the federal government could be doing a lot more, the state and local team insisted. The Feds were not being sufficiently proactive to get ahead of emerging problems in the crisis, for example, by relaxing access to existing programs such as food stamps. For their part, state and local governments were doing what they could to maintain services. They were redeploying those who had recovered from the flu into essential positions, redoubling efforts to mandate telecommuting and other alternative work arrangements, and instituting security measures. They also strengthened

Move 1 was all about containment. The second move was about dealing with the pandemic in the middle of the first wave, basically the first three or four months of the crisis, and focusing stakeholder teams on finding ways to maintain essential government functions, health and business operations, and public order.

their communications efforts, stressing through daily broadcasts the importance of communitywide efforts and respect for law and order. However, there was some evidence that the social compact was fraying, based on injects from the public team. A pharmaceutical company had been stormed by a crowd looking for drugs. Reports of looting were coming in, and there were signs of a developing black market for prescription drugs and consumer products.

The state/local team was communicating regularly with hospitals and other providers of health care. The health-care sector itself was plainly under siege, as that team in our wargame indicated in move 2. Its list of needs was growing as the first wave of the pandemic walloped hospitals. Hospitals needed to use medically trained personnel who were no longer practicing, that is, retired and nonactive nurses and doctors, former paramedics, and others. They needed more oxygen and more ventilators. Nonprofit hospitals needed a system of reimbursement for extraordinary losses because of the pandemic. As the team suggested in move 1, all hospitals needed some kind of criminal and civil indemnification from triage decisions such as the denial of ventilators and resource-intensive services to patients who were likely to die.

Our business teams continued to emphasize how important it was to reassure their principal constituencies—employees, customers, shareholders—but their operations reflected the pandemic's gathering impact. In telecommunications, for example, the surge in demand resulted in a request, which was granted, that the federal Telecommunications Service Priority (TSP) be invoked. TSP gives telecommunications providers the authority to prioritize services, with particular emphasis on national security and emergency preparedness. In transportation and logistics, the team said it could sustain service for essential needs, but at significantly reduced levels of freight-train deliveries and urban commuter service.

All the business teams were desperate for relief provided by the federal government in some shape, manner, or form. The financial component of the financial/telecom team requested and

Our business teams continued to emphasize how important it was to reassure their principal constituencies—employees, customers, shareholders—but their operations reflected the pandemic's gathering impact.

got lower capital ratios from federal bank regulators; the Federal Reserve also eased regulations on repayment of Fed loans and lowered interest rates, increasing bank liquidity. Everyone wanted antitrust waivers because companies were collaborating with competitors on employee practices, production and service issues, and the delivery of manufactured goods. The consumer products and services team got its antitrust waiver from the federal team but was turned down on two other requests: that the federal government impose price controls by executive order and that it nationalize key industries.

Financial and liability issues were also central for the business teams. What if employees who got sick on the job sued their employers? What about companies that failed to satisfy contracts with suppliers or customers?

The scenario for move 3, covering roughly months 4, 5, and 6 of the pandemic, showed a decline in the number of new cases in the United States, but there were fears that another wave might be coming. Hospitals remained understaffed and undersupplied, urban centers were reeling, and rural areas, with acute shortages of health-care workers, appeared to be doing even worse.

Even though we go into wargames with general instructions for teams in each move, we retain the option to improvise as the game progresses. Wargames become learning experiences for the players and are no less than that for us. In this particular wargame, the

Even though we go into wargames with general instructions for teams in each move, we retain the option to improvise as the game progresses. Wargames become learning experiences for the players and are no less than that for us.

teams had ranged far and wide during the first two moves, engaging early and exposing impediments to combating the pandemic. In move 3, we dispensed with a planned set of questions for each team. Instead, we asked each of them to do four things: describe a breakout action your team could take to improve your response to the pandemic, pick another team of your choice and describe a breakout action it could take to improve its response, describe a breakout action the health-care team could take, and give us your key learnings from the game. (We'll get to those lessons at the end of this chapter.)

Well, now. The federal team, which had been slow off the mark earlier in the game, showed up big at the end: It substituted "leadership" for "response" and proposed as its breakout action Washington as the prime mover to "mitigate the catastrophic breakdown of critical social, economic, health, and security systems." Specifically, the president, in consultation with Congress, would modify existing "all-hazards" plans to provide rapid top-down action in circumstances threatening systemic breakdown. Those actions would include preplanned interventions to push resources to the points of the greatest need and immediate consultation with the private sector to resolve regulatory, antitrust, and liability issues. The federal team also would launch a global Manhattan Project, led by the nation's principal research and regulatory institutions, to accelerate vaccine development and production. This neatly encompassed two of the four things we asked the teams to do, since the federal team effectively was picking health care as its other team to play.

Breakout actions suggested by other teams ranged from the predictable and mundane to the offbeat and creative. The state and local group urged a television extravaganza that would be broadcast on all commercial and cable channels and modeled on a "Day After" disaster format. The TV event would emphasize individual education, preparedness, and accountability; explain what viewers should expect from various levels of government, health-care providers, and other sectors of society; and stress community—in the crisis, we are all in it together. The financial services team urged, among other things, the establishment of an emergency debit card that could be activated through existing methods and special financial lines of credit for hospitals in crisis situations. Transportation and logistics wanted to set up a Strategic Transportation Reserve that would design plans to best utilize trains, planes, trucks, and anything else on wheels to move critical goods during the pandemic.

We had developed a dynamic computer model to track the progress of the virus in the wargame against actions taken by the players. It was not a pretty picture. The slow reaction in move 1 relative to the virulent nature of the disease suggested that 9 million people might be infected on the eastern seaboard alone 30 days into the crisis, with perhaps 20 million to 30 million people absent from their jobs.

Designating alternative health-care sites—at companies and in churches, schools, and hotels—was on many team to-do lists. The business teams eagerly coalesced around the idea of a government-industry consortium or roundtable that ideally would meet in anticipation of a crisis to develop plans to protect private-sector supply chains.

We had developed a dynamic computer model to track the progress of the virus in the wargame against actions taken by the players. It was not a pretty picture. The slow reaction in move 1 relative to the virulent nature of the disease suggested that 9 million people might be infected on the eastern seaboard alone 30 days into the crisis, with perhaps 20 million to 30 million people absent from their jobs. Deaths might have reached 200,000 on the East Coast. The steps taken during move 1—social distancing, use of masks, antiviral drugs for health-care workers, limiting travel, and more—did pay off later, during the first big wave of the disease. By mid-January, the infected population on the East Coast peaked at a bit more than 11 million, compared with a baseline of 13 million, and then began to decline over the next three months. The death toll, however, rose steadily through the period; by early spring, more than a million people on the East Coast would have died.

○   ○   ○

Since early 2006, we have designed and conducted several wargames on a flu pandemic. They have ranged from a special three-hour version at the World Economic Forum (WEF) annual meeting in Davos, Switzerland, in January 2006 to a "Pandemic Flu Exercise" sponsored by the U.S. Treasury Department and several financial services associations that took three weeks to complete. The catch: The exercise, with more than 2,700 banks, credit unions, security firms, insurers, and other organizations participating, was conducted entirely online.

Dr. David Nabarro, the Senior United Nations System Coordinator for Avian and Human Influenza, attended and participated in the WEF presentation and delivered closing remarks to the participants in the longer game described in this chapter. His perceptive insights from Davos, which were repeated in part after the game two months later, are shown in the sidebar following.

The lessons from the March 2006 wargame were not identical to Nabarro's, but they touched many common themes:

- **In scale and complexity, an influenza pandemic will be unlike any crisis government and business have experienced.** An effective response must include immediate coordination among multiple sectors of society, with organizations prepared to deal with extraordinary consequences and shortages over several months. Decisive federal guidance and communications will be required, not just at the beginning but throughout the crisis.

TEN THINGS I LEARNED

By Dr. David Nabarro of the United Nations

1. The response needs to be both strategic and opportunistic.
2. The emphasis has to be as much on the people as on the virus.
3. Quite likely by day 28, all systems will have fallen apart. We need a plan to improve infrastructure to support the response.
4. Engaging business from the start is not a luxury. It is essential and perhaps the most important factor of all.
5. Media are an essential part of the response, and you need to learn to work with them.
6. Encourage joint work by government, business, and community organizations at all levels.
7. Martial law is not an end but a means, and you need to understand the end state you are working toward when using it. People are precious; martial law should be used to protect the people.
8. We need to define a pandemic state and how business and government will work in that state; we must do this now.
9. "Flu-casters" need a dashboard to track flu statistics and progress around the world.
10. The military must be involved in the response to help keep the peace and deliver essential goods and services.

- **The U.S. health-care system—its staffing, physical resources, and financial reserves—probably will be overwhelmed by a prolonged spike in a severely ill population.** Its supply chains, highly vulnerable to workforce shortages and transportation disruptions, will suffer, and the situation will be complicated by reliance on just-in-time inventories. All supplies will fall short of demand. It would behoove planners to think now about alternative health-care sites such as schools, universities, community centers, and churches.

- **A flu pandemic could result in a health-care regime of "haves" and "have-nots."** Assuming some rationing of limited supplies of antiviral drugs, get ready for some difficult bioethical decisions as health-care providers are forced to decide who gets treatment and who does not. Treatment protocols promulgated at the national level will be needed.

- **Special care will be required to protect the mental health of the population during and after the pandemic.** If the next pandemic is as vicious as some experts believe it could be, a death toll in the hundreds of thousands or 1, 2, or 3 million is not out of the question. Trauma among the living is sure to be widespread, and grief counseling will be an essential part of the nation's recovery. Attention also should be paid to health-care providers who are forced to make life-and-death triage decisions on a daily basis over a long period.

- **Employers should address workforce and workplace issues now, not in hurried response to the event itself.** Ideally, companies will have prioritized production and services in advance of a health crisis. In the straitened circumstances of a flu pandemic, which employees would be essential? Would nonessential employees be sent home? With full pay and benefits or partial compensation? It is unlikely that federal and state governments would mandate business behavior in such matters, and so companies would be wise to have a plan in place.

- **Liability relief will be a crucial element in the response to a flu pandemic.** The health-care sector will need it both for providers making tough life-and-death decisions and for personnel—volunteers, trainees, and others—who may not have proper licenses. Other organizations—companies, educational institutions, community centers—that open their facilities for use as clinics, shelters, or adjunct hospitals also may need liability

relief. If the government actually led a crash program to accelerate the development of a flu vaccine, some federal waivers from
liability claims might have to be granted to scientific institutions
and drug companies collaborating in the effort.

Perhaps above all else, leaders at every level of government,
business, and the nonprofit sector must prepare to communicate
to multiple constituencies and must do so knowing that their messages will be difficult and emotionally challenging. That was the
sobering bottom line for participants in our flu pandemic wargame, which gave them the opportunity to collaborate, reach conclusions, and learn lessons about an imagined world they and all
of us hope will never occur.

CHAPTER 15

MEGACOMMUNITIES AT WORK

A s we have seen in the last three chapters, the success of a global crisis wargame depends in no small measure on assembling in one place people with different talents and backgrounds to confront dynamic and complex issues. Think of this group of people as a "megacommunity": a network of organizations, drawn from the business, government, and civil sectors, that comes together to engage critical problems of mutual interest that are too big for any one of them to solve alone. You may be unfamiliar with the term, but a megacommunity is a concept that people at our firm have pioneered and promulgated, including in book form (*Megacommunities: How Leaders of Government, Business and Non-Profits Can Tackle Today's Global Challenges Together*, Palgrave Macmillan, March 2008). In this chapter, we want to give you a taste of three more megacommunities, each one tackling a difficult and in some cases emotionally sensitive problem.

The first of these examples also shows that a wargame on global crisis issues does not always involve frightening scenarios

Think of this group of people as a "megacommunity": a network of organizations, drawn from the business, government, and civil sectors, that comes together to engage critical problems of mutual interest that are too big for any one of them to solve alone.

developed by our staff. Sometimes the real world provides a baseline scenario that is compelling enough to command the attention of our participants. That was the way it was with a wargame we designed and conducted on Alzheimer's disease.

If you do not already know of someone who is a victim of this terrible and heartbreaking disease, you probably will soon enough. Today, nearly 5 million people in the United States have Alzheimer's, as many as 10 percent of them under the age of 65 who are living with early-onset symptoms. With the baby boom generation reaching retirement age over the next few years and with no cure or effective treatment in sight, the number of Alzheimer's victims is expected to rise significantly. By some estimates, 7.7 million people age 65 or older may have the disease in the year 2030. Even now, Alzheimer's claims almost as many lives each year as breast cancer and prostate cancer combined.

As is widely understood because of the media attention Alzheimer's has attracted in recent years, the disease affects memory, language and communication skills, reasoning and judgment, the ability to plan, and a person's sense of time and space. In later stages, it leads to personality and behavioral changes: apathy and anxiety, depression, delusions. Daily activities—eating, bathing, dressing—become problematic; motor skills deteriorate, and the simple act of swallowing is impaired. The victim no longer recognizes family and friends (see Figure 15.1). After the onset of symptoms, a person can live another 20 years. It is no wonder that the decline in quality of life, especially in the advanced stages, makes Alzheimer's the most feared disease—more than cancer and stroke—in surveys of those 55 years of age and older.

FIGURE 15.1

The progression of Alzheimer's disease

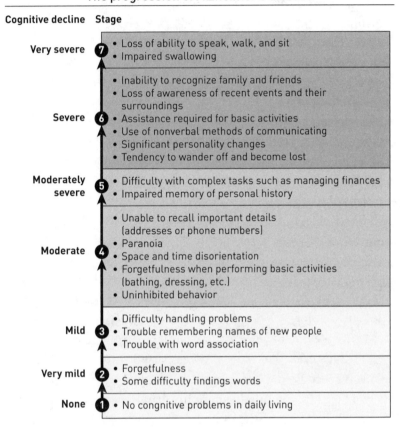

Cognitive decline   Stage

Very severe ⑦
- Loss of ability to speak, walk, and sit
- Impaired swallowing

Severe ⑥
- Inability to recognize family and friends
- Loss of awareness of recent events and their surroundings
- Assistance required for basic activities
- Use of nonverbal methods of communicating
- Significant personality changes
- Tendency to wander off and become lost

Moderately severe ⑤
- Difficulty with complex tasks such as managing finances
- Impaired memory of personal history

Moderate ④
- Unable to recall important details (addresses or phone numbers)
- Paranoia
- Space and time disorientation
- Forgetfulness when performing basic activities (bathing, dressing, etc.)
- Uninhibited behavior

Mild ③
- Difficulty handling problems
- Trouble remembering names of new people
- Trouble with word association

Very mild ②
- Forgetfulness
- Some difficulty findings words

None ①
- No congnitive problems in daily living

Source: B. Reisberg et al., "Global Deterioration Scale," *American Journal of Psychiatry*, 139 (1982):1136–1139.

For our simulation in September 2007, we again partnered with Newt Gingrich's Center for Health Transformation, our co-sponsor for the pandemic flu wargame 18 months earlier, and with the Alzheimer's Association. This particular wargame aimed to identify the priorities and concerns of the key actors in the Alzheimer's drama and explore how collaboration among those stakeholders could enhance prevention, detection, treatment, and care to blunt the impact of the disease on patients, caregivers, and society. The participants in the game reflected our choice of stakeholder

This particular wargame aimed to identify the priorities and concerns of the key actors in the Alzheimer's drama and explore how collaboration among those stakeholders could enhance prevention, detection, treatment, and care to blunt the impact of the disease on patients, caregivers, and society. The participants in the game reflected our choice of stakeholder teams, although many of them played on a team outside their area of expertise.

teams, although many of them played on a team outside their area of expertise. There were eight teams in all, representing patients and families, public advocates, insurance companies, healthcare providers, the U.S. Department of Health and Human Services, the National Institutes of Health and other research organizations and academia, pharmaceutical companies, and diagnostics companies and makers of medical devices. As usual, a control team oversaw the game, introduced external elements, and assessed the play. It was to be a three-move game, with move 1 covering the five years through September 2012, move 2 accounting for the next five years, and move 3 focusing on insights and recommendations.

We departed from form, however, in one respect: Before the first move, we asked one participant with early-onset Alzheimer's to share his experiences with the entire group. Similarly, before the second move, we invited someone whose husband had the disease in its early stages to share her experiences as a caregiver. Their stories essentially described a wilderness of mirrors for patients and their loved ones: missed diagnoses, the loss of jobs and disability insurance, the absence of any financial model to reimburse for care in the home, and signals from every quarter that victims and caregivers are on their own. Those talks helped shape many of the discussions that followed and certainly shaped the learnings at the day's end. "The public fear is in losing memory," said one member of the public advocacy team. "They don't understand the other implications of Alzheimer's disease."

Our instructions to the teams for move 1 were to identify the top three challenges related to Alzheimer's disease from your team's perspective and state how you would address those challenges over a five-year period. Move 2, covering the subsequent five-year period (2012–2017), followed up: What actions are you taking now to address new or continuing challenges, and how has collaboration helped you in your work?

Four overriding themes emerged from team discussions and from exchanges between and among stakeholder teams: the need to recognize and understand the nature of Alzheimer's disease, the need to transform the care model, the need to empower the patient and caregiver, and the need to find a cure. How to get there from here? Several recommendations and next steps helped point the way:

- **Creation of a comprehensive patient registry would be valuable in filling in some of the missing data critical to finding effective treatments and perhaps a cure.** Developing both "disease-modifying and preventive treatments" is imperative, said a participant on the pharmaceuticals team. To that end, what could grow out of a registry would be an epidemiological study yielding important information on common characteristics that contribute to Alzheimer's in the same way, for example, that cholesterol contributes to heart disease. Indeed, the best model, participants felt, was the Framingham Heart Study, which began 60 years ago and over three generations has contributed to our understanding of cardiovascular disease, including the impact of cholesterol.

- **A single Web site or portal for information would assist everyone in the larger Alzheimer's megacommunity.** Patients and caregivers could use it to learn about treatment options, community-support organizations, available clinical trials, recent research results, government funding and assistance, and much more. Physicians and other medical providers could use it too, because they do not know nearly as much about Alzheimer's as we or they may think.

- **We need a new, integrated model of assistance with the patient and caregiver at its center.** Everything we know suggests that patients cared for at home generally enjoy a better quality of life and live longer. However, most families lack the resources—financial, emotional, and physical—to manage home care without help. In-home services can be expensive, ranging from an average of $17 an hour for respite care, in which someone comes into the home for a few hours to relieve the otherwise full-time caregiver, to $150 or more per day for more complete home health help that includes personal care, meals, and household chores. Medicare will pay for a portion of that but not all of it. Outside the home, Medicare and Medicaid pay an average of 62 percent of nursing home costs. However, with a private room at a nursing home running more than $75,000 a year, that would still mean an out-of-pocket cost of nearly $30,000 a year.

- **Someone or some organization must take ownership of what needs to be a collaborative effort across all sectors of society.** One thought was designating the Alzheimer's Association, already a strong organization, as the singular voice of the disease. Another suggestion had the president of the United States or the secretary of the Department of Health and Human Services (HHS) appointing an Alzheimer's czar. In the wargame, the team playing HHS flirted with "I'm in charge" but shied away when the idea got little support from others. The best model for this role may well be the Susan G. Komen Breast Cancer Foundation; its drive, fund-raising abilities, and lobbying skills have led to big increases in breast cancer research, changes in medical examination patterns, higher rates of detection, and a spike in the number of breast cancer survivors.

- **A communications strategy is of paramount importance.** Patients and families want early diagnosis of Alzheimer's even in the absence of a cure or effective treatment, because it gives them more time to prepare themselves for a wide range of decisions on financial and legal matters, care options, and emotional and psychological issues. Awareness and education efforts are important parts of the communications effort, and putting real faces on the disease would help enormously. Enlisting early-onset Alzheimer's patients to serve as spokesmen and spokeswomen in such efforts would prove powerful and effective.

Federal spending on Alzheimer's research has grown steadily this decade, reaching around $650 million a year. A rough estimate of private-sector research adds another $1 billion to the mix. Patient care for Alzheimer's sufferers now costs the federal government more than $100 billion a year. An accurate cost-benefit analysis would be impossible to develop. If you had to bet, however, you'd probably wager that higher spending on basic and applied research might yield a reduction in Alzheimer's-related Medicare and Medicaid costs.

That spending ought to be a part of a larger collaborative effort involving the private sector and civil society: nonprofits such as the Alzheimer's Association and Gingrich's Center for Health Transformation. In other words, as our wargame demonstrated, it takes more than a village. Sometimes it takes a megacommunity.

○   ○   ○

On December 26, 2004, a gigantic earthquake and the resulting tsunami in the Indian Ocean devastated coastal areas in a vast region that included islands and nations in Southeast Asia, South Asia, and Africa. In what was the largest natural disaster in recorded history, an estimated 230,000 people perished, perhaps a third of them children. Indonesia was the hardest hit, with an estimated 167,000 deaths; the list of affected countries included India, Sri Lanka, Thailand, and Tanzania, among many others.

The tragedy, with its immediate aftermath carried live nearly 24/7 by the world's cable news networks, triggered a huge outpouring of sympathy and aid. Thousands of businesses, dozens of nongovernmental organizations (NGOs), and more than 50 governments pledged $6.7 billion in immediate and long-term aid. College students from the Americas, Australia, Europe, and elsewhere chucked their Christmas breaks—and in some cases the rest of the academic year—and headed for the affected areas to help with the relief effort. But the welcome global response, with the former U.S. presidents George H. W. Bush and Bill Clinton playing important symbolic roles, bumped up against an uncomfortable reality. This second tsunami of cash and in-kind donations overwhelmed the agencies, institutions, and countries charged with coordinating what would have been a difficult recovery even in the best and most efficient circumstances. After six months, barely one-third of the money had been disbursed. Was this the inevitable outcome of a vast and complex endeavor, or could the organizations involved in such efforts do better?

We thought they could, but we wanted to test the proposition in one of our wargames. To that end, we partnered with the U.S. Chamber of Commerce's Center for Corporate Citizenship (now known as the Business Civic Leadership Center) and brought together 70 government, business, and nonprofit leaders to participate in a global disaster relief simulation. The date was July 11, 2005. Seven weeks later, Hurricane Katrina churned across the Gulf of Mexico and swept ashore, laying waste to New Orleans and exposing some of the shortcomings addressed by the findings in our wargame.

The primary objective of this simulation was to explore ways to improve the coordination of disaster relief and recovery among the many sectors that want to help. How can they ramp up the quality of their planning, delivery, and communications? The participants were grouped into four stakeholder teams representing the business community; U.S. government agencies, particularly those, such as USAID, with specific relief missions; NGOs and international organizations (IOs); and the government of the Dominican Republic. Why that nation in the Caribbean? Because it was central to the simulation. We posited as an opening scenario that a category five hurricane—Hurricane Ophelia—was battering the northern coast of the Dominican Republic, which occupies the eastern two-thirds of the island of Hispaniola. Thousands of lives were lost, property destruction was widespread, and the country's infrastructure was badly damaged. The teams were supposed to respond to the crisis, mitigating its impact if possible; discuss how to improve future preparedness; and coordinate with other stakeholders.

We partnered with the U.S. Chamber of Commerce's Center for Corporate Citizenship (now known as the Business Civic Leadership Center) and brought together 70 government, business, and nonprofit leaders to participate in a global disaster relief simulation. The date was July 11, 2005. Seven weeks later, Hurricane Katrina churned across the Gulf of Mexico and swept ashore, laying waste to New Orleans and exposing some of the shortcomings addressed by the findings in our wargame.

The gaps in institutional culture and perceptions became clear almost immediately. For example, government agencies of the United States and the Dominican Republic and the NGOs and IOs naturally tended to focus their attention on public health and safety issues during disasters. Businesses in a disaster zone, in contrast, were interested mainly in protecting their employees and restarting operations, and big foreign companies eager to help in relief efforts tended to hesitate, waiting for the right signals to move. To be effective, the participants argued, they would need to find ways to merge their interests; otherwise, coordination of relief and recovery work would be much more difficult.

The nonprofits and international organizations were also at odds with business on another front. They perceived the business community to be profit-motivated to a fault. The business community, meanwhile, thought there should be more accountability from the NGOs and IOs on their use of donated resources: In effect, they wanted to know more about how the nonprofits got a bang for the buck.

In the end, though, the teams came up with a set of insights that deepened everyone's understanding of ways to improve the co-ordination of relief to disaster victims, from individuals to entire countries. Here are some examples:

- The degree and nature of intervention in disaster relief should be dictated by the leadership and will of host government entities. The donor-stakeholders—international agencies, non-governmental organizations, other governments, and the private sector—should cede primacy, assuming that the basic governmental infrastructure remains intact after the disaster hits. If it is not intact, international organizations can be more proactive.

- The donor-stakeholders must understand each other's strengths, weaknesses, and interests. That understanding, established in collaborative agreements before a disaster hits, would be essential if one or more donor-stakeholders became overwhelmed or incapacitated—by a critical interruption in its supply chain, for example—during the relief effort. In that event, others might be able to step in if not seamlessly, at least with a minimum of disruption.

- Avoid at all costs the coals-to-Newcastle syndrome. International aid should support local policy, and assistance that is insensitive to local cultural or economic considerations can violate a principal guideline: First, do no harm. For example, it might seem like a fine idea to send canned fish to a devastated community, but not if that community relies on a local fishing industry for its economic livelihood.

- Transparency, transparency, transparency. In all policies, practices, and actions, transparency is absolutely crucial to building trust among donor-stakeholders and fostering efficient delivery of assistance. The NGOs and IOs need to know what foreign governments, businesses, and business organizations are doing; government agencies and businesses similarly must have a clear sense of nonprofit operations.

- Donor-stakeholders must understand their strengths and limitations. Some organizations—for example, those which are expert at food and clean-water distribution—probably are better suited to provide immediate help. Others can play a bigger role assisting in long-term recovery.

- It's important that the public message evolve with the situation on the ground. In soliciting contributions from their constituencies, donor-stakeholders may begin with an "emergency plea for help." But as progress is made, they must communicate that success even as they address continuing needs. When contributors feel their money or other aid is well spent or well used, they are more inclined to keep giving. One big red flag: Dissembling on this point—saying relief is going well when it is not in the misguided belief that no one will notice or call you on it—will backfire both on an organization and on a population in need of help.

- Nongovernmental organizations should partner with other donors, such as the business community, in advance of a disaster. Such strategic partnerships and information sharing will speed up the donation process during a disaster because NGOs will have a much better idea of what resources are available to them. Participants in the simulation suggested creating a master list of general disaster relief and recovery needs, juxtaposed against likely available resources, as a way to streamline information gathering and sharing.

- Proactive preparedness can mitigate the effects of a disaster. Some of the recommendations developed by the participants in the wargame included vaccinating citizens against diseases likely to emerge in a disaster, establishing building codes to improve structural integrity, and developing a plan for the employment of displaced workers in recovery and reconstruction.

Would these kinds of recommendations, based on collaboration and preplanning among donor-stakeholders, have helped in the immediate aftermath of Hurricane Katrina? It is impossible to know, but we do know that the *absence* of coherent disaster planning at every level of government helped turn a terrible storm and natural disaster into one of the worst human-made catastrophes in U.S. history, one that soiled political reputations, undermined confidence in some prominent NGOs, and almost destroyed a great American city.

It is worth noting a related disaster-relief effort by our corporate family because that work bears on the admirable relief and recovery programs of so many nongovernmental organizations.

World Vision International, one of the largest Christian relief organizations in the world, was a major player in post-tsunami relief, airlifting l, 500 tons of aid into five countries in the first month after the disaster and committing $360 million to a multiyear reconstruction program in affected areas. WVI has massive supply chains, and Booz Allen has a long and well-earned reputation for supply-chain expertise. On a pro bono basis, our people conducted an assessment of WVI's supply chain management. After three months of study and fieldwork, the Booz Allen team gave outstanding grades to WVI's food-distribution supply chains; its nonfood programs, however, required some improvements.

The assessment outlined 20 supply-chain improvements for WVI and a plan for phasing them in over five years. They included installing a chief logistics officer to provide leadership, installing updated supply-chain technology, hiring experienced supply-chain managers to implement proven processes, and creating a council of key decision makers to ensure consensus on critical operating decisions.

○   ○   ○

S cholars already are debating George W. Bush's consequential and controversial presidency and its place in history. One piece of Bush's legacy, however, does not get as much attention as it should: He is the first American president to make a major financial commitment—tens of billions of dollars—to attacking the HIV/AIDS crisis in Africa and in developing countries elsewhere in the world. Meanwhile, major nonprofits, including the Bill & Melinda Gates Foundation and the William J. Clinton Foundation, actively support programs in Africa, India, and elsewhere to reduce infection rates and increase treatment of those who have the disease with antiretroviral drugs. However, the overall battle is not going well: According to the Global HIV Prevention Working Group, a panel of 50 public health experts around the world, six people became infected with HIV in 2006 for every one who started antiretroviral therapy. If current trends continue, the group said in a mid-2007 report, HIV will infect 60 million more people by 2015.

We first got involved in work on the HIV/AIDS crisis earlier in this decade, when we partnered with the Global Business Coalition on HIV/AIDS, Tuberculosis, and Malaria and the Confederation of Indian Industry to do a wargame on the epidemic in India.

We first got involved in work on the HIV/AIDS crisis earlier in this decade, when we partnered with the Global Business Coalition on HIV/AIDS, Tuberculosis, and Malaria and the Confederation of Indian Industry to do a wargame on the epidemic in India. The GBC, which was founded in 2001, is headed by the investment banker and veteran diplomat Richard Holbrooke, who has worked hard and successfully to develop an alliance of international companies to combat the HIV/AIDS epidemic.

The fact that India had an HIV/AIDS problem of serious dimensions was not in doubt. By 2002, the number of HIV/AIDS cases in India was approaching 4.5 million, according to that country's National AIDS Control Organisation. Heterosexual exposure was the primary means of infection, with rates rising sharply in high-risks groups such as intravenous drug users. A significant "bridge population"—that is, a group carrying the disease to the larger population—was thought to consist of so-called mobile workers: in short, truck drivers. These men had unprotected sex

The game was designed to focus on the long-term economic, political, and social effects of HIV/AIDS as well as the impact of potential interventions.

and later brought the disease home to their communities and spouses. HIV/AIDS in India thus was proliferating from high-risk groups to the general population and from urban centers to rural communities. The trend lines were alarming.

Over two days in October 2003, we brought together more than 200 leaders from industry, government, the health-care sector, community organizations, and nongovernmental organizations to address the crisis. The NGOs included representatives from the Gates Foundation, the United Nations, the World Bank, and the World Economic Forum, and the countries that participated included not only India but the United States, Britain, Australia, and Germany as well.

The game was designed to focus on five key objectives. In consultation with our partners, we wanted the participants to better understand the long-term economic, political, and social effects of HIV/AIDS as well as the impact of potential interventions. We asked them to identify areas for collaboration between the public and private sectors and to determine how best to mobilize business and public resources. Finally, we asked them to unearth strategies for all sectors in developing a national HIV/AIDS response for India.

It was a good thing we had a big turnout because we needed to staff nine teams representing India's manufacturing sector, its service sector, the consumer product sector, the pharmaceutical industry, health-care providers, the Indian national government, Indian state governments, non-Indian donor organizations and governments, and Indian field community organizations (see Figure 15.2). A control team was there to structure the game, introduce the external shocks or injects, arbitrate the play, and play other stakeholders, such as the press.

The game consisted of three moves, simulating a 10-year period moving forward. The teams were to discuss among themselves and with other teams the choices before them and the decisions they

FIGURE 15.2

The simulation explored he stakeholders' interdependencies
in response to the AIDS epidemic.

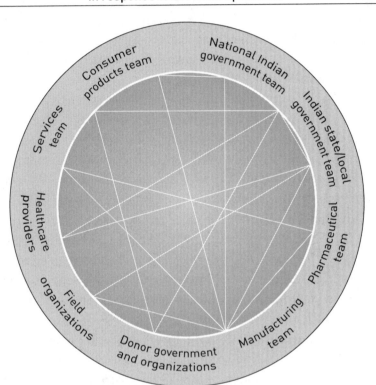

wanted to make to mitigate the impact of the epidemic. The control team would rule on proposals, with just one pregame stipulation: Only initiatives that had common agreement and adequate funding would be recognized in the simulation. We wanted to ground this wargame in reality as much as possible. The idea was to demand not only effective interventions but strategies that actually could be implemented.

As one might imagine, that was the hard part. The players quickly discovered that no single sector could tackle the problem without leveraging the know-how, talents, and resources of others. Early on, five problems got in the way of solutions.

First, there was a lack of trust among the teams, with various sectors or organizations preoccupied with their own constituencies rather than with the larger issue. Early in the game, for example, the business-sector teams developed HIV/AIDS programs that focused exclusively on their own employees and customers. But failing to address the needs of high-risk and marginalized groups such as commercial sex workers undermined the effectiveness of those business teams' responses.

Second, there was the social and cultural stigma associated with HIV/AIDS. Individuals worried about learning their HIV status for fear of being ostracized by their families, friends, and communities if they tested positive. Health-care workers feared the loss of other patients if it was known that they were treating HIV. Open discussion of risk factors was culturally taboo, making it difficult to education the population even about the basics of prevention.

Third, people were reluctant to be tested for another reason: Treatment for those testing positive was inadequate. However, when antiretroviral therapy was available, people were more willing to use voluntary counseling and testing services to learn their HIV status.

Fourth, the entire health-care infrastructure in India was insufficiently sized to deal with the potential scale of the epidemic. As the simulation progressed, teams became more aggressive in proposing programs to combat the spread of the disease, but they quickly encountered big roadblocks. Many of the business teams, for instance, wanted to implement voluntary counseling and testing programs for their employees but lacked the trained staff needed to make such programs work.

Fifth, the teams bumped up against a sad irony: Long-term treatment of HIV/AIDS, transforming it from a fatal disease to a chronic illness, increased demand on already overburdened health-care infrastructure and available resources. That in turn raised a new set of challenges.

Early game play reflected those problems. In the first move, the teams responded to the opening scenario—the crisis as it was at the time—with caution, approving broad and well-accepted aware-ness campaigns headed by top leaders and limited voluntary coun-seling and testing programs on a national basis. For the most part, however, teams were insisting they knew how to do their work and did not much countenance advice from or collaboration with oth-ers. However, two injects during the move added a sense of ur-gency to the participants' deliberations. First, the control team reported that the prevalence of HIV infection among India's grow-ing middle class was rising rapidly. Second, there were news re-ports of blood supplies contaminated with HIV.

Soon the walls separating the teams began to collapse. One team sent an e-mail to another asking for assistance: "Would the federal government team be willing to flow the majority of funds to state regions where they are needed?" Another team weighed in: "Could we use corporate facilities to help others in the surround-ing region?" Then another: "Treatment options need to be linked with counseling, but the drugs are too expensive. Could we develop lower-cost solutions together?"

In move 2, covering the years 2008–2013, the teams started to collaborate more effectively. In addition to general awareness pro-grams, health-care providers, pharmaceutical companies, national and state teams, and others increased the production and distribu-tion of antiretroviral drugs, and that helped boost voluntary coun-seling and testing. Business teams and nonprofits ramped up donations to boost counseling, testing, and health-care infrastruc-ture; led by the government and health-care teams, there was an ef-fort to target high-risk populations for testing.

Move 3 was a continuation of the 2008–2013 time frame and the kinds of programs initiated in move 2, but there remained sig-nificant gaps between the prevention and treatment programs the teams wanted and the funding available to support those programs. As a result, in move 3 the teams started to prioritize programs.

When it was over, the participants generally agreed that the job before them—containing India's HIV/AIDS epidemic—was even harder than they had imagined at the beginning of the wargame. But they also felt that the simulation had yielded a better understanding of the crisis and equipped them with the strategic insights necessary to tackle this threat to India's social, medical, and economic well-being. The overriding lessons reflected that greater understanding:

- Leadership from the top—in government, business, or community groups—is essential to laying the groundwork for broad participation across all sectors of society. In the game, for example, India's prime minister put together a national government task force on HIV/AIDS that included specific assignments for cabinet ministers and attempted to engage top politicians, business leaders, and celebrities. In an effort to destigmatize the disease, the national government strongly and publicly affirmed that HIV/AIDS was not a moral issue; meanwhile, legislation was introduced to protect the privacy of those tested and treated for the disease. Those steps by the national government during the wargame provided a context for business leaders to support antidiscrimination policies in both employment and health insurance.

- Effective solutions, balance prevention, testing, care, and treatment on the basis of the needs of the community. Targeted early actions often prove to be the least expensive interventions, reducing the long-term costs of delivering treatment and care to people living with the disease. Proactive measures to target high-risk groups, for example, can prevent HIV/AIDS from spreading to the general population. During the game, the pharmaceutical industry proposed a social marketing initiative aimed at truck drivers and other migrant workers; the manufacturing sector suggested implementing early HIV detection programs for high-risk groups.

- Collaboration is critical to maximizing impact, but it requires careful management and clear communication. In cross-sector collaborations, successful strategies leverage the unique capabilities, resources, and skills of each group. In the simulation, for example, telecommunications companies provided an HIV/AIDS toll-free help line, with tech support from the information technologies industry and management by NGOs. In another step, industry teams offered to collaborate with the government and open their health-care facilities to provide voluntary counseling and testing, treatment, and care to the larger community. In effective partnerships, communication and a common language are critical; each party must understand the motivations of its partners and what they have to gain or lose.

- Clear priorities must be established in the funding of programs, and innovative approaches must be encouraged because of the constraints on financial resources. One recommendation was for a centralized body to identify criteria for the funding of programs and develop performance benchmarks by which to monitor progress, but teams also stressed the need for decentralized funding to deliver cash to end users as quickly as possible. Innovation? Businesses offered to provide training to medical and health-care professionals. The team representing donor organizations and governments proposed a basket-funding approach in which donors would coordinate their funding decisions to ensure that programs supported India's national strategy for combating HIV/AIDS.

In all, the teams in this wargame initiated and explored dozens of partnerships and proposed 100 new initiatives that ranged from awareness and testing and treatment programs to national outreach programs. Our computer modeling staff had developed what we called the HOPE Model—HIV operation planning environment—to measure the effectiveness of what the teams proposed. At the beginning of the wargame, the prevalence of HIV/AIDS infection was expected to grow from 0.5 percent of India's population to 4.5 percent by 2025; by the end of the simulation, the strategies proposed by the teams had reduced that projection to 2 percent by

2025. Projected cumulative deaths, as a result, declined from more than 70 million to around 30 million by 2025. The saving of human life also had a beneficial economic impact: Our model estimated that the steps taken had prevented a simulated loss of $31.5 billion in gross domestic product.

Some of the partnerships and collaborations envisioned in the wargame were realized in the subsequent years. HIV/AIDS remains a huge problem in India, although new and more accurate estimates suggest that the infection rate is lower than was thought when we did our simulation in October 2003. According to the United Nations, as many as 3.1 million people in India were living with the disease in 2006.

CHAPTER 16

THE PERSIAN GULF, REVISITED

This book began with a summons and a challenge from Andrew Marshall of the Pentagon's Office of Net Assessment. We had talked about quick-reaction wargames, Marshall reminded us. Now Iraq had invaded Kuwait and was threatening the entire Middle East. Could there be a better time to convert talk into action and conduct a wargame, preferably today?

That wargame on August 2, 1990, was followed by work for the U.S. Defense Department before and during Operation Desert Storm in 1991. Since that time, Marshall and others at the Pentagon and in the uniformed military have called on us to design and stage wargames on Iraq-related matters. One, the 1999 wargame called Desert Crossing discussed in Chapter 3, exposed some of the potential difficulties that might derive from a U.S. military invasion of Iraq, particularly during an occupation phase after the fall of Saddam Hussein's regime.

We have continued to assist the U.S. Defense Department by providing Iraq wargaming services in more recent years. Some of these games have been quick-reaction tactical games that have addressed specific issues raised by the Army serving in Iraq. These are not real-time exercises, but they are about as close as we get. Usually, our military games require at least two to four months of design and preparation. In these tactical games, the lead time is considerably less: two or three days between the time we receive a request for support and the actual staging of the game, then another two or three days before the results of the game are conveyed to commanders in the field—in short, a week or less between engagement and deployment.

Let us give you an example. In 2007, the Army was setting up new security posts and wanted to wargame their effectiveness in the event of an attack by insurgents or another hostile force. The message from the Army to our wargamers was simple: Here's where we're setting this up, and here's the force we're thinking about putting there to defend it. We believe the chances of being attacked are pretty high. If there are vulnerabilities, we want to expose them before our men and women are placed in harm's way.

Thank goodness for advances in computer modeling, graphics, and simulation. In this particular game, there were only two teams—Red, representing the bad guys, and Blue, representing the good guys—with our people acting as control.

Red moved first. Its team members were given information that a new kind of security facility was about to be put in place. We also showed them, using a three-dimensional visualization on computers, what they probably would see and learn about it through routine ground reconnaissance.

Red could see with little difficulty where Blue had arrayed its defenses and came up with a plan of attack that involved a vehicle-borne improvised explosive device and follow-on small arms fire. The Red team chose as the point of attack an area of fencing that the original designers of the security post had not anticipated as a zone worthy of serious defense. In the computer simulation, Red penetrated the area, which was not covered by the field of fire from Blue's primary weapons systems. The IED exploded, and the rest of the attack also went as the Red team had planned.

Now it was Blue's turn. We ran the game simulation and the subsequent modeling we had done to reflect Red's success and showed it to the Blue team. Blue was all shades of red with embarrassment because its weapons had been arrayed poorly and its troops had been caught flat-footed. Furthermore, we had simulated what the Blue response would be, whether they could counterattack successfully. They could not.

If it had been the real deal, not a drill executed on a computer's three-dimensional battlefield in suburban Washington, D.C., American lives would have been lost, and the security post might have been overrun.

Our wargaming is objective and unbiased. It is about problem solving or, at a minimum, problem exposing. This is especially critical in military wargames because civilian leaders and commanders in the field make difficult decisions in the real world that risk blood and treasure. In other words, the stakes are very high.

That could have been the end of it if we had accepted the initial outcome as evidence that the security post's original design was fatally flawed. Instead, we braced the Blue team: Is this just a dumb idea or, in light of how you saw the game play out, can changes be made to make such facilities defensible in these particular threat environments?

Blue regrouped, rearranged its force deployment, and reinforced soft spots in the walls of its compound. Red attacked again, this time unsuccessfully. Could Red try another approach? The Red team did, but Blue was a much tougher target because of the adjustments it had made.

Bottom line: The Army made changes in the security post design that reflected the results of the wargame. That facility is not bulletproof or miraculously protected by some sort of Star Trek shield, but it's significantly more secure than it otherwise would have been.

And yes, it's worth saying again: American lives were saved. The U.S. military and the Office of the Secretary of Defense are clients we serve as professionally as we can. Our wargaming is objective and unbiased. It is about problem *solving* or, at a minimum, problem *exposing*. We have written often about the power of what we do to create an imagined future in which players can observe, work together, make decisions, and learn from outcomes in a risk-free environment. This is especially critical in military wargames because civilian leaders and commanders in the field make difficult decisions in the real world that risk blood and treasure. In other words, the stakes are very high whether it's a strategic wargame planned over many months and played by hundreds of military men and women at the Army War College or a tactical wargame designed and played in less than a week on a computerized front line in Iraq.

◇   ◇   ◇

As of this writing, U. S. forces continue to occupy Iraq and to fight insurgent elements in Afghanistan. However, at some point, a new administration and a new president—Republican or Democrat—probably will begin to reduce American troop levels and in other ways scale back the U.S. profile in Iraq and perhaps in Afghanistan as well. In the wake of this partial disengagement, a new post-Iraq strategic environment is bound to emerge.

With that in mind, it seemed appropriate to end this book with a wargame that looked ahead to a world we could glimpse in small flashes of insight but whose larger strategic meaning remained understandably elusive.

How will that new environment be shaped by and affect U.S. security interests? That was the question we wanted to address in the wargame. Its central objective, in short, was to gain a deeper understanding of the changing priorities and budget implications within the defense and intelligence communities as a result of a new and evolving strategic environment.

This was to be an internal wargame, with participants drawn not only from the firm's wargamers, computer modelers, and simulation experts but from Booz Allen's extended family as well. The list of our colleagues included a few retired generals and admirals; Jim Woolsey, head of the Central Intelligence Agency under President Clinton; and Dov Zakheim, comptroller of the Department of Defense and its chief financial officer during George W. Bush's first term. To put it mildly, there was a lot of talent and experience in the room.

We wanted the game to expose shifting funding priorities in this new world, major organizational changes that might occur, the way the rise of irregular warfare missions would meld with the traditional roles of the military services, and whether the intelligence community needed to be rethought, in part or in its entirety, in light of the altered strategic environment.

These were our people, but in most respects we treated them no differently than we would treat a corporate or military client. Also, we added an important instruction that should be familiar to you by now: Do not fight the game or its scenarios. We stressed, as we always do, that the wargame would represent a simplified version of reality. It was designed to be plausible, not predictive, although it was possible that the game's outcomes one day might be reflected in amazing things in the real world. Many of the players knew what we meant. They had read the recently declassified reports of the 1999 "Desert Crossing" wargame we did for General Tony Zinni, then the chief of Central Command, and knew it revealed some of the stumbling blocks that had tripped up the Bush administration since Saddam Hussein's regime was taken down in spring 2003.

The game's organization—part of that simplified version of reality—featured five competing teams: one for each of the three services (Army, Navy/Marines, and Air Force), one representing the intelligence community, and one representing the Department of Homeland Security. The control team served as the president and the secretary of defense and their advisors, in effect, the "customers" for the initiatives and programs the other teams would try to sell. Control also acted for consumers and all others (the media and Congress, for example) and introduced the injects: the external shocks which in this game as in so many others would prove especially important in the second move.

We played the game in early November 2007, but the scenario for move 1 began 18 months into the future.

It was June 1, 2009, and a new administration in Washington had focused much of its attention on efforts to resolve the Iraq conflict and reexamine American national security interests. Three months earlier, an unclassified version of a new National Security Estimate (NIE) had been released. It argued that the nation continued to face significant security challenges. Those challenges included threats from terrorists eager to target U.S. interests at home and abroad, find sanctuary in ungoverned or undergoverned areas, and employ irregular warfare to subvert and overthrow weak governments or failing states. The NIE also recognized the dangers posed by potentially hostile nuclear powers (North Korea and, soon, Iran), an increasingly assertive and militarily capable China, and the proliferation of weapons of mass destruction and the advanced technology to deliver them.

About the same time, the new administration released its National Security Strategy (NSS), which was praised at home and abroad for its expressed interest in engaging enemies and developing global coalitions to attack terrorism and deal with climate change and other transnational issues. Under the NSS umbrella, key strategy documents were published: one each on the stabilization of Iraq, the military, the intelligence community, and homeland protection.

○   ○   ○

With that as the backdrop, each team, armed with budget documents and strategic guidance created for the game, was asked in the first move to identify its three top priorities/strategies and its three major challenges.

In the breakout sessions, most of the teams were tentative. "After Iraq, we've got to come back and reset the force," a participant on the Army team asserted to general agreement among his team-mates. But exactly how? "Will we ever see an old-fashioned tank-on-tank battle, the kind we had in World War II?" another participant wondered aloud. Maybe not, but a conventional land force proba-bly would be needed, provided that it was part of a very mobile Army that would be able to move quickly in certain kinds of trouble spots.

That raised another issue: How should the Army balance its force between conventional missions and irregular missions? "We need programs to ensure full-spectrum capability," said one Army team member. But in a new age of asymmetric warfare, what would be the trade-offs?

Furthermore, all the services faced budget limitations imposed in part by an explosion in their health-care costs as well as increases in pay and housing allowances. In short, maintaining a fit and happy volunteer military, even with no growth in the size of the force, now came with a growing price tag for health care and other benefits that was bound to affect budgets for big-ticket purchases. Increase the size of the force, and those costs figured to grow expo-nentially.

Later, when the Army team briefed its "customers" in the exec-utive branch, it set as its top priority out of move 1 a gradual in-crease in personnel done in concert with a reexamination of the Army's Force Combat Structure. TRADOC—the training and doc-trine command that "thinks for the Army," as it says on its Web site—would lead the way.

The U.S. Navy team, meanwhile, was struggling. "It'll be an-other generation or more before there's another major ground war," argued one participant, "so there ought to be relatively more em-phasis on the Navy and the Marine Corps." The Navy's major pro-grams in its budget still included big carrier groups and its stealthy boats: the nuclear submarines that patrolled the world's oceans, generally impervious to detection. But even though the carriers and the subs would continue to provide maritime security and "domain awareness," they did not really reflect and address the changing nature of real and potential threats to the United States. As one participant conceded, "The Navy and Marines have insufficient amphibious assets right now." The Marine Corps would have to grow, the team members thought, to help confront hostile nonstate actors, and wouldn't that require greater reliance on new tools for force projections?

"Joint seabasing will drive modernization," said one participant. Heads nodded affirmatively. By that, they meant greater use of sea-based integrated forces rather than land bases overseas. But Navy team members conceded that interservice rivalries would have to be overcome if the Pentagon was serious about joint seabasing.

The Air Force seemed to be flying blind too. Participants ticked off several priorities: defense of the homeland, modernization of its fleet of aging aircraft, improved airlift and long-range strike capabilities, and better ISR: intelligence, surveillance, and reconnaissance. Air superiority, the Air Force team insisted, was essential, and that meant the acquisition of state-of-the-art fighter jets.

But it was the Department of Homeland Security, a creation of the post-9/11 era that consolidated old or retooled agencies from across the government into a new arm of the executive branch, that was having the toughest time responding to control's request for priorities and challenges. DHS has about 20 different arms, but its top five agencies account for roughly 80 percent of its budget. Those agencies are the U.S. Coast Guard and four agencies that have become familiar to Americans from their abbreviations: the Federal Emergency Management Agency (FEMA), the Transportation Security Administration (TSA), Immigration and Customs Enforcement (ICE), and Customs and Border Protection (CBP).

Its priorities and strategies in move 1 were both elementary and revealing. Preparedness, for example, generally was agreed to be an essential priority; that struck a few team members as something of a "duh" insight in light of the reason for DHS's creation in the first place. In fact, much of the DHS team's deliberations focused on the department's perceived shortcomings, such as the need for greater interagency collaboration and integration.

The intelligence team, in contrast, was the one most willing to marry traditional priorities—doing its part to prevent and disrupt terrorist attacks—to new, creative possibilities. In the long war against terrorism, for example, it might make sense to outsource the prosecution of targets once they were identified by U.S. intelligence.

Looking ahead, we told the teams that the new administration was thinking about fewer people and more technology as the players approached move 2. The second move, we thought, should push them to think bigger.

Overall, when the teams finally briefed control after their deliberations in move 1, it was plain that much work needed to be done.

The players' verdict on DHS: It needs organizational reexamination. It also needs to be part of a debate about the mission of the National Guard and establish better links to the intelligence community.

The Air Force: It was not paying enough attention to unmanned aircraft, and its emphasis on new fighter jets did not fly with control. What enemy, exactly, is building all the tactical fighters that the United States needs to confront with an expanded force of its own? That question, raised by control, went unanswered by the Air Force team.

The Navy: Yes, joint sea basing was important looking forward, so why the emphasis on what is still, at its core, a Cold War–era fleet?

The Army: You're raising some of the big questions, and we'll be giving you more money to reset the force. But you need to drill down and get more specific.

The intelligence community: Kudos on some creative thinking. In this budget round, you get a nice "plus up" for your good work.

The overall assessment, shared by everyone on control, was that the players were still in their stovepipes. That was understandable: They were dealing with the here and now, not the medium-term and long-term future. Looking ahead, we told the teams that the new administration was thinking about fewer people and more technology as the players approached move 2. The second move, we thought, should push them to think bigger.

○　　○　　○

Move 2: The date is June 1, 2014, and the world is at once familiar and terra incognita. The United States still has 60,000 troops in Iraq, but a steady drawdown continues as terrorist attacks diminish and the country functions essentially as a weak central government with three semiautonomous regions: one Sunni, one Shia, and one Kurd. However, U.S. foreign and defense policymakers have much more than Iraq on their plates. Nearly 30,000 U.S. troops, mainly Army and Marines, are deployed around the world in small-scale contingency situations and irregular warfare missions.

This includes 10,000 troops assigned to the tribal areas of northwestern Pakistan in an effort to eliminate Al-Qaida strongholds in that area. Prime Minister Benazir Bhutto, who took over in 2011, had initiated political reforms even though former President Pervez Musharraf remained a powerful figure in Pakistani affairs through his control of the country's intelligence services. But on July 26, 2012, both Bhutto and Musharraf were assassinated by Al-Qaida in nearly simultaneous suicide bomber attacks. As a consequence, Pakistan seemed to be slipping into civil war as its uneasy neighbor India began to prepare for the worst: the possibility that Al-Qaida would gain control of Pakistan's nuclear arsenal. (Note: Benazir Bhutto was assassinated in Pakistan on December 27, 2007, about seven weeks after this wargame was played.)

The year 2012 was eventful in other ways as well. In late September, a truck exploded at the Queens entrance of New York City's Midtown Tunnel; within minutes, the authorities determined that the truck had carried radioactive material. The explosion killed 27 people and injured 200 others; the level of panic in New York and the nation at the release of a "dirty bomb" was high. It turned out the truck was driven by a native of Chechnya who had entered the country from Canada a year earlier on a French passport. Relations with Canada and France grew strained. Nine months later, in mid-2013, the United States began the construction of a fence along its northern border: a seven-year project estimated to cost at least $1 billion per year.

In December 2012, Iran test fired a new long-range ballistic missile with a range of 1,200 miles, putting almost the entire Middle East, Turkey, Pakistan, and parts of India and Russia within its potential crosshairs. Still, Iran had yet to develop a viable nuclear capability.

The next two years provided little respite from global turmoil. In January 2013, Colombian terrorists struck the Panama Canal in suicide attacks that severely damaged the canal's operation. A Panamanian businessman of Syrian descent appeared to be involved, investigators believed.

Elsewhere, relations between Poland and Ukraine deteriorated because of aggressive Ukrainian actions, including a series of statements about reclaiming territory in Poland and Belarus that once had been part of Ukraine. Poland requested NATO help, and 2,000 U.S. troops were dispatched as part of a NATO stabilization force.

In Africa, international stabilization forces, including U.S. Army troops, sailors, and Marines, were deployed in several countries to quell violence (Nigeria), intercede in a civil war (Libya after Muammar Qadhafi's death), fight pirates threatening shipping interests (Somalia), and help in large refugee camps (southern Egypt was filling up with Sudanese fleeing turmoil at home).

Our instructions to our stakeholder teams: How have your priorities and strategies evolved? What are the biggest changes your team faced in this 2009–2114 time frame as a result of the "injects" in the scenario? And how do the actions of others help or hinder you in an irregular warfare environment?

Team Army. "Is Pakistan now the enemy? No? Well, what is it?" That set of questions, raised by one of the participants, launched the Army team's discussion of the move 2 scenarios and how to respond to them. The Pakistan situation, moreover, suggested a whole new set of questions about the nature of warfare looking forward. Did the United States face one big war—the long war against terrorism—or a seemingly endless string of smaller wars? Did the nation's armed forces, reconstituted after the Iraqi drawdown began, need to be retooled yet again to face the kinds of threats revealed by the scenario injects? The Army, in short, still was struggling with the composition of its force and the doctrine guiding it.

Team Navy. "What are the game changers for us?" That was what one participant wanted to know at the beginning of the Navy's deliberations. One game changer, several people said, would be unmanned naval aircraft entering the fleet. Another could be greater cooperation with the intelligence community on information sharing, part of a revamped and upgraded Navy capability for ISR (intelligence, surveillance, and reconnaissance). The Navy still was emphasizing big carriers and submarines, but its team was beginning to recognize bigger possibilities. The "thousand-ship Navy," an objective of the period covered in move 1, still might be feasible, but only if it included major contributions by allied navies and the smaller vessels required for brown- and green-water operations, that is, operations in rivers, lakes, and other waterways close to shore.

Team Air Force. This team still seemed to be locked into its move 1 mode: air superiority, more fighter jets, more long-range bombers. The Air Force had not yet realized that the larger mission was changing. For example, transport aircraft to get personnel and equipment from point A to point B to engage in irregular warfare or join peacekeeping, stabilization, and reconstruction missions were becoming more important. They might not have much sex appeal, but big transports were necessary in the new world, and the Air Force had to be central to that effort. The wall under construction along the nation's northern border—part of the move 2 scenario—prompted one player on the Air Force team to quip:

"If we're going to be responsible for patrolling it, there better not be East and West Coast walls too, because we won't have any planes left."

Team DHS. Slowly but surely, the DHS team was starting to get it. The participants finally were raising the right questions: Should the department, jerry-built quickly in response to the legislation creating it, be restructured? If so, another question needed to be addressed: What is DHS supposed to be? The department, everyone agreed, desperately required mission clarity. To get from here to there, DHS would have to reexamine the department top-down and bottom-up. Players also thought the DHS should do a better job of collaborating with other parts of the government with the responsibility for homeland security, especially the Air Force and agencies falling under the Director of National Intelligence (DNI).

Team Intel. The intelligence team, under the DNI umbrella, was beginning to shine. It recognized that it needed to modernize its information technology, engage more global partners, build up its human-intelligence capabilities, and focus on developing language skills among its operatives in the field. Intel's players also discussed intelligence needs within the United States and settled on what certainly would be a controversial proposal. "We need our own MI5," said one participant to general agreement. "The FBI can't do the job."

MI5 is Britain's century-old domestic security service, "responsible for protecting the country against covertly organized threats to national security," as the service states on its Web site. Contemporary threats include terrorism, espionage, and weapons of mass destruction. In the post-9/11 era, Washington policymakers and any number of national security experts have debated whether the FBI, primarily a crime-fighting organization, can make the transition and also become a sophisticated domestic spy service roughly modeled on MI5. Thus far, concerns about privacy violations and other potential excesses have trumped efforts to press the case for an American version of MI5, but the debate has not disappeared.

○   ○   ○

The intelligence team got high marks from the control group serving as the "customer" for the five teams; control, holding the budget strings, gave DNI fresh funds to foster its "single information environment" and seed money to design a domestic security service that might be presented to Congress for debate and consideration. DHS, control said, finally had begun the process of mission integration, with an eye on ridding itself of redundancy in an agency with too many moving parts. Its principal priorities and strategies had to revolve around preparedness, prevention, protection, response, and recovery. Its budget would get a bump so that it could complete the job. Other team budgets were flatlined into move 3, which was designed to look back and forward: to review move 2, in effect, and to project what new steps might be contemplated.

We got some provocative stuff. There was widespread agreement that a review of the overall national security architecture was essential to ensure effective strategies for both conventional and irregular warfare missions. "What if you could reverse engineer the Army?" asked one Army team participant. "If you contemplated this world we've posed, what kind of Army would you design?" What would be the balance between capabilities for conventional war and irregular war?

Another key learning was that the National Guard was due for a total transformation. But that could not happen without broad consultation and agreement among all the stakeholders: not only the Office of the Secretary of Defense and the Army but DHS, Congress, and state governors as well. The Air Force and Navy? One big takeaway was that both services would be forced to transform as strategy changes to meet evolving security threats and as the focus begins to shift toward mission support and away from the acquisition of costly platforms.

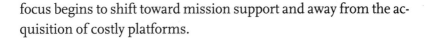

As you read this book, the post-Iraq period for the U.S. defense and intelligence communities already may have begun. It's just possible that some elements of what has been suggested as plausible in this chapter have come to pass or are under intense discussion in the real world.

Such is the power of wargames: They create a virtual world players can experience, learn from, and integrate into their tactical and strategic decision making. Let's repeat what we said at the outset. If you had the opportunity to probe the future, make strategic choices, and view the consequences of those choices in a risk-free environment before making expensive and irrevocable decisions, wouldn't you take advantage of it?

INDEX

ABOUT THE AUTHORS

MARK HERMAN

Mark Herman is a Booz Allen Hamilton vice president based in McLean, Virginia, who leads the firm's modeling, simulation, wargaming, and analysis work. He has more than 30 years of experience designing and de-  veloping wargames on a variety of strategic and boardroom topics for the U.S. Department of Defense and Fortune 500 companies.

Mr. Herman is a leader in the development of wargame and simulation methodologies emphasizing strategic planning, the development of measures of effectiveness, and economic analysis. His areas of expertise include:

- Wargaming
- Modeling and simulation
- Architecture analysis
- Information warfare
- Net assessments
- Network centric warfare
- New measures of effectiveness
- Revolution in military affairs (RMA)
- Strategic planning

Mr. Herman has designed more than 50 commercial wargames on topics ranging from the Peloponnesian War to tactical warfare in antiquity, the American Revolution, the American Civil War, World War I, World War II, modern warfare, and science fiction. His 1983 design Gulf Strike, which covered the Iran-Iraq War and a U.S.-led defense of Saudi Arabia, was used in the initial U.S. analytic efforts at the beginning of the Gulf War in August 1990.

Mr. Herman has received two Booz Allen Hamilton Professional Excellence Awards in recognition of outstanding and innovative client service on an assignment for the U.S. Air Force and on a commercial wargaming engagement.

Mr. Herman has been an adjunct professor teaching Strategy and Policy for the U.S. Naval War College, has coauthored books on military history and wargaming, and is a lecturer for the U.S. Naval War College, the University of Maryland, and Georgetown University. He holds an M.A. in National Security Studies from Georgetown University and a B.A. in History from the State University of New York at Stony Brook.

MARK FROST

Mark Frost is a principal with Booz Allen Hamilton in McLean, Virginia, with more than 20 years of experience in military, government, and commercial modeling, simulation, wargaming, and analysis. In the commercial sector, he has pioneered the transfer of military wargaming techniques to assist in developing strategy and managing change for major corporations worldwide. Booz Allen's innovative work in this area has been profiled in numerous business publications, including *Business Week*, the *Wall Street Journal*, and *Forbes*.

At Booz Allen, Mr. Frost leads the development of wargames for commercial and civil sector clients worldwide, addressing some of the most complex problems our governments, businesses, and public face. In addition, he has developed wargames for a myriad of global leadership events such as the World Economic Forum and Aspen Ideas Festival.

Recent wargames have addressed:

- Impact of regulations to reduce carbon emissions
- Resilience of global financial networks
- Megacommunities for chronic diseases
- National strategies to fight HIV/AIDS
- Regional crisis preparedness and response
- Frameworks for international development
- Product launch strategies in highly competitive markets
- Impact of disruptive change on businesses
- Battle for consumer relationships
- Implementation of new operating models (organizational change)
- Due diligence for mergers and acquisitions

Mr. Frost has received two Booz Allen Hamilton Professional Excellence Awards, given in recognition of outstanding and innovative client service, for the AIDS Epidemic Strategic Simulation to build a megacommunity to fight the HIV/AIDS epidemic in India and for pioneering the application of wargaming to business strategy.

Before joining Booz Allen, Mr. Frost served in the U.S. Navy in antisubmarine warfare patrol aircraft and the aircraft carrier *Carl Vinson* and taught in the Mathematics Department at the U.S. Naval Academy. He holds an M.S. in Operations Research from the Naval Post Graduate School and a B.S. from the United States Naval Academy (1974).

ROBERT KURZ

Robert Kurz is a principal with Booz Allen Hamilton in McLean, Virginia, with 30 years of experience in governmental strategy and operations. For the last 15 years, he has supported government and commercial clients with consulting services in strategy, analysis, and wargaming.

At Booz Allen, Mr. Kurz leads the firm's wargames and simulations for defense, security, and civil sector clients that address strategic, operational, and tactical issues addressing some of the most complex challenges that confront governmental leaders, from action officers to cabinet officers.

Some recent wargames and simulations have addressed:

- Opportunities for expanding interagency coordination and co-operation for complex national security issues
- Innovative governmental acquisition strategies and implementation options
- Enhancements of organizational structures and strategies for improved government effectiveness
- Expanded education for senior leaders to improve force protection
- Improved resilience of financial service organizations
- Implementation of new governmental enterprise-level management strategies
- New technologies to improve military operations
- Options for addressing cyberspace challenges and opportunities
- Improved bilateral relationships and greater understanding of difficult international issues

Before joining Booz Allen, Mr. Kurz served in the office of the governor of Wisconsin and on the staffs of several committees and offices in the U. S. House of Representatives. He has been a guest scholar at the Brookings Institution, an international affairs Fellow with the Council on Foreign Relations, and an adjunct faculty member at Georgetown University. He holds an M.A. in Government from Georgetown University and a B.A. in Political Science from the University of Wisconsin–Madison.